FIRST WORLD WAR ATLAS

BOOKS BY MARTIN GILBERT

American History Atlas
British History Atlas
Jewish History Atlas
Recent History Atlas: 1860 to 1960
The Appeasers *(with Richard Gott)*
The European Powers: 1900–1945
The Roots of Appeasement
Winston Churchill *(Clarendon Biographies)*

FIRST WORLD WAR ATLAS

Martin Gilbert
Fellow of Merton College, Oxford

Introduction by
VISCOUNT MONTGOMERY OF ALAMEIN

Cartography by ARTHUR BANKS

The Macmillan Company
New York, New York

The Macmillan Company
866 Third Avenue, New York, N.Y. 10022
Collier-Macmillan Canada Ltd., Toronto, Ontario

First World War Atlas was first published in Great Britain in 1970 by Weidenfeld and Nicolson, London.

Library of Congress Catalog Card Number: 76-151695

First American Edition 1971

Printed in the United States of America

Table of Contents

Introduction
Field-Marshal The Viscount Montgomery of Alamein

The idea of teaching history by a series of maps was new to me until
Martin Gilbert's historical atlas of British history had come my way. I was
at once intensely interested and later studied those of other countries and
nations which he published. Such visual pictures of historical facts cannot
fail to be of real value to students in schools and universities; they would
look through a window, as it were, at the subject before getting down to a
detailed study—which is, of course, essential.

My own study of history has proved to me, a soldier, that the verdict
of war has been, time and again, a deciding factor in the process of
historical change—though, of course, not the only one. But it has always
been the arbiter when other methods of reaching agreement have failed.

This atlas of the 1914–18 war is therefore of particular interest to me,
since I led my platoon of some 30 men into battle against the German
army in August 1914, and remained on the western front in Europe until
the war ended. It was an honour when my friend Martin Gilbert asked me
to write an introduction to this atlas.

I look forward eagerly to his atlas of the 1939–45 war in which I fought
on the battlefields of Africa and Europe—but by then being somewhat
more senior in rank than in 1914.

MONTGOMERY OF ALAMEIN

Preface

This Atlas is intended as an introductory guide to as many aspects of the First World War as can reasonably be put in map form: the military, the naval, the aerial, the diplomatic, the technical, the economic, and pervading all, the human. The principal books upon which I have drawn for both facts and ideas are listed in the bibliography at the end of the volume. Two of the maps are constructed entirely from material which I have found in the recently opened British Government archives at the Public Record Office in London: *A Plan for the Middle East 1915* (map 34) from a Cabinet paper entitled "The Spoils" written in March 1915 by the Colonial Secretary, Lewis Harcourt, which contained the first formal proposals for the post-war future of Palestine; and *British Defences Against a Possible German Invasion 1915* (map 44) from the facts given to the members of the War Council at the beginning of January 1915. I have tried to build up each map by a detailed study of the available evidence, some of it extremely well known, some obscure, and some, as with the two maps above, previously unpublished.

Many of the subjects mapped here, although written about elsewhere, have not been put in map form before. But it is my hope that the visual aspect of a map such as *German War Aims in the West 1914–1918* (map 124), or *British Supplies to the Allies 1914–1918* (map 140) can be as useful, and as revealing, as the printed form; and that the putting together of normally scattered and diverse facts such as *Food Riots in Germany 1916* (map 77), *British Labour Corps 1914–1918* (map 136) or *Gold Gains 1914–1918* (map 143) can give an unexpected interest to problems which, because of their unfamiliarity, do not always find a place in general histories of the war.

During the four years in which I have been compiling these maps and preparing the drafts, I have been fortunate in the advice given by colleagues and friends. The Imperial War Museum, and in particular Dr Christopher Dowling and Mr Vernon Rigby, gave me the benefit of their wide knowledge and critical skills. Dr Immanuel Geiss gave me the advantage of his careful study of German war aims and policy; Mr Michael Glenny gave the Russian maps the benefit of his unique blend of scholarship and zeal; Mr and Mrs Tsvi Hercberg accompanied me to several battlefields on the western front and encouraged me with their enthusiasm and suggestions; Madame Taillandier gave me a vivid insight into the effect of the war on a French village cruelly thrust into the front line. The Commonwealth (formerly Imperial) War Graves Commission provided me with excellent detailed maps of the western front on which over two thousand British graveyards mark the savage progress and preserve a sombre echo of the fighting of over fifty years ago. Mr Norman Pemberton, the Commonwealth War Graves representative at Çanakkale, kindly took me to the cemeteries which he guards with such care upon the Gallipoli Peninsula; Mr A. G. Major accompanied me to the summit of Sari Bair from where, gazing down at the Aegean Sea across the whole Anzac area, we felt almost in the living presence of the aspirations, the folly, the suffering and the heroism of mankind. The Mayor of Eceabat (the town of Maidos on maps 35 and 38), Mr Vedat Okay, and the Governor of Çanakkale, Mr Celâlettin Tüfekçi, gave me every help while I was at the Dardanelles, and Mr Okay not only put a jeep at my disposal, but gave up his own time to ensure that my visit to the battlefields was as comprehensive as it could be. My visit there was made possible by the generosity of the Turkish Government which invited me to Turkey in connection with my work on the Official Biography of Sir Winston Churchill, and enabled me to pursue simultaneously my researches both as a historian and as a historical geographer.

Mr Arthur Banks once more supervised with his usual skill the activities of his team of cartographers, of whom Mr T. A. Bicknell deserves a special mention for his high standard of cartography. Jane Cousins supervised the final cartographic corrections. Mr Joseph Robinson examined the maps with the thorough professional eye of a former member of the diplomatic service. Mrs Jean Kelly again gave the maps the advantage of her geographic expertise; and Sarah Graham, as well as typing all the preparatory matter, the bibliography and the index, subjected the maps to a further critical scrutiny. I am deeply grateful to all those who have helped to eliminate errors and ambiguities, but for those which

x

remain I bear the sole responsibility.

I should welcome suggestions for future maps, and for corrections or additions to the existing ones.

Ten years have passed since Mr A. J. P. Taylor gave me my last undergraduate tutorial in his room overlooking the Deer Park at Magdalen. Since then I have never ceased to benefit by his extraordinary enthusiasm for history and by his advice. It is he, for example, who, by urging me to include graphs in this Atlas, led me to prepare *Casualties and Prisoners on the British Front 1918* (map 119) and *British Merchant Shipping Losses 1917–1918* (map 85), as well as for the graph which appears on *Allied Losses Off North America 1917* (map 86). Likewise, it was his railway enthusiasm which made me look more closely at the rail and transport problems of the First World War and to draw *The Berlin–Bagdad Railway by 1914* (map 4), *Communications at Ypres by 1918* (map 22) and *Railway Communications of the Central Powers 1916* (map 61).

I wish above all to thank my father, Mr Peter Gilbert, for his constant interest and true enthusiasm. By his questionings he led me to many searches which I might otherwise have neglected. Twice during my work on the Atlas he came with me to the Ypres Salient and together we would listen to the Last Post as it was sounded every night under the Menin Gate. He also tramped with me over Flanders' fields in search of the mine craters of *Messines: The Mines* (map 90) and in order to find the precise location of the farms and fortifications of *Churchill in Flanders 1916* (map 58). It is therefore with a sense of gratitude for this as for so many other things that I dedicate this volume to him.

The Map House   MARTIN GILBERT
Harcourt Hill
Oxford
Christmas 1969

List of Maps

Section One

PRELUDE TO WAR

It is a painful and terrible thing to think how easy
it is to stir up a nation to war . . . and you will find
that wars are always supported by a class of arguments
which, after the war is over, the people find were
arguments they should not have listened to.

> JOHN BRIGHT
> *House of Commons*
> *31 March 1854*

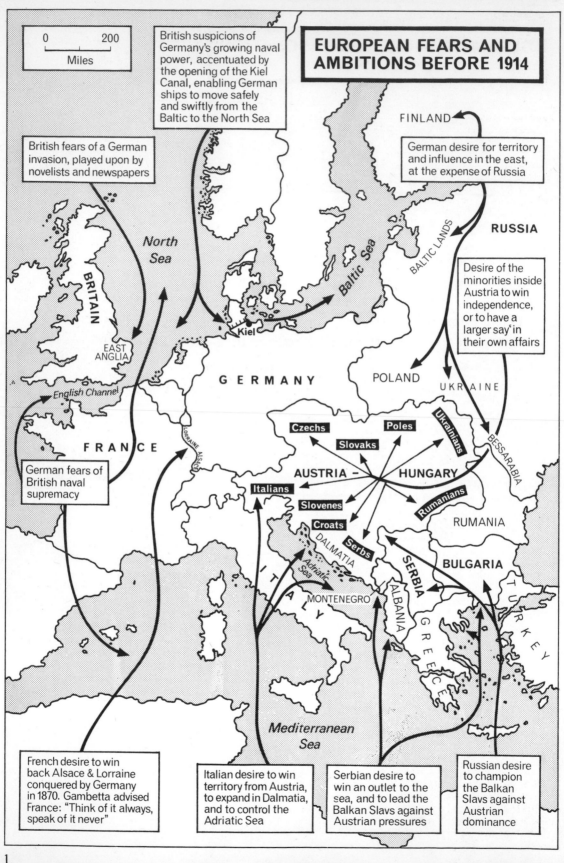

0
200
Miles

EUROPEAN FEARS AND AMBITIONS BEFORE 1914

British suspicions of Germany's growing naval power, accentuated by the opening of the Kiel Canal, enabling German ships to move safely and swiftly from the Baltic to the North Sea

British fears of a German invasion, played upon by novelists and newspapers

German desire for territory and influence in the east, at the expense of Russia

Desire of the minorities inside Austria to win independence, or to have a larger say in their own affairs

German fears of British naval supremacy

French desire to win back Alsace & Lorraine conquered by Germany in 1870. Gambetta advised France: "Think of it always, speak of it never"

Italian desire to win territory from Austria, to expand in Dalmatia, and to control the Adriatic Sea

Serbian desire to win an outlet to the sea, and to lead the Balkan Slavs against Austrian pressures

Russian desire to champion the Balkan Slavs against Austrian dominance

FINLAND

RUSSIA

North Sea

Baltic Sea

BALTIC LANDS

BRITAIN

EAST ANGLIA

Kiel

English Channel

GERMANY

POLAND

UKRAINE

BESSARABIA

FRANCE

LORRAINE ALSACE

Czechs
Poles
Slovaks
Ukrainians

AUSTRIA – HUNGARY

Italians
Slovenes
Croats
Serbs
Rumanians

RUMANIA

ITALY

DALMATIA

Adriatic Sea

SERBIA

BULGARIA

MONTENEGRO

ALBANIA

GREECE

TURKEY

Mediterranean Sea

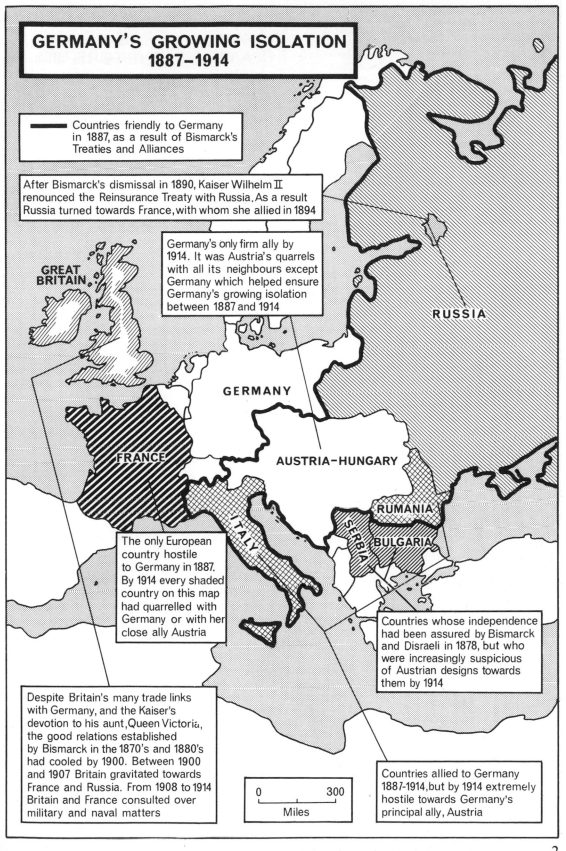

GERMANY'S GROWING ISOLATION 1887–1914

—— Countries friendly to Germany in 1887, as a result of Bismarck's Treaties and Alliances

After Bismarck's dismissal in 1890, Kaiser Wilhelm II renounced the Reinsurance Treaty with Russia. As a result Russia turned towards France, with whom she allied in 1894

Germany's only firm ally by 1914. It was Austria's quarrels with all its neighbours except Germany which helped ensure Germany's growing isolation between 1887 and 1914

GREAT BRITAIN

RUSSIA

GERMANY

FRANCE

AUSTRIA-HUNGARY

ITALY

RUMANIA

SERBIA

BULGARIA

The only European country hostile to Germany in 1887. By 1914 every shaded country on this map had quarrelled with Germany or with her close ally Austria

Countries whose independence had been assured by Bismarck and Disraeli in 1878, but who were increasingly suspicious of Austrian designs towards them by 1914

Despite Britain's many trade links with Germany, and the Kaiser's devotion to his aunt, Queen Victoria, the good relations established by Bismarck in the 1870's and 1880's had cooled by 1900. Between 1900 and 1907 Britain gravitated towards France and Russia. From 1908 to 1914 Britain and France consulted over military and naval matters

0   300
Miles

Countries allied to Germany 1887–1914, but by 1914 extremely hostile towards Germany's principal ally, Austria

2

THE MINORITIES OF THE CENTRAL POWERS IN 1914

Belgians

FRANCE

Baltic Sea

Danes

GERMANY

Metz

Strassburg

French

Posen

Prague

Czechs

Poles

RUSSIA

Italians

ITALY

Slovenes

Trieste

AUSTRIA - HUNGARY

Pressburg

Ukrainians

Croats

Slovaks

Serbs

Sarajevo

The three central Empires each contained large minority groups who wished for eventual independence. Many of these groups hoped that an Allied victory might lead to their liberation. The Allies encouraged such hopes, and offered to support the minorities if they turned against their imperial masters

Adriatic Sea

SERBIA

RUMANIA

Rumanians

GREECE

Aegean Sea

Constantinople

Black Sea

RUSSIA

Greeks

TURKEY

Russians

Kars

Armenians

Mediterranean Sea

Arabs

Kurds

Arabs & Jews

Jerusalem

Arabs

0   100

Miles

THE BERLIN-BAGDAD RAILWAY BY 1914

Germany hoped to gain important trade and political influence in Turkey and Persia by the construction of the Berlin-Bagdad railway. With the exception of 175 miles in Serbia, its 1,875 miles ran through countries sympathetic to Germany. But British traders could make as much use of it as they wished, and French investors had a strong financial interest. The railway was in no sense a cause of war, although British public opinion saw it as evidence of German and Austrian expansionist tendencies

0   200
Miles

SWITZERLAND
GERMANY
Berlin
Dresden
Prague
ITALY
Vienna
AUSTRIA-HUNGARY
Budapest
Belgrade
ALBANIA
SERBIA
Nish
Sofia
RUMANIA
RUSSIA
GREECE
BULGARIA
Constantinople
Haidarpasha
Afion-Karahissar
TURKEY
Konya
Adana
Alexandretta
Aleppo
Mardin
RUSSIA
EGYPT
Gaza
Damascus
Mosul
Tabriz
Russian sphere of influence
PERSIA
Bagdad
Kermanshah

— The Berlin-Bagdad railway. The Adana-Aleppo and Mardin-Mosul sections were not completed on the outbreak of war in 1914

■ Serbia: the only country on the Berlin-Bagdad railway not associated with Germany, and also hostile to Austria-Hungary

+++ Branch line completed by 1914

- - - Branch line proposed to the Persian oilfields

Directors of the railway in 1914	
German	11
French	8
Turkish	4
Swiss	2
Austrian	1

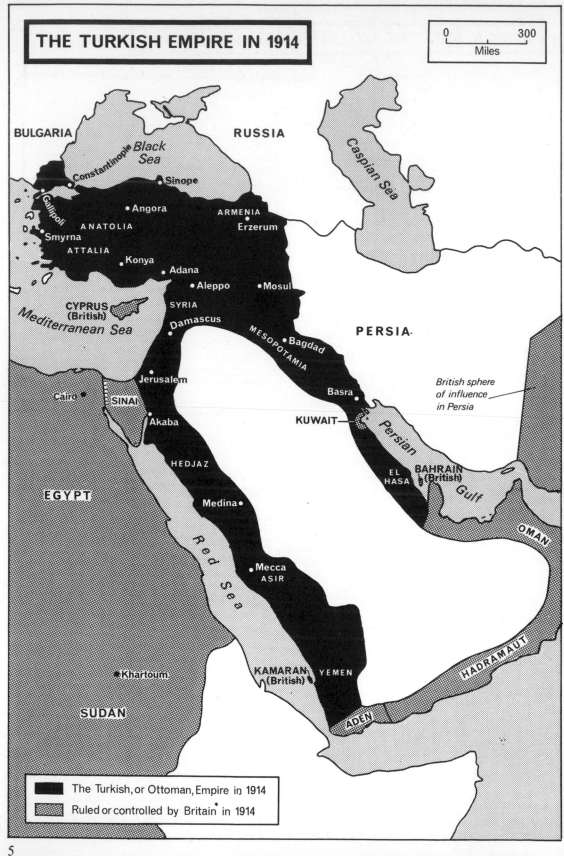

THE TURKISH EMPIRE IN 1914

0   300
Miles

BULGARIA

RUSSIA

Black Sea

Constantinople

Sinope

Angora

ARMENIA

Gallipoli

ANATOLIA

Erzerum

Smyrna

ATTALIA

Konya

Adana

Aleppo

Mosul

Caspian Sea

CYPRUS
(British)

SYRIA

Mediterranean Sea

Damascus

MESOPOTAMIA

Bagdad

PERSIA

Jerusalem

*British sphere
of influence
in Persia*

Cairo

SINAI

Akaba

Basra

KUWAIT

HEDJAZ

EGYPT

Medina

EL
HASA

BAHRAIN
(British)

Persian

Gulf

OMAN

Red Sea

Mecca

ASIR

Khartoum

KAMARAN
(British)

YEMEN

HADRAMAUT

SUDAN

ADEN

The Turkish, or Ottoman, Empire in 1914

Ruled or controlled by Britain in 1914

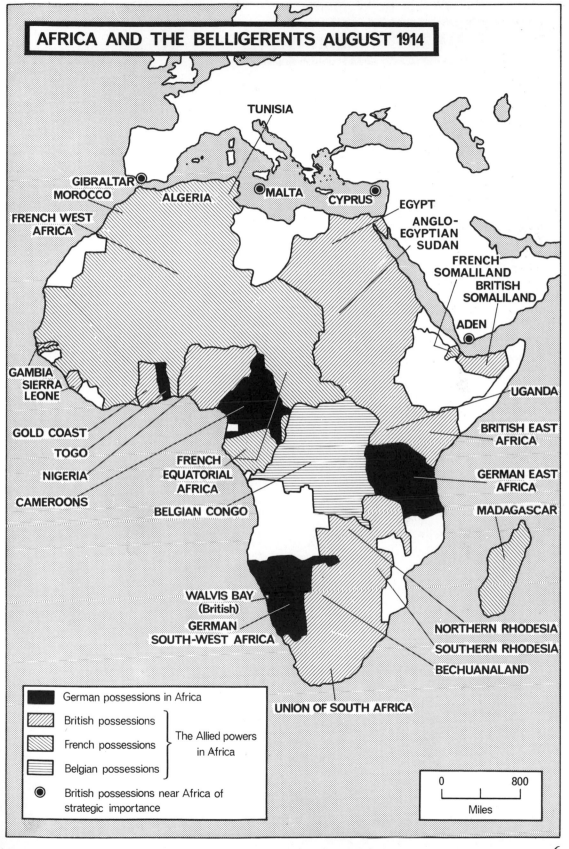

AFRICA AND THE BELLIGERENTS AUGUST 1914

TUNISIA

GIBRALTAR

MOROCCO

ALGERIA

MALTA

CYPRUS

EGYPT

ANGLO-EGYPTIAN SUDAN

FRENCH WEST AFRICA

FRENCH SOMALILAND

BRITISH SOMALILAND

ADEN

GAMBIA
SIERRA LEONE

UGANDA

GOLD COAST

BRITISH EAST AFRICA

TOGO

NIGERIA

FRENCH EQUATORIAL AFRICA

GERMAN EAST AFRICA

CAMEROONS

MADAGASCAR

BELGIAN CONGO

WALVIS BAY
(British)

GERMAN
SOUTH-WEST AFRICA

NORTHERN RHODESIA

SOUTHERN RHODESIA

BECHUANALAND

UNION OF SOUTH AFRICA

German possessions in Africa

British possessions

French possessions } The Allied powers in Africa

Belgian possessions

British possessions near Africa of strategic importance

0   800

Miles

6

ITALY AND THE MEDITERRANEAN 1911-1914

Legend:
- Italy in 1911
- Annexed by Italy in 1912, after war with Turkey
- Turkish, Austrian and Albanian territory which Italy hoped to annex either by the defeat of the Central Powers or by agreement with Austria-Hungary

TYROL

AUSTRIA–HUNGARY

Milan

Turin

Trieste
ISTRIA

ITALY

DALMATIA

ALBANIA

TURKEY

Rome

Naples

SARDINIA

Smyrna

Konya

ATTALIA

SICILY

Rhodes

DODECANESE ISLANDS

TUNISIA
(French)

Tripoli

TRIPOLITANIA

Benghazi
CYRENAICA

EGYPT
(British)

LIBYA

FEZZAN

0   200
Miles

SERBIA AND ITS NEIGHBOURS 1878 – 1914

0 — 100 Miles

2 The Serbs of Bosnia looked to Serbia for their future, as Austrian rule was oppressive

11 Austria feared unrest among its 23 million subject Slavs if Serbia were allowed to build up its power and prestige

10 Serbia's only active ally among the Great Powers. Russia disliked Austria's growing influence in the Balkans. The Balkan Slavs looked to Russia as their champion

1 Independent from Turkey, 1878, after nearly 500 years of Turkish rule

3 Austria ruled Dalmatia, a Serb outlet to the sea, including the ports of Spalato and Cattaro

MONTENEGRO
4 Serbia's only Balkan ally, a mountainous country with no easy access to the sea, and only one port

5 Created from Turkish territory as a result of Austrian pressure in 1912, deliberately cutting Serbia off from the sea

8 Bulgaria, anxious to annex Serbian Macedonia

6 Conquered from Turkey by Greece during the Balkan war 1912-1913. Serbia had hoped to expand to Salonika and the sea

9 Novibazar and Macedonia, conquered by Serbia from Turkey 1912-1913

7 Conquered from Turkey by Bulgaria 1912-1913, again frustrating Serb ambitions seaward

RUSSIA
Odessa
AUSTRIA – HUNGARY
DALMATIA
Adriatic Sea
Spalato
BOSNIA
Sarajevo
Belgrade
SERBIA
Nish
MONTENEGRO
NOVIBAZAR
Cattaro
Dulcigno
ALBANIA
Skopje
Durazzo
MACEDONIA
Ochrid
Valona
Salonika
Prevesa
GREECE
Athens
Mediterranean Sea
Aegean Sea
RUMANIA
Bucharest
BULGARIA
Sofia
Dedeagatch
Kavalla
Constantinople
TURKEY
Black Sea

■ Serbia in 1878
□ Conquered by Serbia in 1913
▨ Serbia's allies

8

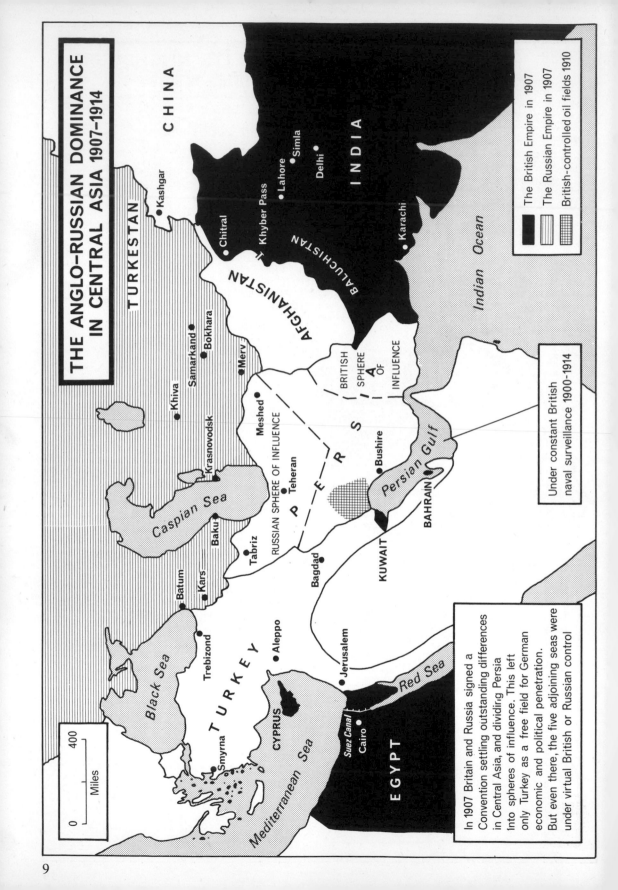

THE ANGLO-RUSSIAN DOMINANCE IN CENTRAL ASIA 1907-1914

The British Empire in 1907
The Russian Empire in 1907
British-controlled oil fields 1910

C H I N A

TURKESTAN

Kashgar

Chitral

Khyber Pass

Simla
Lahore
Delhi

I N D I A

Karachi

BALUCHISTAN

AFGHANISTAN

Samarkand
Bokhara
Khiva
Merv

Krasnovodsk

Meshed

Caspian Sea

Teheran

RUSSIAN SPHERE OF INFLUENCE

P E R S I A

BRITISH SPHERE OF INFLUENCE

Bushire

Persian Gulf

BAHRAIN

KUWAIT

Baku

Tabriz

Batum
Kars

Bagdad

Black Sea

Trebizond

Aleppo

T U R K E Y

Smyrna

Jerusalem

CYPRUS

Mediterranean Sea

Suez Canal
Cairo

Red Sea

E G Y P T

Indian Ocean

Under constant British naval surveillance 1900-1914

In 1907 Britain and Russia signed a Convention settling outstanding differences in Central Asia, and dividing Persia into spheres of influence. This left only Turkey as a free field for German economic and political penetration. But even there, the five adjoining seas were under virtual British or Russian control

0   400
Miles

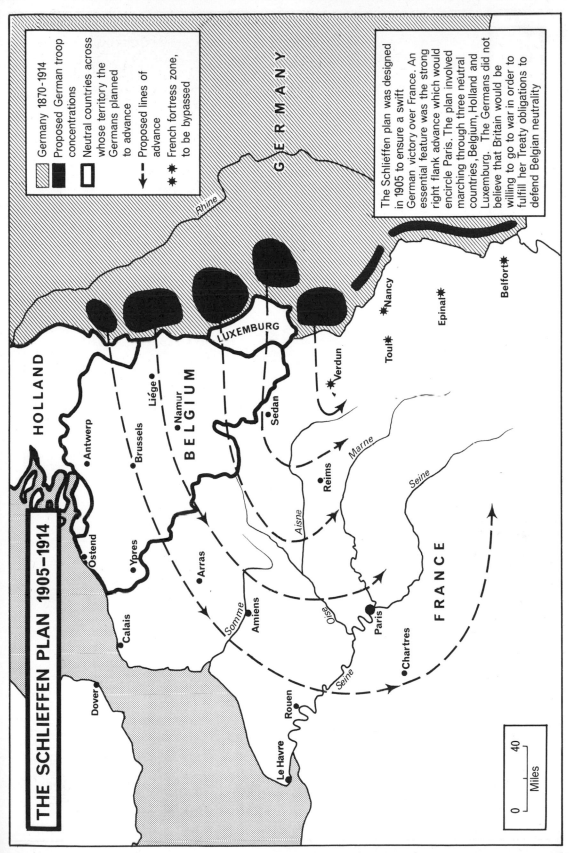

THE SCHLIEFFEN PLAN 1905–1914

Legend:

- Germany 1870-1914
- Proposed German troop concentrations
- Neutral countries across whose territory the Germans planned to advance
- Proposed lines of advance
- French fortress zone, to be bypassed

The Schlieffen plan was designed in 1905 to ensure a swift German victory over France. An essential feature was the strong right flank advance which would encircle Paris. The plan involved marching through three neutral countries, Belgium, Holland and Luxemburg. The Germans did not believe that Britain would be willing to go to war in order to fulfill her Treaty obligations to defend Belgian neutrality.

GERMANY

Rhine

LUXEMBURG

HOLLAND

BELGIUM

Antwerp

Brussels

Liége

Namur

Sedan

Verdun

Nancy

Toul

Epinal

Belfort

Ypres

Arras

Somme

Amiens

Oise

Aisne

Reims

Marne

Seine

Paris

Chartres

FRANCE

Ostend

Calais

Dover

Le Havre

Rouen

Seine

0   40
Miles

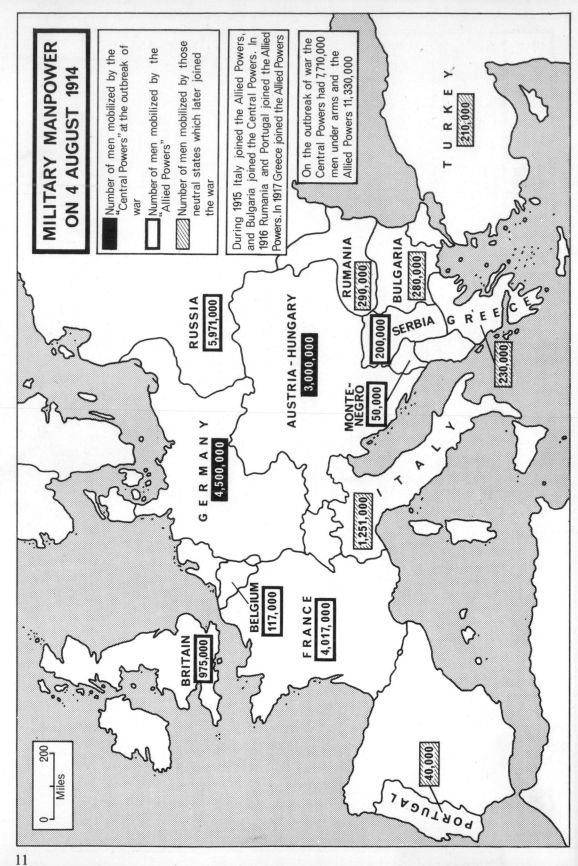

MILITARY MANPOWER ON 4 AUGUST 1914

Number of men mobilized by the "Central Powers" at the outbreak of war

Number of men mobilized by the "Allied Powers"

Number of men mobilized by those neutral states which later joined the war

During 1915 Italy joined the Allied Powers, and Bulgaria joined the Central Powers. In 1916 Rumania and Portugal joined the Allied Powers. In 1917 Greece joined the Allied Powers

On the outbreak of war the Central Powers had 7,710,000 men under arms and the Allied Powers 11,330,000

TURKEY 210,000

RUSSIA 5,971,000

RUMANIA 290,000

BULGARIA 280,000

SERBIA 200,000

GREECE 230,000

AUSTRIA - HUNGARY 3,000,000

MONTE-NEGRO 50,000

GERMANY 4,500,000

ITALY 1,251,000

BELGIUM 117,000

FRANCE 4,017,000

BRITAIN 975,000

PORTUGAL 40,000

200

0

Miles

11

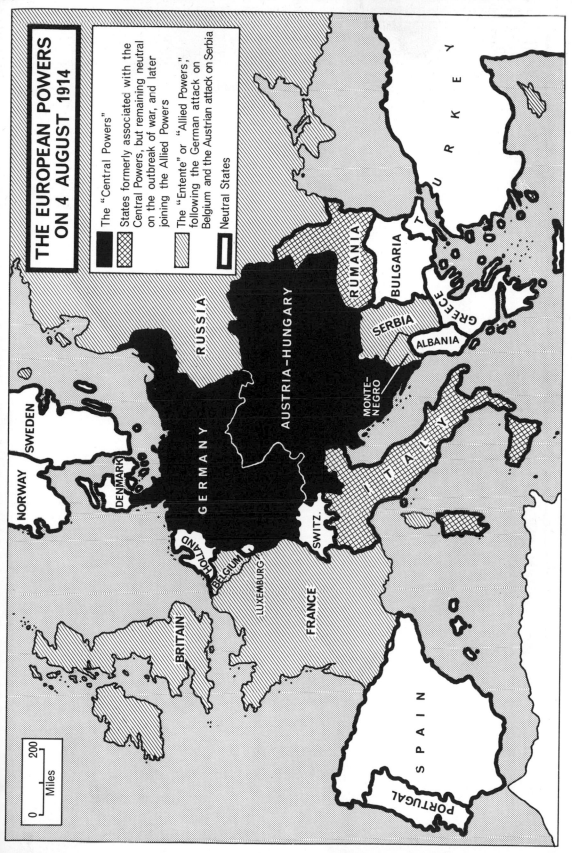

THE EUROPEAN POWERS ON 4 AUGUST 1914

The "Central Powers"

States formerly associated with the Central Powers, but remaining neutral on the outbreak of war, and later joining the Allied Powers

The "Entente" or "Allied Powers," following the German attack on Belgium and the Austrian attack on Serbia

Neutral States

200
0
Miles

NORWAY
SWEDEN
DENMARK
RUSSIA
GERMANY
AUSTRIA–HUNGARY
HOLLAND
BELGIUM
LUXEMBURG
SWITZ.
FRANCE
BRITAIN
ITALY
SPAIN
PORTUGAL
MONTE-NEGRO
ALBANIA
SERBIA
RUMANIA
BULGARIA
GREECE
TURKEY

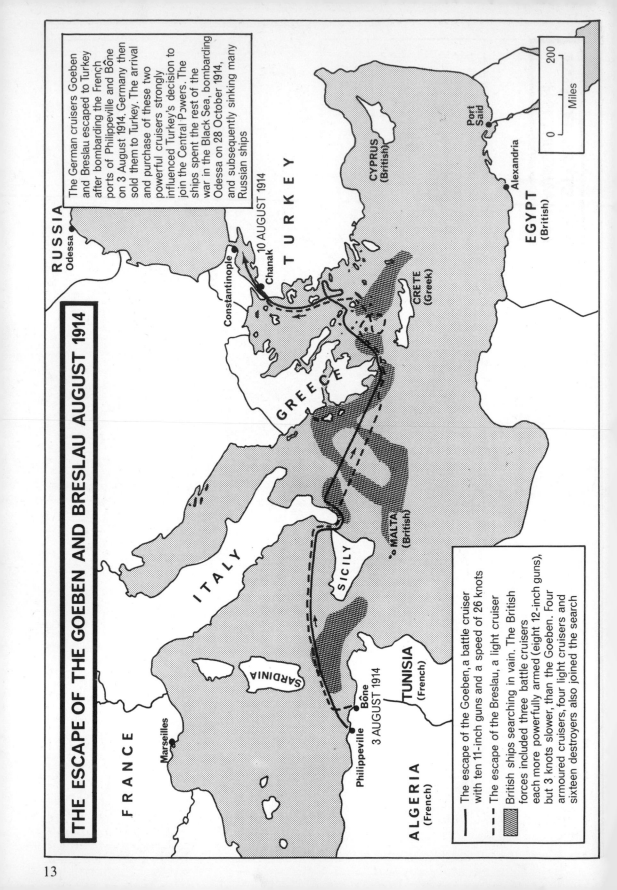

THE ESCAPE OF THE GOEBEN AND BRESLAU AUGUST 1914

The German cruisers Goeben and Breslau escaped to Turkey after bombarding the French ports of Philippeville and Bône on 3 August 1914. Germany then sold them to Turkey. The arrival and purchase of these two powerful cruisers strongly influenced Turkey's decision to join the Central Powers. The ships spent the rest of the war in the Black Sea, bombarding Odessa on 28 October 1914, and subsequently sinking many Russian ships

RUSSIA
Odessa

TURKEY

10 AUGUST 1914

Chanak

Constantinople

GREECE

CRETE (Greek)

CYPRUS (British)

Port Said

Alexandria

EGYPT (British)

FRANCE

Marseilles

ITALY

SARDINIA

MALTA (British)

SICILY

Philippeville
Bône
3 AUGUST 1914

TUNISIA (French)

ALGERIA (French)

0   200
Miles

───── The escape of the Goeben, a battle cruiser with ten 11-inch guns and a speed of 26 knots

----- The escape of the Breslau, a light cruiser

▨ British ships searching in vain. The British forces included three battle cruisers each more powerfully armed (eight 12-inch guns), but 3 knots slower, than the Goeben. Four armoured cruisers, four light cruisers and sixteen destroyers also joined the search

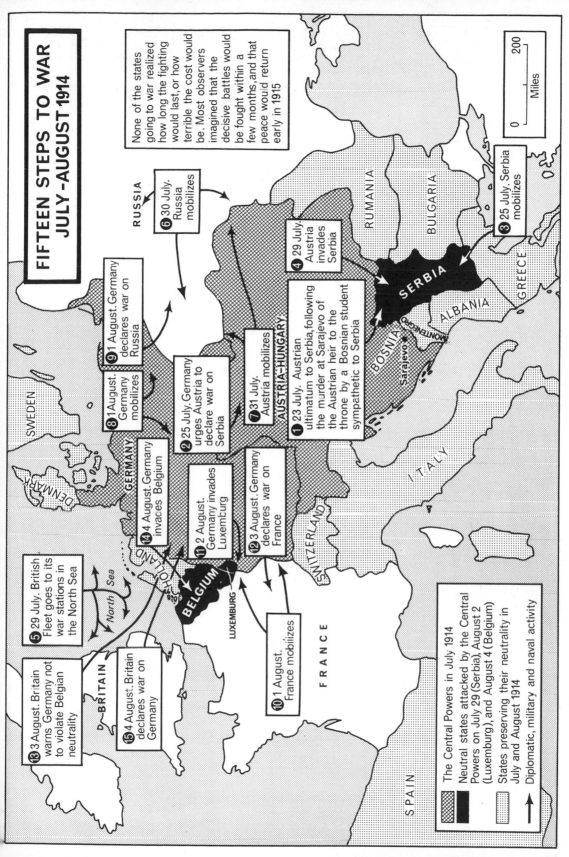

FIFTEEN STEPS TO WAR JULY-AUGUST 1914

None of the states going to war realized how long the fighting would last, or how terrible the cost would be. Most observers imagined that the decisive battles would be fought within a few months, and that peace would return early in 1915.

6 30 July. Russia mobilizes

4 29 July, Austria invades Serbia

3 25 July. Serbia mobilizes

9 1 August. Germany declares war on Russia

8 1 August. Germany mobilizes

2 25 July. Germany urges Austria to declare war on Serbia

7 31 July. Austria mobilizes

1 23 July. Austrian ultimatum to Serbia, following the murder at Sarajevo of the Austrian heir to the throne by a Bosnian student sympathetic to Serbia

14 4 August. Germany invaces Belgium

11 2 August. Germany invades Luxemburg

12 3 August. Germany declares war on France

5 29 July. British Fleet goes to its war stations in the North Sea

13 3 August. Britain warns Germany not to violate Belgian neutrality

15 4 August. Britain declares war on Germany

10 1 August. France mobilizes

RUSSIA

RUMANIA

BULGARIA

GREECE

ALBANIA

SERBIA

MONTENEGRO

BOSNIA

Sarajevo

AUSTRIA-HUNGARY

ITALY

SWEDEN

DENMARK

GERMANY

HOLLAND

BELGIUM

LUXEMBURG

SWITZERLAND

FRANCE

SPAIN

BRITAIN

North Sea

0   200
Miles

The Central Powers in July 1914

Neutral states attacked by the Central Powers on July 29 (Serbia), August 2 (Luxemburg), and August 4 (Belgium)

States preserving their neutrality in July and August 1914

Diplomatic, military and naval activity

14

Section Two

1914

Now, God be thanked Who has matched us with His hour,
   And caught our youth, and wakened us from sleeping,
With hand made sure, clear eye, and sharpened power,
   To turn, as swimmers into cleanness leaping,
Glad from a world grown old and cold and weary,
   Leave the sick hearts that honour could not move,
And half-men, and their dirty songs and dreary,
   And all the little emptiness of love! . . .

RUPERT BROOKE
"1914"

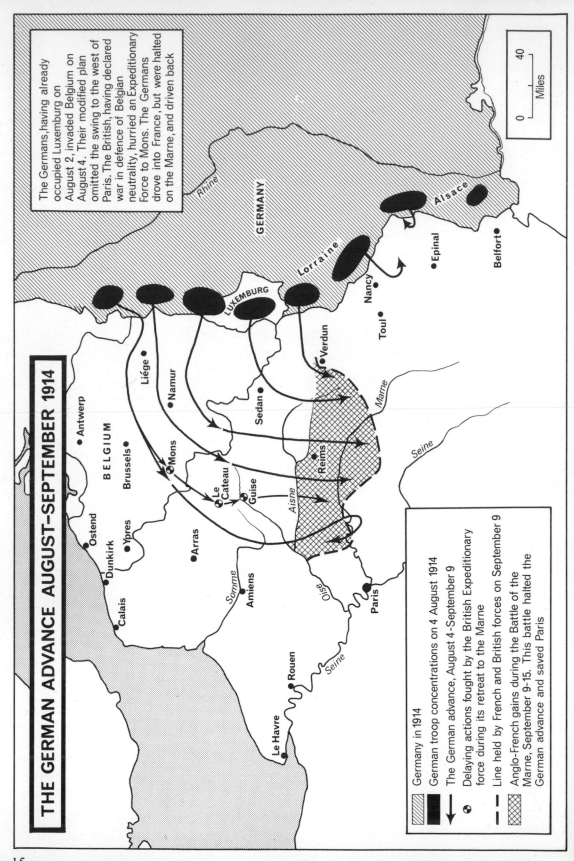

THE GERMAN ADVANCE AUGUST–SEPTEMBER 1914

The Germans, having already occupied Luxemburg on August 2, invaded Belgium on August 4. Their modified plan omitted the swing to the west of Paris. The British, having declared war in defence of Belgian neutrality, hurried an Expeditionary Force to Mons. The Germans drove into France, but were halted on the Marne, and driven back

GERMANY

Rhine

Alsace

Lorraine

LUXEMBURG

• Epinal

Belfort •

Nancy •

Toul •

Verdun •

• Liége

• Namur

Sedan •

Marne

Reims •

BELGIUM

Antwerp •

Brussels •

• Mons

Le Cateau

Guise •

Aisne

Seine

Ypres •

Ostend

Dunkirk •

• Arras

Somme

Amiens •

Oise

Calais •

Seine

PARIS ●

Rouen •

Le Havre •

Germany in 1914

German troop concentrations on 4 August 1914

The German advance, August 4–September 9

Delaying actions fought by the British Expeditionary force during its retreat to the Marne

Line held by French and British forces on September 9

Anglo-French gains during the Battle of the Marne, September 9–15. This battle halted the German advance and saved Paris

0   40
Miles

15

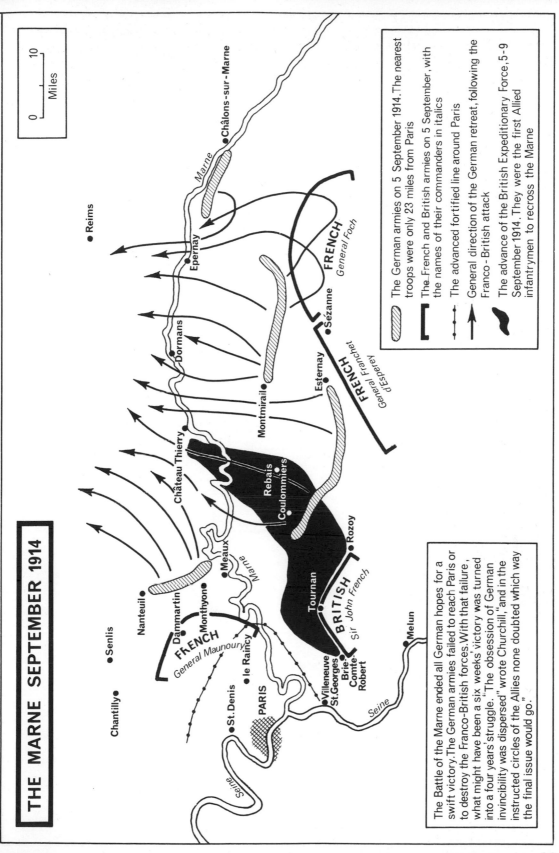

THE MARNE SEPTEMBER 1914

Scale:
0 — 10 Miles

• Châlons-sur-Marne
Marne

• Reims

• Epernay

FRENCH
General Foch

• Dormans

• Sézanne

FRENCH
General Franchet d'Esperey

• Esternay

• Montmirail

• Château Thierry

Rebais •
Coulommiers •

• Rozoy

BRITISH
Sir John French

• Tournan

• Chantilly

• Senlis

• Nanteuil

• Dammartin
• Monthyon

FRENCH
General Maunoury

Marne
• Meaux

• St. Denis

• le Raincy

PARIS

Villeneuve •
St. Georges •
Brie- •
Comte- •
Robert

• Melun

Seine

Seine

The German armies on 5 September 1914. The nearest troops were only 23 miles from Paris

The French and British armies on 5 September, with the names of their commanders in italics

The advanced fortified line around Paris

General direction of the German retreat, following the Franco-British attack

The advance of the British Expeditionary Force, 5-9 September 1914. They were the first Allied infantrymen to recross the Marne

The Battle of the Marne ended all German hopes for a swift victory. The German armies failed to reach Paris or to destroy the Franco-British forces. With that failure, what might have been a six weeks' victory was turned into a four years' struggle. "The obsession of German invincibility was dispersed" wrote Churchill, "and in the instructed circles of the Allies none doubted which way the final issue would go."

16

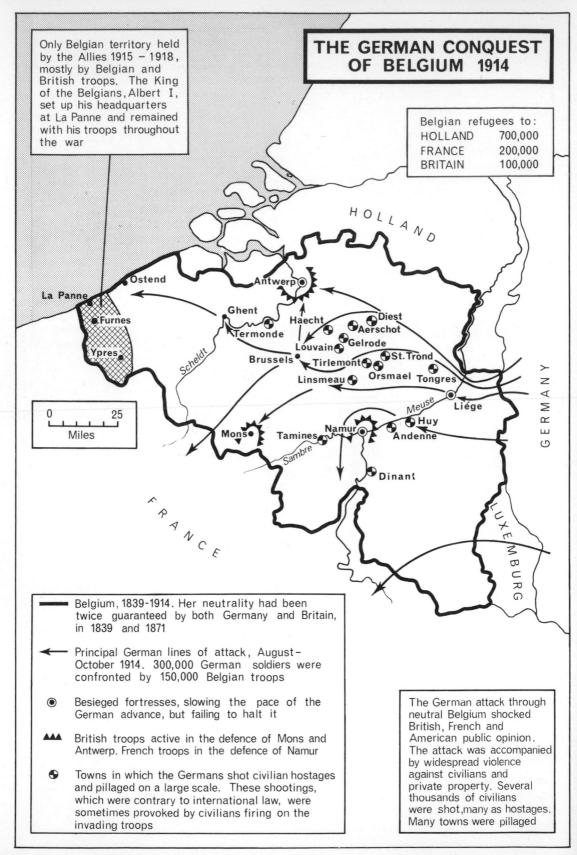

THE GERMAN CONQUEST OF BELGIUM 1914

Only Belgian territory held by the Allies 1915 – 1918, mostly by Belgian and British troops. The King of the Belgians, Albert I, set up his headquarters at La Panne and remained with his troops throughout the war

Belgian refugees to:
HOLLAND	700,000
FRANCE	200,000
BRITAIN	100,000

HOLLAND

La Panne
Ostend
Antwerp
Furnes
Ghent
Ypres
Termonde
Haecht
Diest
Aerschot
Gelrode
Louvain
St. Trond
Brussels
Tirlemont
Linsmeau
Orsmael
Tongres
Scheldt
Liége
Meuse
Huy
Mons
Tamines
Namur
Andenne
Sambre
Dinant

GERMANY

FRANCE

LUXEMBURG

0 ____ 25
Miles

Belgium, 1839-1914. Her neutrality had been twice guaranteed by both Germany and Britain, in 1839 and 1871

Principal German lines of attack, August– October 1914. 300,000 German soldiers were confronted by 150,000 Belgian troops

⊙ Besieged fortresses, slowing the pace of the German advance, but failing to halt it

▲▲▲ British troops active in the defence of Mons and Antwerp. French troops in the defence of Namur

⊕ Towns in which the Germans shot civilian hostages and pillaged on a large scale. These shootings, which were contrary to international law, were sometimes provoked by civilians firing on the invading troops

The German attack through neutral Belgium shocked British, French and American public opinion. The attack was accompanied by widespread violence against civilians and private property. Several thousands of civilians were shot, many as hostages. Many towns were pillaged

17

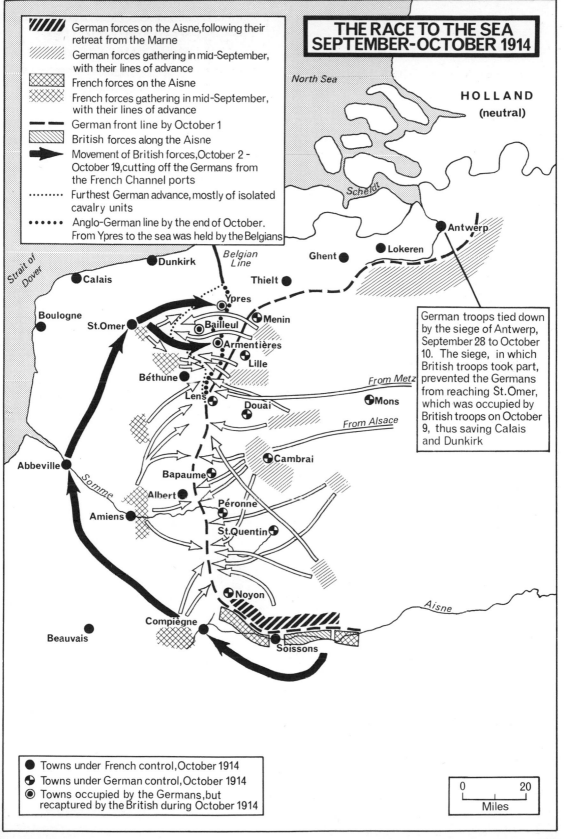

THE RACE TO THE SEA
SEPTEMBER-OCTOBER 1914

German forces on the Aisne, following their retreat from the Marne

German forces gathering in mid-September, with their lines of advance

French forces on the Aisne

French forces gathering in mid-September, with their lines of advance

German front line by October 1

British forces along the Aisne

Movement of British forces, October 2 - October 19, cutting off the Germans from the French Channel ports

Furthest German advance, mostly of isolated cavalry units

Anglo-German line by the end of October. From Ypres to the sea was held by the Belgians

North Sea

HOLLAND
(neutral)

Scheldt

Belgian Line

Antwerp

Ghent   Lokeren

Dunkirk

Thielt

Strait of Dover

Calais

Ypres

Menin

Boulogne

St.Omer

Bailleul

Armentières

Lille

Béthune

Lens

Douai

From Metz

Mons

From Alsace

Abbeville

Somme

Cambrai

Bapaume

Albert

Péronne

Amiens

St.Quentin

German troops tied down by the siege of Antwerp, September 28 to October 10. The siege, in which British troops took part, prevented the Germans from reaching St.Omer, which was occupied by British troops on October 9, thus saving Calais and Dunkirk

Noyon

Aisne

Compiègne

Beauvais

Soissons

Towns under French control, October 1914

Towns under German control, October 1914

Towns occupied by the Germans, but recaptured by the British during October 1914

0   20
Miles

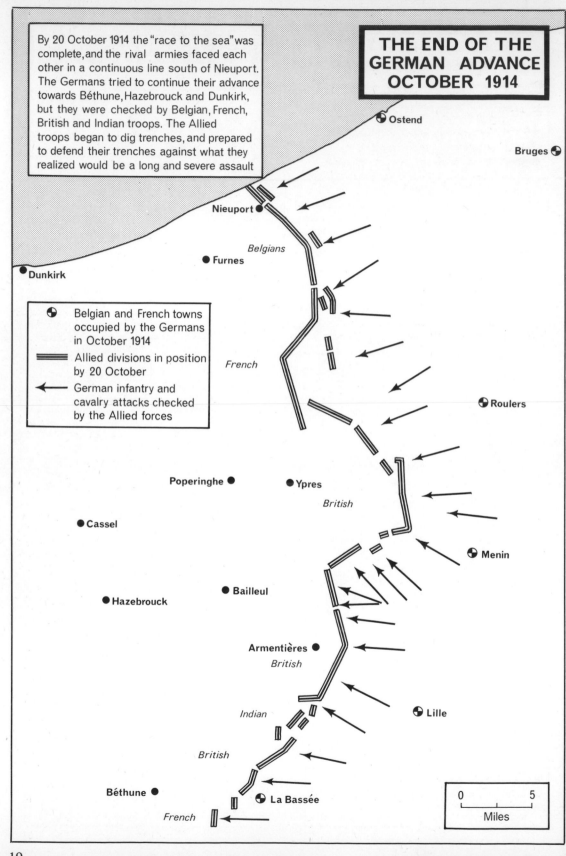

By 20 October 1914 the "race to the sea" was complete, and the rival armies faced each other in a continuous line south of Nieuport. The Germans tried to continue their advance towards Béthune, Hazebrouck and Dunkirk, but they were checked by Belgian, French, British and Indian troops. The Allied troops began to dig trenches, and prepared to defend their trenches against what they realized would be a long and severe assault

THE END OF THE GERMAN ADVANCE OCTOBER 1914

Ostend

Bruges

Nieuport

Belgians

Furnes

Dunkirk

⊕ Belgian and French towns occupied by the Germans in October 1914

▦ Allied divisions in position by 20 October

← German infantry and cavalry attacks checked by the Allied forces

French

Roulers

Poperinghe

Ypres

British

Cassel

Menin

Bailleul

Hazebrouck

Armentières
British

Lille

Indian

British

Béthune

La Bassée

French

```
0            5
|___|___|___|___|___|
      Miles
```

19

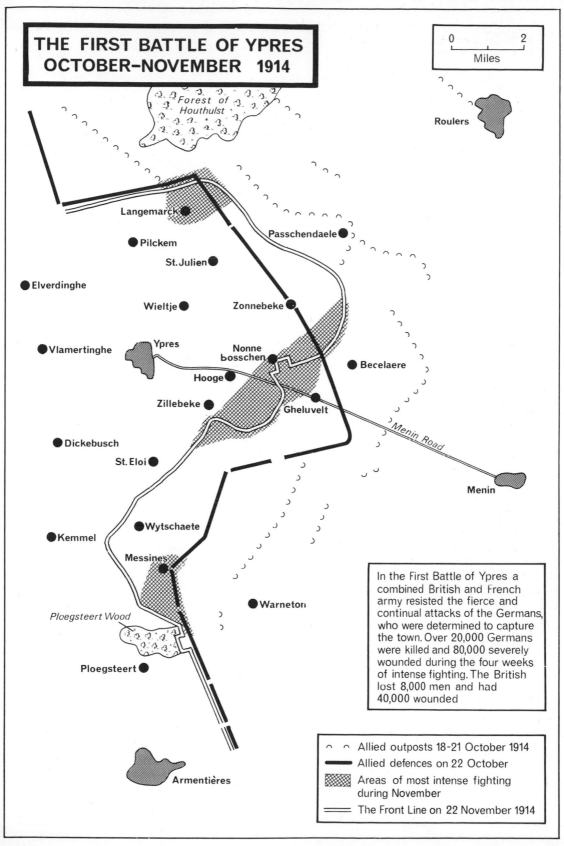

THE FIRST BATTLE OF YPRES OCTOBER–NOVEMBER 1914

0   2
Miles

Forest of Houthulst

Roulers

Langemarck

Pilckem

St. Julien

Passchendaele

Elverdinghe

Wieltje

Zonnebeke

Vlamertinghe

Ypres

Nonne bosschen

Becelaere

Hooge

Zillebeke

Gheluvelt

Menin Road

Dickebusch

St. Eloi

Menin

Wytschaete

Kemmel

Messines

Ploegsteert Wood

Warneton

Ploegsteert

Armentières

In the First Battle of Ypres a combined British and French army resisted the fierce and continual attacks of the Germans, who were determined to capture the town. Over 20,000 Germans were killed and 80,000 severely wounded during the four weeks of intense fighting. The British lost 8,000 men and had 40,000 wounded

⌒ ⌒   Allied outposts 18-21 October 1914

━━━   Allied defences on 22 October

▨   Areas of most intense fighting during November

═   The Front Line on 22 November 1914

20

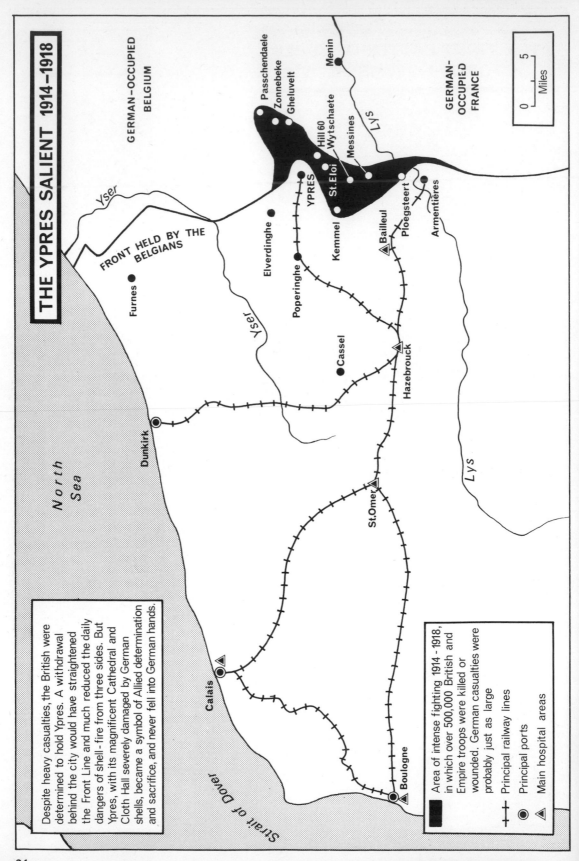

THE YPRES SALIENT 1914–1918

Despite heavy casualties, the British were determined to hold Ypres. A withdrawal behind the Front Line would have straightened the city would have reduced the daily dangers of shell-fire from three sides. But Ypres, with its magnificent Cathedral and Cloth Hall severely damaged by German shells, became a symbol of Allied determination and sacrifice, and never fell into German hands.

North Sea

GERMAN-OCCUPIED BELGIUM

Yser

FRONT HELD BY THE BELGIANS

Furnes

Elverdinghe

Passchendaele
Zonnebeke
Gheluvelt

Menin

Hill 60
Wytschaete

Messines

YPRES

St.Eloi

Lys

Kemmel

Bailleul

Ploegsteert

Armentières

Poperinghe

Yser

Cassel

Dunkirk

Hazebrouck

St.Omer

Calais

Boulogne

Strait of Dover

Lys

GERMAN-OCCUPIED FRANCE

Area of intense fighting 1914 - 1918, in which over 500,000 British and Empire troops were killed or wounded. German casualties were probably just as large

┼┼┼ Principal railway lines

◉ Principal ports

▲ Main hospital areas

0   5
Miles

21

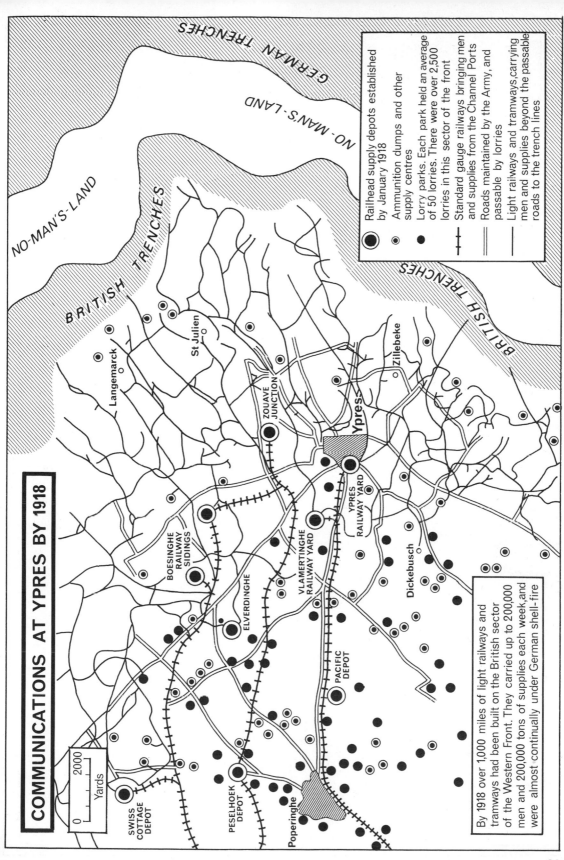

COMMUNICATIONS AT YPRES BY 1918

GERMAN TRENCHES

NO-MAN'S-LAND

NO-MAN'S-LAND

BRITISH TRENCHES

BRITISH TRENCHES

Langemarck

St Julien

ZOUAVE JUNCTION

Zillebeke

Ypres

YPRES RAILWAY YARD

BOESINGHE RAILWAY SIDINGS

ELVERDINGHE

VLAMERTINGHE RAILWAY YARD

Dickebusch

PACIFIC DEPOT

SWISS COTTAGE DEPOT

PESELHOEK DEPOT

Poperinghe

Railhead supply depots established by January 1918

Ammunition dumps and other supply centres

Lorry parks. Each park held an average of 50 lorries. There were over 2,500 lorries in this sector of the front

Standard gauge railways bringing men and supplies from the Channel Ports

Roads maintained by the Army, and passable by lorries

Light railways and tramways, carrying men and supplies beyond the passable roads to the trench lines

0   2000
Yards

By 1918 over 1,000 miles of light railways and tramways had been built on the British sector of the Western Front. They carried up to 200,000 men and 200,000 tons of supplies each week, and were almost continually under German shell-fire

22

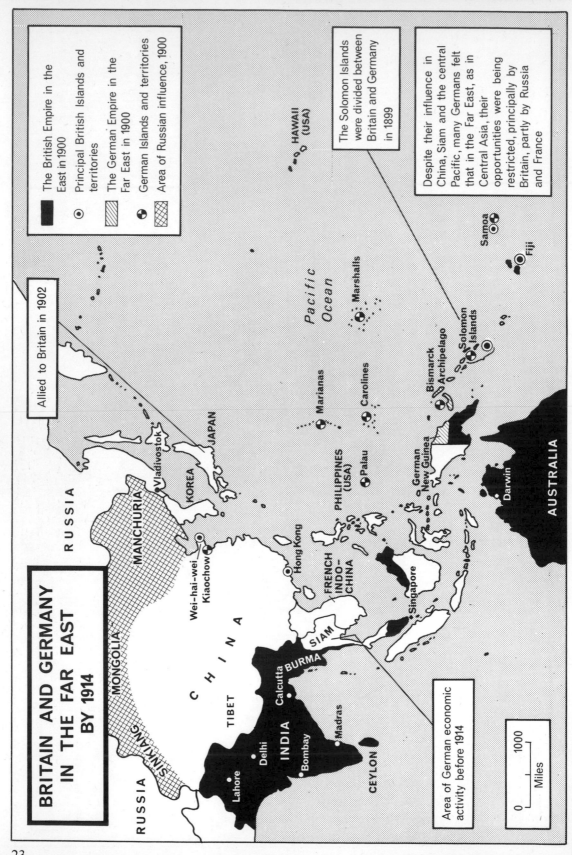

BRITAIN AND GERMANY IN THE FAR EAST BY 1914

Legend:

The British Empire in the East in 1900

Principal British Islands and territories

The German Empire in the Far East in 1900

German Islands and territories, 1900

Area of Russian influence, 1900

Allied to Britain in 1902

The Solomon Islands were divided between Britain and Germany in 1899

Despite their influence in China, Siam and the central Pacific, many Germans felt that in the Far East, as in Central Asia, their opportunities were being restricted, principally by Britain, partly by Russia and France

Area of German economic activity before 1914

0   1000
Miles

HAWAII (USA)

Samoa

Fiji

Marshalls

Pacific Ocean

Marianas

Carolines

Palau

Solomon Islands

Bismarck Archipelago

German New Guinea

Darwin

AUSTRALIA

PHILIPPINES (USA)

Singapore

Vladivostok

JAPAN

KOREA

Wei-hai-wei

Kiaochow

Hong Kong

FRENCH INDO-CHINA

SIAM

BURMA

CHINA

MANCHURIA

MONGOLIA

SINKIANG

TIBET

RUSSIA

RUSSIA

Lahore

Delhi

Bombay

Calcutta

Madras

INDIA

CEYLON

23

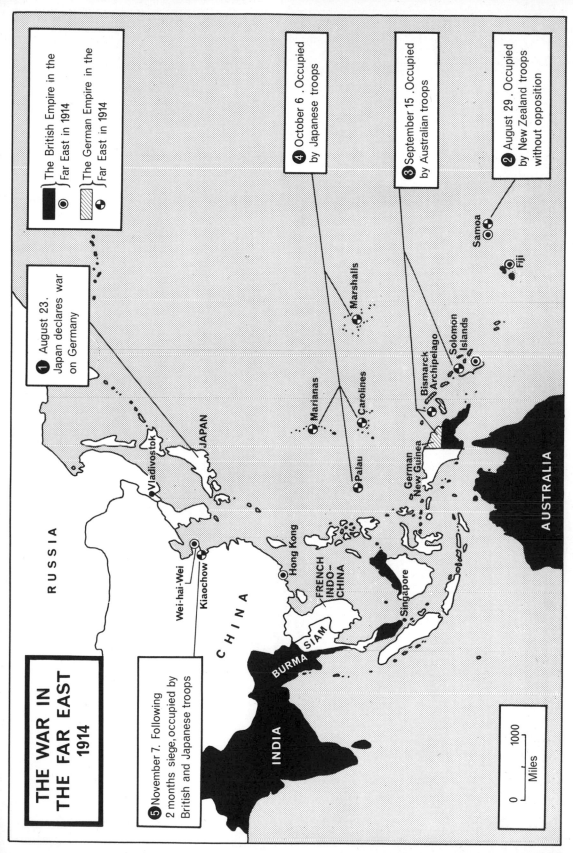

THE WAR IN
THE FAR EAST
1914

1 August 23.
Japan declares war
on Germany

5 November 7. Following
2 months siege, occupied by
British and Japanese troops

4 October 6 . Occupied
by Japanese troops

3 September 15. Occupied
by Australian troops

2 August 29 . Occupied
by New Zealand troops
without opposition

◉ | The British Empire in the
Far East in 1914

⊕ | The German Empire in the
Far East in 1914

RUSSIA

CHINA

INDIA

BURMA

SIAM

FRENCH
INDO–
CHINA

Singapore

Hong Kong

Wei-hai-Wei

Kiaochow

Vladivostok

JAPAN

Marianas

Palau

Carolines

Marshalls

German
New Guinea

Bismarck
Archipelago

Solomon
Islands

Fiji

Samoa

AUSTRALIA

0   1000
Miles

24

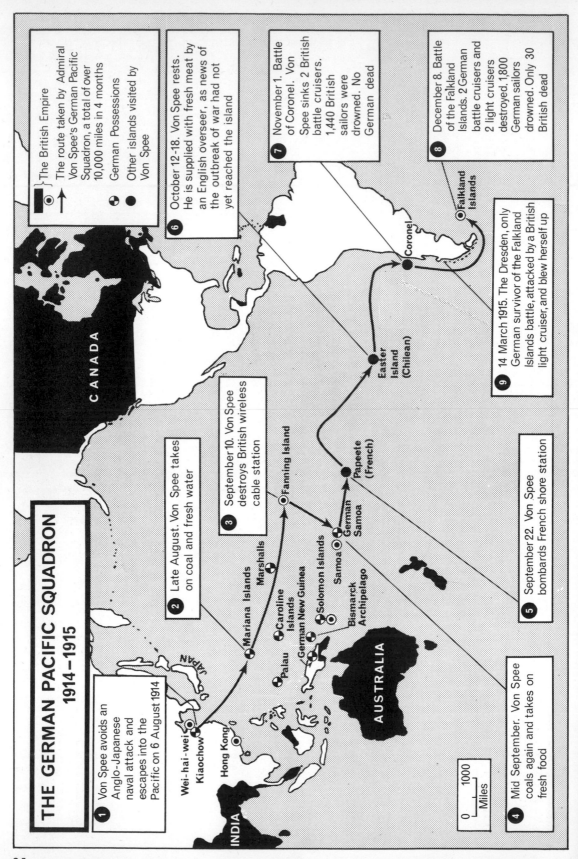

THE GERMAN PACIFIC SQUADRON
1914–1915

Legend:
- The British Empire
- The route taken by Admiral Von Spee's German Pacific Squadron, a total of over 10,000 miles in 4 months
- German Possessions
- Other islands visited by Von Spee

1 Von Spee avoids an Anglo-Japanese naval attack and escapes into the Pacific on 6 August 1914

2 Late August. Von Spee takes on coal and fresh water

3 September 10. Von Spee destroys British wireless cable station

4 Mid September. Von Spee coals again and takes on fresh food

5 September 22. Von Spee bombards French shore station

6 October 12–18. Von Spee rests. He is supplied with fresh meat by an English overseer, as news of the outbreak of war had not yet reached the island

7 November 1. Battle of Coronel. Von Spee sinks 2 British battle cruisers. 1,440 British sailors were drowned. No German dead

8 December 8. Battle of the Falkland Islands. 2 German battle cruisers and 2 light cruisers destroyed. 1,800 German sailors drowned. Only 30 British dead

9 14 March 1915. The Dresden, only German survivor of the Falkland Islands battle, attacked by a British light cruiser, and blew herself up

Map labels: CANADA, JAPAN, INDIA, AUSTRALIA, Wei-hai-wei, Kiaochow, Hong Kong, Mariana Islands, Marshalls, Palau, Caroline Islands, German New Guinea, Solomon Islands, Bismarck Archipelago, Samoa, German Samoa, Fanning Island, Papeete (French), Easter Island (Chilean), Coronel, Falkland Islands

Scale: 0 — 1000 Miles

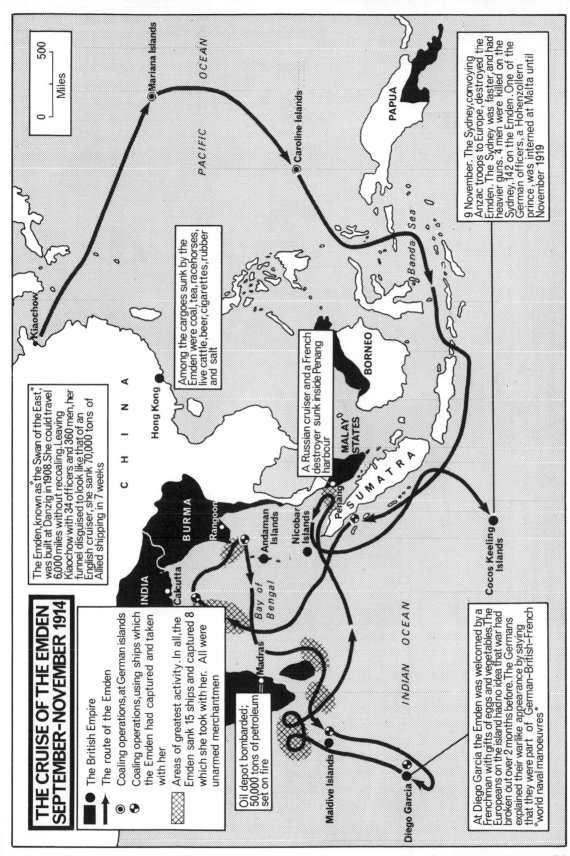

THE CRUISE OF THE EMDEN
SEPTEMBER–NOVEMBER 1914

● The British Empire

↑ The route of the Emden

◉ Coaling operations, at German islands

◔ Coaling operations, using ships which the Emden had captured and taken with her

▨ Areas of greatest activity. In all, the Emden sank 15 ships and captured 8 which she took with her. All were unarmed merchantmen

The Emden, known as the "Swan of the East", was built at Danzig in 1908. She could travel 6,000 miles without recoaling. Leaving Kiaochow with 34 officers and 360 men, her funnel disguised to look like that of an English cruiser, she sank 70,000 tons of Allied shipping in 7 weeks

Among the cargoes sunk by the Emden were coal, tea, racehorses, live cattle, beer, cigarettes, rubber and salt

A Russian cruiser and a French destroyer sunk inside Penang harbour

9 November. The Sydney, convoying Anzac troops to Europe, destroyed the Emden. The Sydney was faster, and had heavier guns. 4 men were killed on the Sydney, 142 on the Emden. One of the German officers, a Hohenzollern prince, was interned at Malta until November 1919

Oil depot bombarded; 50,000 tons of petroleum set on fire

At Diego Garcia the Emden was welcomed by a Frenchman with gifts of eggs and vegetables. The Europeans on the island had no idea that war had broken out over 2 months before. The Germans explained their warlike appearance by saying that they were part of "German–British–French world naval manoeuvres"

0 _____ 500
Miles

PACIFIC OCEAN

Mariana Islands

Caroline Islands

PAPUA

Banda Sea

Kiaochow

CHINA

Hong Kong

BURMA

Rangoon

INDIA

Calcutta

Bay of Bengal

Madras

Andaman Islands

Nicobar Islands

Penang

SUMATRA

MALAY STATES

BORNEO

Maldive Islands

Diego Garcia

Cocos Keeling Islands

INDIAN OCEAN

26

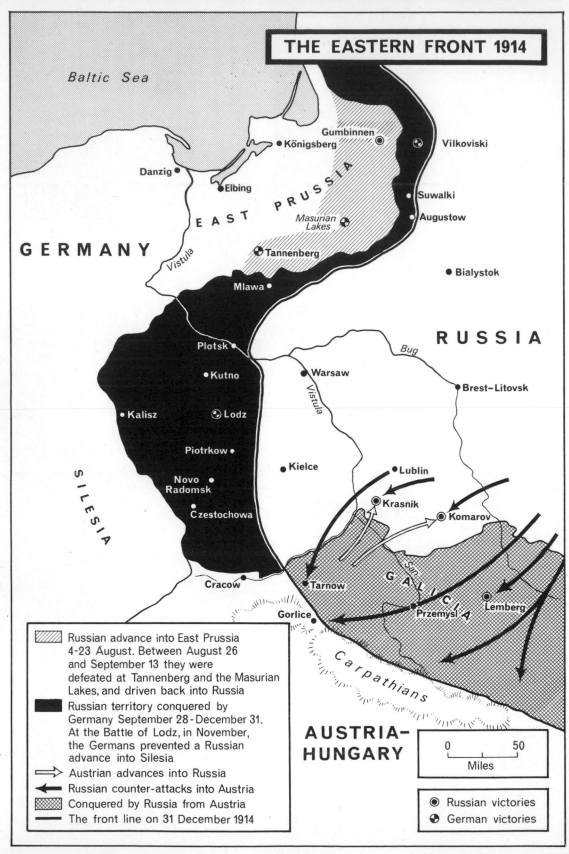

THE EASTERN FRONT 1914

Baltic Sea

GERMANY

EAST PRUSSIA

- Danzig
- Königsberg
- Gumbinnen ⊙
- Vilkoviski ⊕
- Elbing
- Suwalki
- Augustow
- *Masurian Lakes* ⊕
- Tannenberg ⊕
- Mlawa
- Bialystok

Vistula

RUSSIA

Bug

- Plotsk
- Kutno
- Warsaw
- Brest–Litovsk
- Kalisz
- Lodz ⊙
- *Vistula*
- Piotrkow
- Novo Radomsk
- Kielce
- Czestochowa
- Lublin
- Krasnik ⊙
- Komarov ⊙

SILESIA

- Cracow
- Tarnow
- Gorlice
- Przemysl
- Lemberg ⊙

G A L I C I A

San

Carpathians

AUSTRIA-
HUNGARY

0   50
Miles

	Russian advance into East Prussia 4-23 August. Between August 26 and September 13 they were defeated at Tannenberg and the Masurian Lakes, and driven back into Russia
▉	Russian territory conquered by Germany September 28 - December 31. At the Battle of Lodz, in November, the Germans prevented a Russian advance into Silesia
⇨	Austrian advances into Russia
←	Russian counter-attacks into Austria
▨	Conquered by Russia from Austria
──	The front line on 31 December 1914

⊙ Russian victories
⊕ German victories

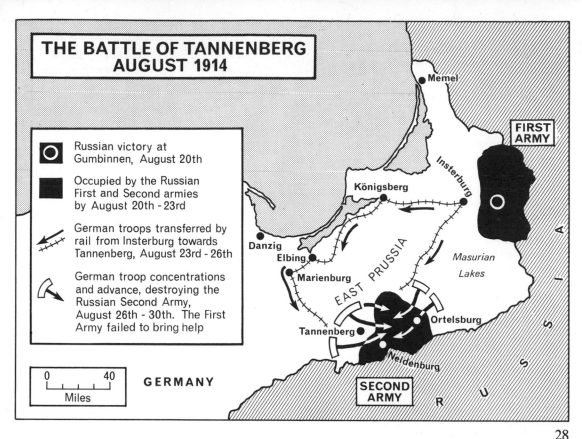

THE BATTLE OF TANNENBERG AUGUST 1914

Legend:

◎ Russian victory at Gumbinnen, August 20th

■ Occupied by the Russian First and Second armies by August 20th - 23rd

↞ German troops transferred by rail from Insterburg towards Tannenberg, August 23rd - 26th

↱ German troop concentrations and advance, destroying the Russian Second Army, August 26th - 30th. The First Army failed to bring help

0 — 40 Miles

GERMANY

Memel

FIRST ARMY

Insterburg

Königsberg

Danzig

Elbing

Marienburg

EAST PRUSSIA

Masurian Lakes

Tannenberg

Ortelsburg

Neidenburg

SECOND ARMY

R U S S I A

28

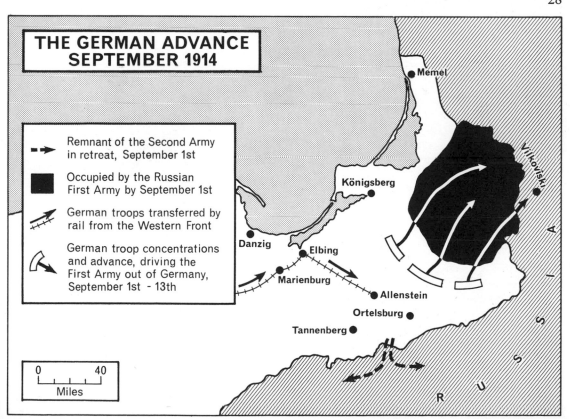

THE GERMAN ADVANCE SEPTEMBER 1914

Legend:

⇢ Remnant of the Second Army in retreat, September 1st

■ Occupied by the Russian First Army by September 1st

↠ German troops transferred by rail from the Western Front

↱ German troop concentrations and advance, driving the First Army out of Germany, September 1st - 13th

0 — 40 Miles

Memel

Königsberg

Vilkoviski

Danzig

Elbing

Marienburg

Allenstein

Ortelsburg

Tannenberg

R U S S I A

29

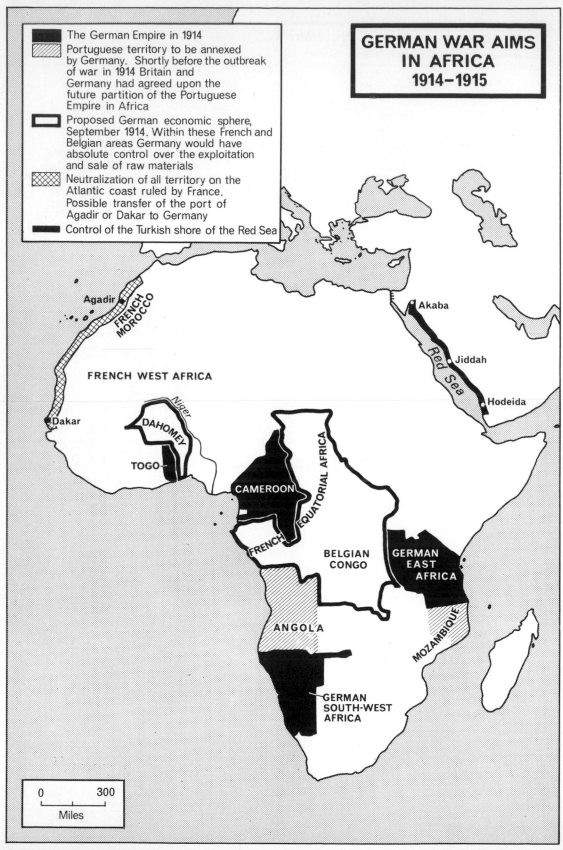

GERMAN WAR AIMS IN AFRICA 1914–1915

The German Empire in 1914

Portuguese territory to be annexed by Germany. Shortly before the outbreak of war in 1914 Britain and Germany had agreed upon the future partition of the Portuguese Empire in Africa

Proposed German economic sphere, September 1914. Within these French and Belgian areas Germany would have absolute control over the exploitation and sale of raw materials

Neutralization of all territory on the Atlantic coast ruled by France. Possible transfer of the port of Agadir or Dakar to Germany

Control of the Turkish shore of the Red Sea

Agadir

FRENCH MOROCCO

Akaba

Red Sea

Jiddah

Hodeida

FRENCH WEST AFRICA

Niger

Dakar

DAHOMEY

TOGO

CAMEROON

FRENCH EQUATORIAL AFRICA

BELGIAN CONGO

GERMAN EAST AFRICA

ANGOLA

MOZAMBIQUE

GERMAN SOUTH-WEST AFRICA

0   300

Miles

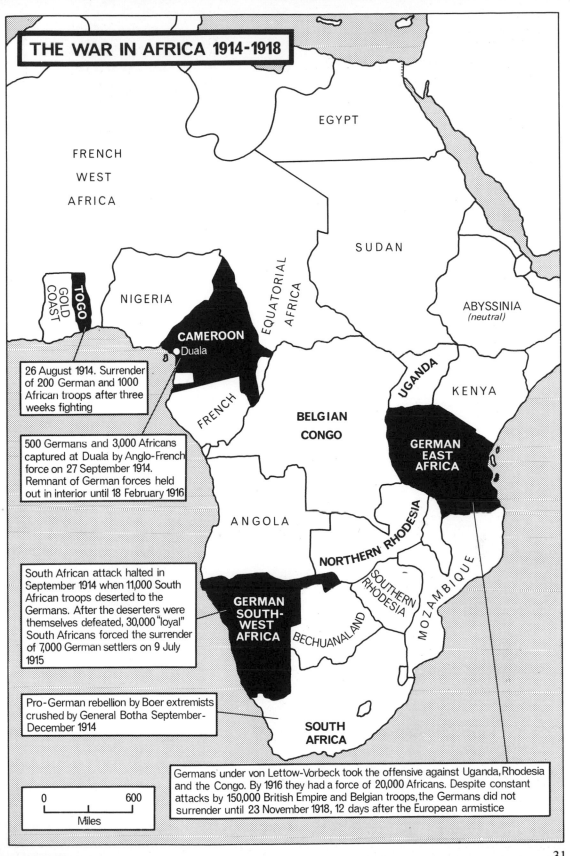

THE WAR IN AFRICA 1914-1918

EGYPT

FRENCH

WEST

AFRICA

SUDAN

GOLD COAST

TOGO

NIGERIA

EQUATORIAL AFRICA

ABYSSINIA
(neutral)

CAMEROON
●Duala

FRENCH

UGANDA

KENYA

BELGIAN
CONGO

GERMAN
EAST
AFRICA

26 August 1914. Surrender
of 200 German and 1000
African troops after three
weeks fighting

500 Germans and 3,000 Africans
captured at Duala by Anglo-French
force on 27 September 1914.
Remnant of German forces held
out in interior until 18 February 1916

ANGOLA

NORTHERN RHODESIA

SOUTHERN RHODESIA

MOZAMBIQUE

South African attack halted in
September 1914 when 11,000 South
African troops deserted to the
Germans. After the deserters were
themselves defeated, 30,000 "loyal"
South Africans forced the surrender
of 7,000 German settlers on 9 July
1915

GERMAN
SOUTH-
WEST
AFRICA

BECHUANALAND

Pro-German rebellion by Boer extremists
crushed by General Botha September-
December 1914

SOUTH
AFRICA

0   600
Miles

Germans under von Lettow-Vorbeck took the offensive against Uganda, Rhodesia
and the Congo. By 1916 they had a force of 20,000 Africans. Despite constant
attacks by 150,000 British Empire and Belgian troops, the Germans did not
surrender until 23 November 1918, 12 days after the European armistice

Section Three

1915

A hundred thousand million mites we go
Wheeling and tacking o'er the eternal plain,
Some black with death—and some are white with woe.
Who sent us forth? Who takes us home again?

And there is sound of hymns of praise—to whom?
And curses—on whom curses?—snap the air.
And there is hope goes hand in hand with gloom,
And blood and indignation and despair. . . .

    CHARLES SORLEY
    "A HUNDRED THOUSAND MILLION MITES WE GO"

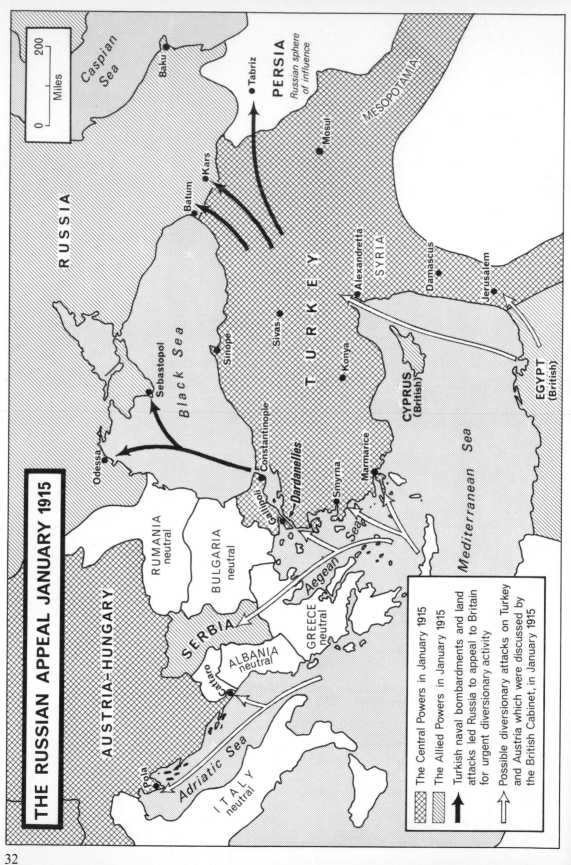

THE RUSSIAN APPEAL JANUARY 1915

200

Miles

0

Caspian Sea

Baku

PERSIA

Russian sphere of influence

Tabriz

MESOPOTAMIA

Mosul

RUSSIA

Kars

Batum

SYRIA

Alexandretta

Damascus

Jerusalem

Sivas

Konya

CYPRUS (British)

EGYPT (British)

Sebastopol

Black Sea

Sinope

Odessa

Constantinople

Dardanelles

TURKEY

Smyrna

Marmarice

Mediterranean Sea

Gallipoli

Aegean Sea

RUMANIA
neutral

BULGARIA
neutral

GREECE
neutral

SERBIA

ALBANIA
neutral

AUSTRIA–HUNGARY

Cattaro

Adriatic Sea

Pola

ITALY
neutral

The Central Powers in January 1915

The Allied Powers in January 1915

Turkish naval bombardments and land attacks led Russia to appeal to Britain for urgent diversionary activity

Possible diversionary attacks on Turkey and Austria which were discussed by the British Cabinet, in January 1915

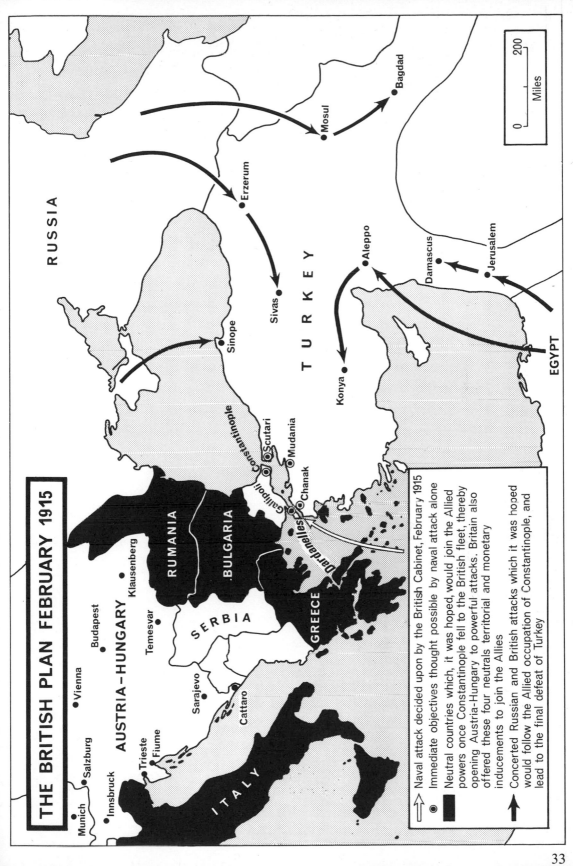

THE BRITISH PLAN FEBRUARY 1915

RUSSIA

TURKEY

AUSTRIA–HUNGARY

ITALY

SERBIA

RUMANIA

BULGARIA

GREECE

EGYPT

Munich
Salzburg
Innsbruck
Vienna
Budapest
Klausenberg
Temesvar
Trieste
Fiume
Sarajevo
Cattaro

Constantinople
Scutari
Mudania
Chanak
Gallipoli
Dardanelles

Sinope
Sivas
Erzerum
Mosul
Bagdad
Konya
Aleppo
Damascus
Jerusalem

0   200
Miles

Naval attack decided upon by the British Cabinet, February 1915

Immediate objectives thought possible by naval attack alone

Neutral countries which, it was hoped, would join the Allied powers once Constantinople fell to the British fleet, thereby opening Austria–Hungary to powerful attacks. Britain also offered these four neutrals territorial and monetary inducements to join the Allies

Concerted Russian and British attacks which it was hoped would follow the Allied occupation of Constantinople, and lead to the final defeat of Turkey

33

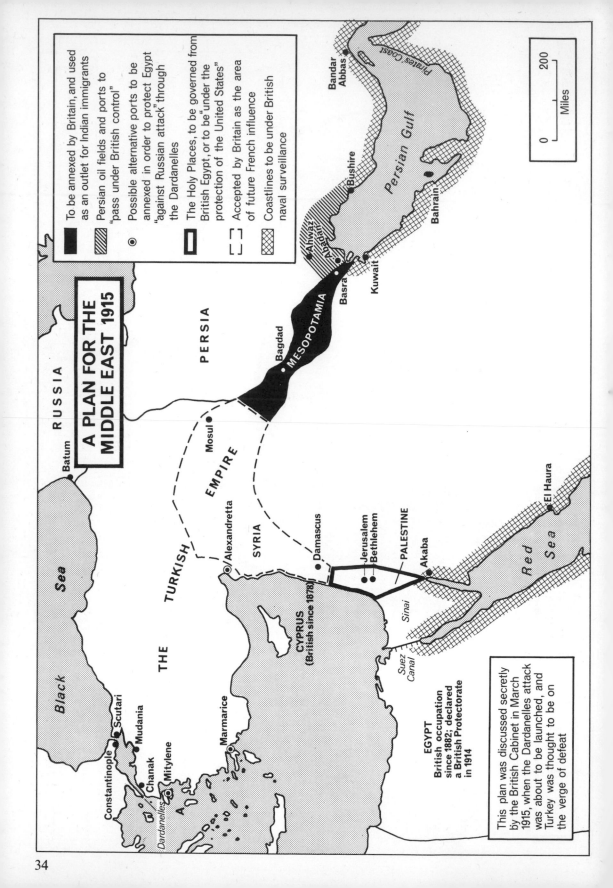

A PLAN FOR THE MIDDLE EAST 1915

Legend:

- ■ To be annexed by Britain, and used as an outlet for Indian immigrants
- ▨ Persian oil fields and ports to "pass under British control"
- ⊙ Possible alternative ports to be annexed in order to protect Egypt "against Russian attack" through the Dardanelles
- ▭ The Holy Places, to be governed from British Egypt, or to be "under the protection of the United States"
- ⊏⊐ Accepted by Britain as the area of future French influence
- ▨ Coastlines to be under British naval surveillance

0   200
Miles

RUSSIA

Batum

PERSIA

Mosul

THE TURKISH EMPIRE

Black Sea

Constantinople
Scutari
Mudania
Chanak
Mitylene
Dardanelles
Marmarice

SYRIA

Alexandretta

Damascus

Jerusalem
Bethlehem
PALESTINE
Akaba

CYPRUS
(British since 1878)

Sinai

Suez Canal

Red Sea

El Haura

EGYPT
British occupation since 1882; declared a British Protectorate in 1914

Bagdad

MESOPOTAMIA

Basra

Kuwait

Ahwaz
Abadan

Bushire

Bahrain

Bandar Abbas

Persian Gulf

Pirates' Coast

This plan was discussed secretly by the British Cabinet in March 1915, when the Dardanelles attack was about to be launched, and Turkey was thought to be on the verge of defeat

34

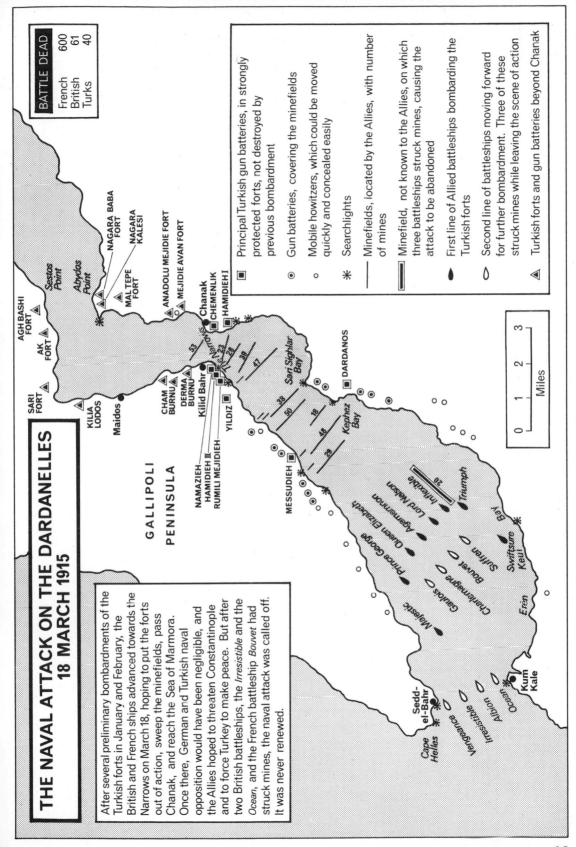

THE NAVAL ATTACK ON THE DARDANELLES 18 MARCH 1915

After several preliminary bombardments of the Turkish forts in January and February, the British and French ships advanced towards the Narrows on March 18, hoping to put the forts out of action, sweep the minefields, pass Chanak, and reach the Sea of Marmora. Once there, German and Turkish naval opposition would have been negligible, and the Allies hoped to threaten Constantinople and to force Turkey to make peace. But after two British battleships, the *Irresistible* and the *Ocean*, and the French battleship *Bouvet* had struck mines, the naval attack was called off. It was never renewed.

BATTLE DEAD	
French	600
British	61
Turks	40

Principal Turkish gun batteries, in strongly protected forts, not destroyed by previous bombardment

Gun batteries, covering the minefields

Mobile howitzers, which could be moved quickly and concealed easily

Searchlights

Minefields, located by the Allies, with number of mines

Minefield, not known to the Allies, on which three battleships struck mines, causing the attack to be abandoned

First line of Allied battleships bombarding the Turkish forts

Second line of battleships moving forward for further bombardment. Three of these struck mines while leaving the scene of action

Turkish forts and gun batteries beyond Chanak

GALLIPOLI PENINSULA

Miles
0   1   2   3

NAGARA BABA FORT
NAGARA KALESI
MAL TEPE FORT
ANADOLU MEJIDIE FORT
MEJIDIE AVAN FORT
Sestos Point
Abydos Point

AGH BASHI FORT
AK FORT
SARI FORT
KILIA LODOS
Maidos

Chanak
CHEMENLIK
HAMIDIEH I
The Narrows
CHAM BURNU
DERMA BURNU
Kilid Bahr
YILDIZ
NAMAZIEH
HAMIDIEH II
RUMILI MEJIDIEH

Sari Sighlar Bay
DARDANOS
Kephez Bay
MESSUDIEH

Majestic
Vengeance
Irresistible
Albion
Ocean
Cape Helles
Sedd-el-Bahr

Prince George
Gaulois
Charlemagne
Bouvet
Suffren
Queen Elizabeth
Agamemnon
Lord Nelson
Inflexible
Triumph

Swiftsure
Keul
Eren Bey
Kum Kale

35

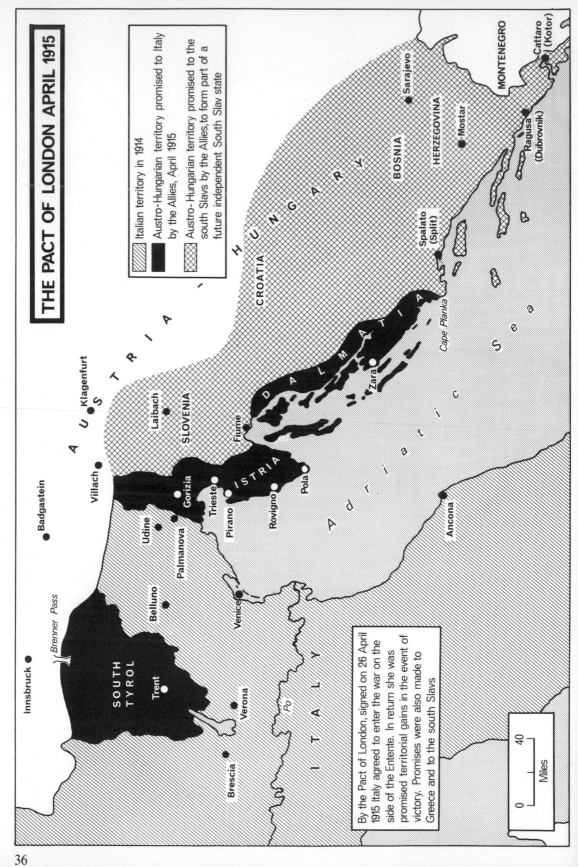

THE PACT OF LONDON APRIL 1915

Italian territory in 1914

Austro-Hungarian territory promised to Italy by the Allies, April 1915

Austro-Hungarian territory promised to the south Slavs by the Allies, to form part of a future independent South Slav state

MONTENEGRO

Cattaro (Kotor)

Sarajevo

BOSNIA

HERZEGOVINA

Mostar

Ragusa (Dubrovnik)

A U S T R I A - H U N G A R Y

CROATIA

DALMATIA

Spalato (Split)

Cape Planka

Klagenfurt

Laibach

SLOVENIA

Fiume

Zara

Villach

Badgastein

Gorizia

Trieste

ISTRIA

Pirano

Pola

Rovigno

A d r i a t i c   S e a

Udine

Palmanova

Ancona

Innsbruck

Brenner Pass

Belluno

Venice

SOUTH TYROL

Trent

Po

Verona

I T A L Y

Brescia

By the Pact of London, signed on 26 April 1915 Italy agreed to enter the war on the side of the Entente. In return she was promised territorial gains in the event of victory. Promises were also made to Greece and to the south Slavs

0   40

Miles

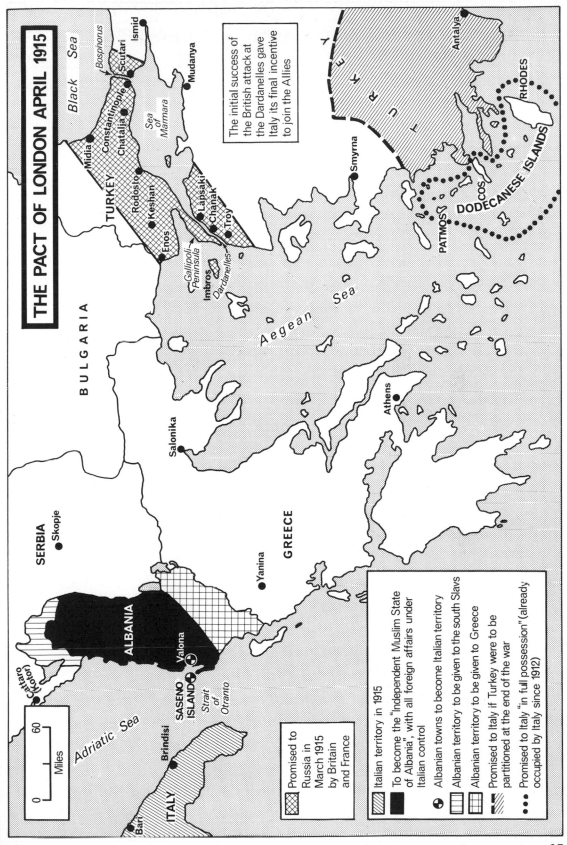

THE PACT OF LONDON APRIL 1915

The initial success of the British attack at the Dardanelles gave Italy its final incentive to join the Allies

Black Sea

Bosphorus

Ismid

Scutari

Mudanya

TURKEY

Constantinople

Chatalja

Midia

Sea of Marmara

Rodosto

Keshan

Enos

Lapsaki

Chanak

Troy

Gallipoli Peninsula

Imbros

Dardanelles

Aegean Sea

Smyrna

Antalya

RHODES

DODECANESE ISLANDS

PATMOS

COS

BULGARIA

SERBIA

Skopje

GREECE

Yanina

Salonika

Athens

ALBANIA

Valona

SASENO ISLAND

Strait of Otranto

Cattaro (Kotor)

Adriatic Sea

Brindisi

Bari

ITALY

Miles
0 60

Legend

	Italian territory in 1915
	To become the "Independent Muslim State of Albania", with all foreign affairs under Italian control
	Albanian towns to become Italian territory
	Albanian territory to be given to the south Slavs
	Albanian territory to be given to Greece
	Promised to Italy if Turkey were to be partitioned at the end of the war
••••	Promised to Italy "in full possession"(already occupied by Italy since 1912)

Promised to Russia in March 1915 by Britain and France

37

THE MILITARY LANDINGS ON THE GALLIPOLI PENINSULA APRIL AND AUGUST 1915

Kiretch Tepe

Tekke Tepe

Suvla Point

Anafarta Sagir

Suvla Bay

Biyuk Anafarta

Salt Lake (dry in summer)

Nibrunesi Point

Lala Baba

Hill 60

Sari Bair Ridge

Chunuk Bair 850 ft

Koja Chemen Tepe 971 ft

Ocean Beach

Ari Burnu

Anzac Cove

Hell Spit

Boghali

Mal Tepe 534 ft

Brighton Beach

Gaba Tepe

Maidos

Kilid Bahr Plateau

Kilid Bahr

Chanak

The Narrows

After the failure of the naval attack of 18 March 1915, Allied troops landed on 25 April, hoping to capture the high ground of Achi Baba and Sari Bair, and to reach the shore of the Narrows. But a tenacious Turkish defence kept them pinned down to their tiny beachheads. A second landing on 6 August likewise failed to reach the Narrows. After more than eight months of heroism, frustration, muddle, incompetence, disease and death, the Allied armies withdrew in January 1916 and the enterprise was abandoned. The Turkish successes both in April and August owed much to the military genius of Mustafa Kemal, later, as Atatürk, President of Turkey

The two areas on the Gallipoli Peninsula held by Allied troops were known as 'Helles' (after the Cape) and 'Anzac' (after the colloquial Australian name for the Australian and New Zealand Army Corps, or Anzacs, who took a leading part in the northern landings

ESTIMATED BATTLE DEAD

Turkish	100,000
Allied	46,000

Achi Baba 709 ft

Krithia

Gully Ravine

Kereves Dere

Tekke Burnu

Sedd-el-Bahr

Morto Bay

Cape Helles

● Landing beaches at 'Helles' on April 25

◉ Landing beaches at 'Anzac' on April 25

〰〰 Objectives for April 25, not reached in 8 months of fighting

▨ Ground held at 'Helles' from May 1915 until the evacuation in January 1916

▨ Ground held at 'Anzac' from May 1915 until August 1915

△ Landing beaches at Suvla on August 6

▥ Ground held until evacuated in December

▨ Ground gained at 'Anzac' and 'Suvla' in August 1915 and held until the evacuation in January 1916

▲▲▲ Furthest advance in August, held only for a few hours, when the Turks counter-attacked successfully and drove the Allied troops off the crest of Chunuk Bair

0	1	2

Miles

ALLIED TRENCHES ON GALLIPOLI THE 'HELLES' FRONT IN JULY 1915

Aegean Sea

Fusilier Bluff

Gully Ravine

Ghurka Mule Track

Western Birdcage

Forward Inch

Eastern Birdcage

Eastern Mule Trench

Holborn Circus

Lancashire St

Chelmsford St

Rue de Paris

Munster Terrace

Worcester Barricade

Leith Walk

Princes St

Clapham Junction

No 1 Australian Line

No 2 Australian Line

Oldham Rd.

Ardwick Gn

Wigan Road

Hope St

KRITHIA VILLAGE

The Vineyard

Sauchiehall Street

Oxford Street

Plymouth Ave

Nelson Ave

Main Street

Piccadilly Circus

Central St.

Leicester Square

Park Lane

Regent St

Hyde Park Corner

Avenue de Paris

Avenue de Constantinople

Esplanade

The Haricot

Boyau Central

Withered Tree

N

Dardanelles

0   500
Yards

- - - - Turkish Front Line
〰〰〰 } Allied trenches
⊙ Dressing stations and first aid post

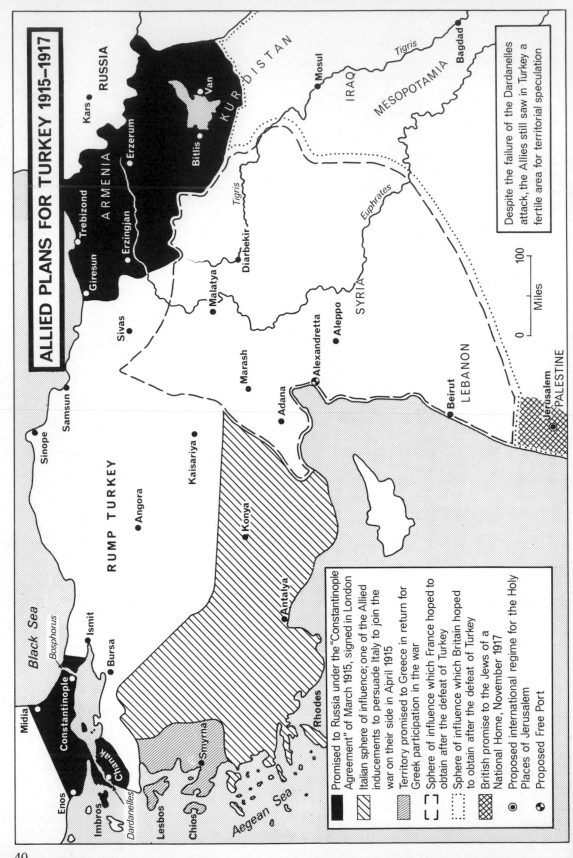

ALLIED PLANS FOR TURKEY 1915–1917

Despite the failure of the Dardanelles attack, the Allies still saw in Turkey a fertile area for territorial speculation

RUSSIA

Kars •
Van ▲
Erzerum ●
Erzingian ●
Bitlis •
ARMENIA
Trebizond ●
Giresun ●

K U R D I S T A N

Mosul •
Bagdad ●
IRAQ
Tigris
MESOPOTAMIA

Diarbekir •
Tigris
Euphrates
Malatya •

Sivas •
Marash •
Adana •
Alexandretta ●
Aleppo •
SYRIA

Beirut ●
LEBANON
Jerusalem ●
PALESTINE

Samsun •
Sinope •

RUMP TURKEY
Angora •
Kaisariya •
Konya ●

Black Sea
Bosphorus
Ismit •
Bursa •
Midia ○
Constantinople
Chanak ○
Dardanelles
Enos ○
Imbros
Lesbos
Chios
Smyrna ●
Rhodes
Aegean Sea

Antalya ●

0   100
Miles

Promised to Russia under the "Constantinople Agreement" of March 1915, signed in London

Italian sphere of influence; one of the Allied inducements to persuade Italy to join the war on their side in April 1915

Territory promised to Greece in return for Greek participation in the war

Sphere of influence which France hoped to obtain after the defeat of Turkey

Sphere of influence which Britain hoped to obtain after the defeat of Turkey

British promise to the Jews of a National Home, November 1917

Proposed international regime for the Holy Places of Jerusalem

Proposed Free Port

40

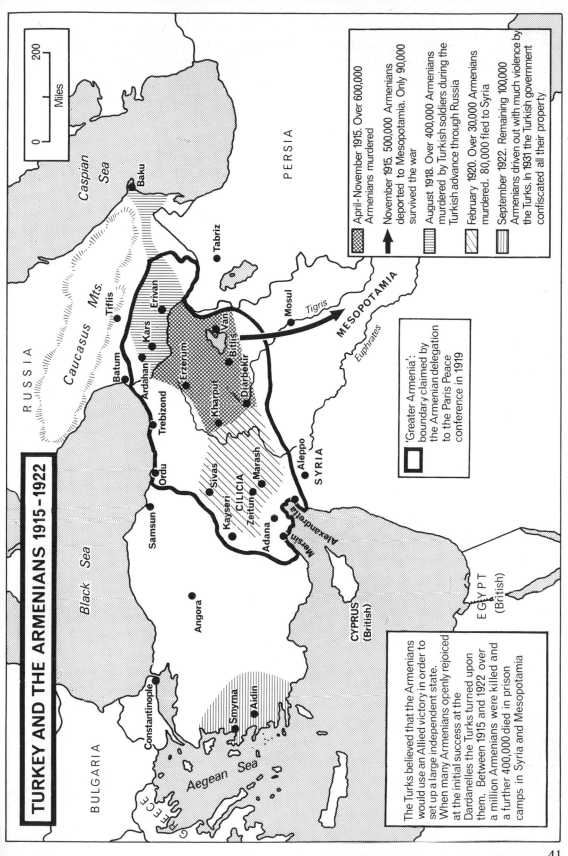

TURKEY AND THE ARMENIANS 1915-1922

Scale: 0 – 200 Miles

Caspian Sea

Baku

PERSIA

Tabriz

RUSSIA

Caucasus Mts.

Tiflis
Erivan
Kars
Ardahan
Batum
Trebizond
Ordu
Samsun

Erzerum
Van
Bitlis
Djarbekir
Kharput

Mosul
Tigris
MESOPOTAMIA
Euphrates

Aleppo
SYRIA

Sivas
Kayseri
Zeitun
Marash
CILICIA
Adana
Mersin
Alexandretta

Black Sea

Angora

Constantinople

Smyrna
Aidin

Aegean Sea

GREECE

BULGARIA

CYPRUS (British)

EGYPT (British)

Legend (top right box):

April–November 1915. Over 600,000 Armenians murdered

November 1915. 500,000 Armenians deported to Mesopotamia. Only 90,000 survived the war

August 1918. Over 400,000 Armenians murdered by Turkish soldiers during the Turkish advance through Russia

February 1920. Over 30,000 Armenians murdered. 80,000 fled to Syria

September 1922. Remaining 100,000 Armenians driven out with much violence by the Turks. In 1931 the Turkish government confiscated all their property

(Right box):

'Greater Armenia': boundary claimed by the Armenian delegation to the Paris Peace conference in 1919

(Bottom box):

The Turks believed that the Armenians would use an Allied victory in order to set up a large independent state. When many Armenians openly rejoiced at the initial success at the Dardanelles the Turks turned upon them. Between 1915 and 1922 over a million Armenians were killed and a further 400,000 died in prison camps in Syria and Mesopotamia

41

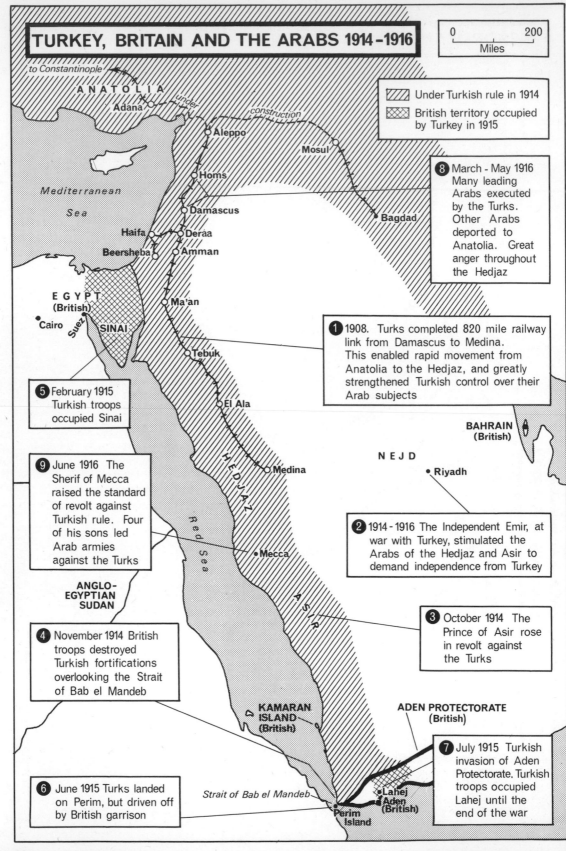

TURKEY, BRITAIN AND THE ARABS 1914-1916

0   200
Miles

to Constantinople

A N A T O L I A

Adana

under

construction

Aleppo

Mosul

Homs

Mediterranean Sea

Damascus

Haifa

Deraa

Beersheba

Amman

Bagdad

E G Y P T (British)

Cairo

SINAI

Suez

Ma'an

Tebuk

El Ala

H E D J A Z

Red Sea

Medina

Mecca

ANGLO-EGYPTIAN SUDAN

A S I R

N E J D

Riyadh

BAHRAIN (British)

KAMARAN ISLAND (British)

ADEN PROTECTORATE (British)

Strait of Bab el Mandeb

Perim Island

Lahej
Aden (British)

☒ Under Turkish rule in 1914

☒ British territory occupied by Turkey in 1915

8 March - May 1916 Many leading Arabs executed by the Turks. Other Arabs deported to Anatolia. Great anger throughout the Hedjaz

1 1908. Turks completed 820 mile railway link from Damascus to Medina. This enabled rapid movement from Anatolia to the Hedjaz, and greatly strengthened Turkish control over their Arab subjects

5 February 1915 Turkish troops occupied Sinai

9 June 1916 The Sherif of Mecca raised the standard of revolt against Turkish rule. Four of his sons led Arab armies against the Turks

2 1914 - 1916 The Independent Emir, at war with Turkey, stimulated the Arabs of the Hedjaz and Asir to demand independence from Turkey

4 November 1914 British troops destroyed Turkish fortifications overlooking the Strait of Bab el Mandeb

3 October 1914 The Prince of Asir rose in revolt against the Turks

7 July 1915 Turkish invasion of Aden Protectorate. Turkish troops occupied Lahej until the end of the war

6 June 1915 Turks landed on Perim, but driven off by British garrison

42

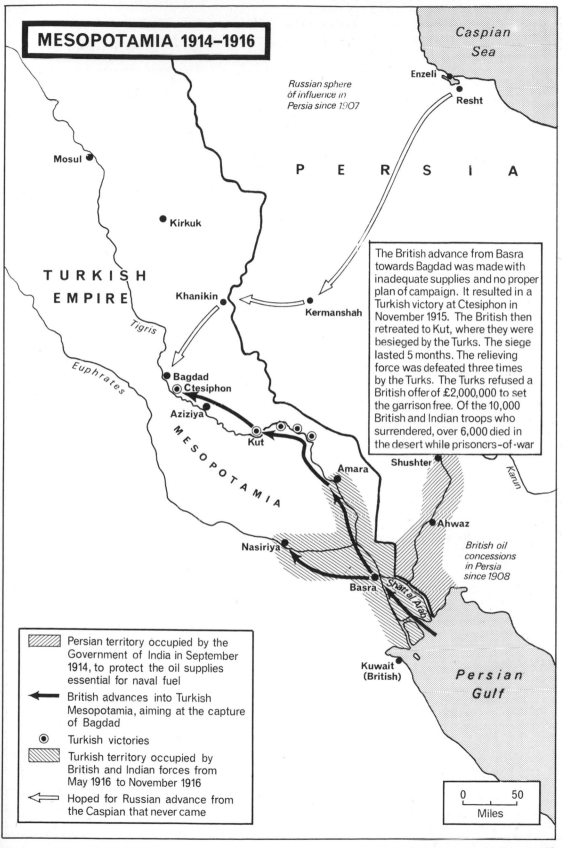

MESOPOTAMIA 1914–1916

Caspian Sea

Enzeli

Resht

Russian sphere of influence in Persia since 1907

P E R S I A

Mosul

Kirkuk

TURKISH EMPIRE

Khanikin

Kermanshah

Tigris

Euphrates

Bagdad
Ctesiphon

Aziziya

M E S O P O T A M I A

Kut

Amara

Shushter

Karun

Nasiriya

Ahwaz

British oil concessions in Persia since 1908

Basra

Shatt al Arab

Kuwait (British)

Persian Gulf

The British advance from Basra towards Bagdad was made with inadequate supplies and no proper plan of campaign. It resulted in a Turkish victory at Ctesiphon in November 1915. The British then retreated to Kut, where they were besieged by the Turks. The siege lasted 5 months. The relieving force was defeated three times by the Turks. The Turks refused a British offer of £2,000,000 to set the garrison free. Of the 10,000 British and Indian troops who surrendered, over 6,000 died in the desert while prisoners-of-war

Persian territory occupied by the Government of India in September 1914, to protect the oil supplies essential for naval fuel

British advances into Turkish Mesopotamia, aiming at the capture of Bagdad

Turkish victories

Turkish territory occupied by British and Indian forces from May 1916 to November 1916

Hoped for Russian advance from the Caspian that never came

0   50
Miles

43

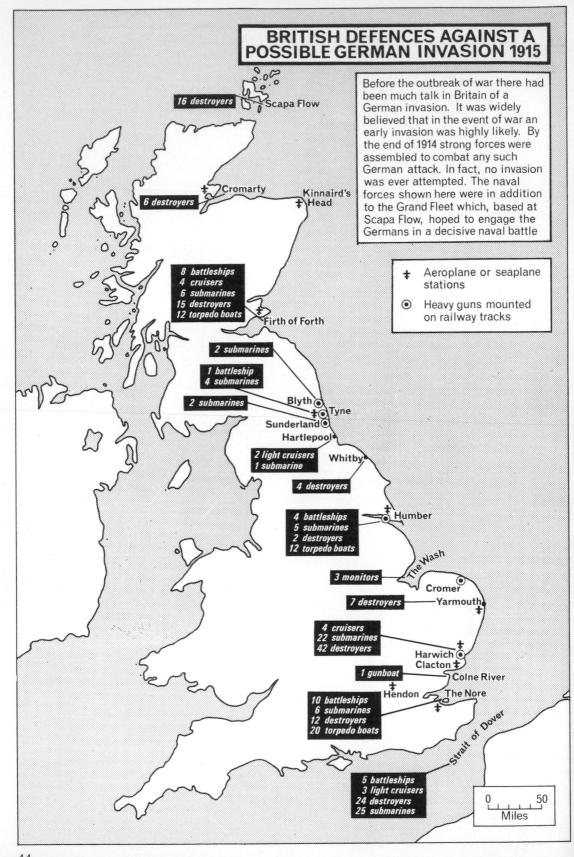

BRITISH DEFENCES AGAINST A POSSIBLE GERMAN INVASION 1915

Before the outbreak of war there had been much talk in Britain of a German invasion. It was widely believed that in the event of war an early invasion was highly likely. By the end of 1914 strong forces were assembled to combat any such German attack. In fact, no invasion was ever attempted. The naval forces shown here were in addition to the Grand Fleet which, based at Scapa Flow, hoped to engage the Germans in a decisive naval battle

✝ Aeroplane or seaplane stations

⊙ Heavy guns mounted on railway tracks

16 destroyers — Scapa Flow

6 destroyers — Cromarty

Kinnaird's Head

8 battleships
4 cruisers
6 submarines
15 destroyers
12 torpedo boats — Firth of Forth

2 submarines

1 battleship
4 submarines

2 submarines — Blyth — Tyne

Sunderland

Hartlepool

2 light cruisers
1 submarine — Whitby

4 destroyers

4 battleships
5 submarines
2 destroyers
12 torpedo boats — Humber

The Wash

3 monitors — Cromer

7 destroyers — Yarmouth

4 cruisers
22 submarines
42 destroyers — Harwich — Clacton

1 gunboat — Colne River

Hendon — The Nore

10 battleships
6 submarines
12 destroyers
20 torpedo boats

Strait of Dover

5 battleships
3 light cruisers
24 destroyers
25 submarines

0   50
Miles

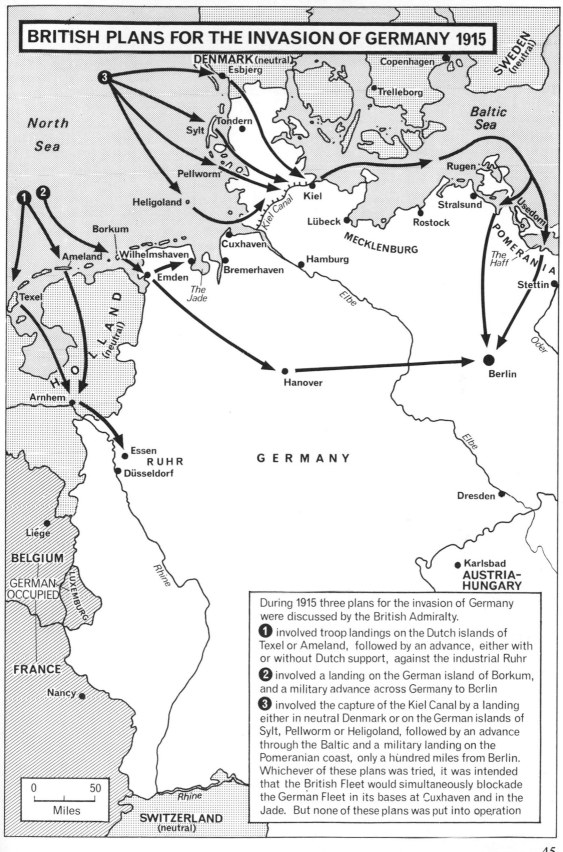

BRITISH PLANS FOR THE INVASION OF GERMANY 1915

During 1915 three plans for the invasion of Germany were discussed by the British Admiralty.

1 involved troop landings on the Dutch islands of Texel or Ameland, followed by an advance, either with or without Dutch support, against the industrial Ruhr

2 involved a landing on the German island of Borkum, and a military advance across Germany to Berlin

3 involved the capture of the Kiel Canal by a landing either in neutral Denmark or on the German islands of Sylt, Pellworm or Heligoland, followed by an advance through the Baltic and a military landing on the Pomeranian coast, only a hundred miles from Berlin. Whichever of these plans was tried, it was intended that the British Fleet would simultaneously blockade the German Fleet in its bases at Cuxhaven and in the Jade. But none of these plans was put into operation

0   50
Miles

45

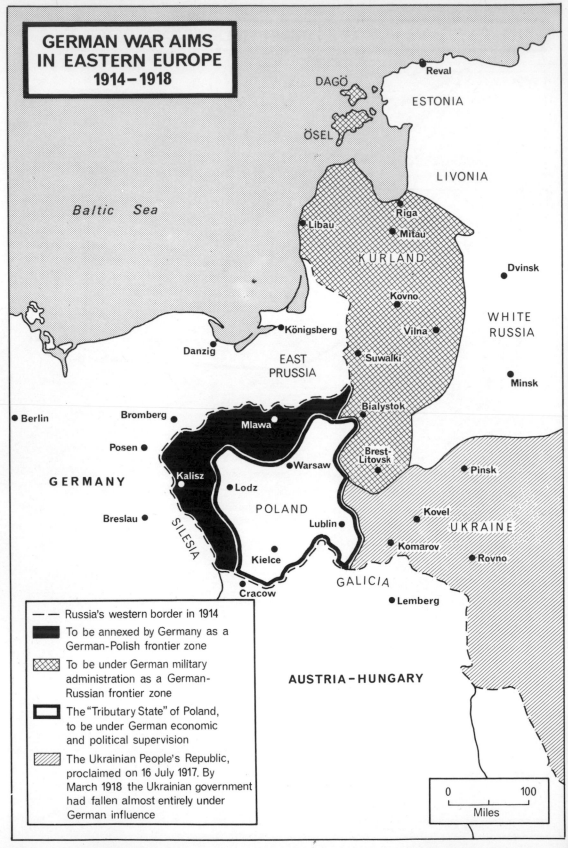

GERMAN WAR AIMS IN EASTERN EUROPE 1914–1918

DAGÖ

ÖSEL

Reval

ESTONIA

LIVONIA

Baltic Sea

Riga

Libau

Mitau

Dvinsk

KURLAND

Kovno

WHITE RUSSIA

Vilna

Königsberg

Danzig

EAST PRUSSIA

Suwalki

Minsk

Berlin

Bromberg

Mlawa

Bialystok

Posen

Kalisz

Warsaw

Brest-Litovsk

Pinsk

GERMANY

Lodz

Kovel

UKRAINE

POLAND

SILESIA

Breslau

Lublin

Komarov

Rovno

Kielce

GALICIA

Cracow

Lemberg

AUSTRIA–HUNGARY

— — — Russia's western border in 1914

To be annexed by Germany as a German-Polish frontier zone

To be under German military administration as a German-Russian frontier zone

The "Tributary State" of Poland, to be under German economic and political supervision

The Ukrainian People's Republic, proclaimed on 16 July 1917. By March 1918 the Ukrainian government had fallen almost entirely under German influence

0   100

Miles

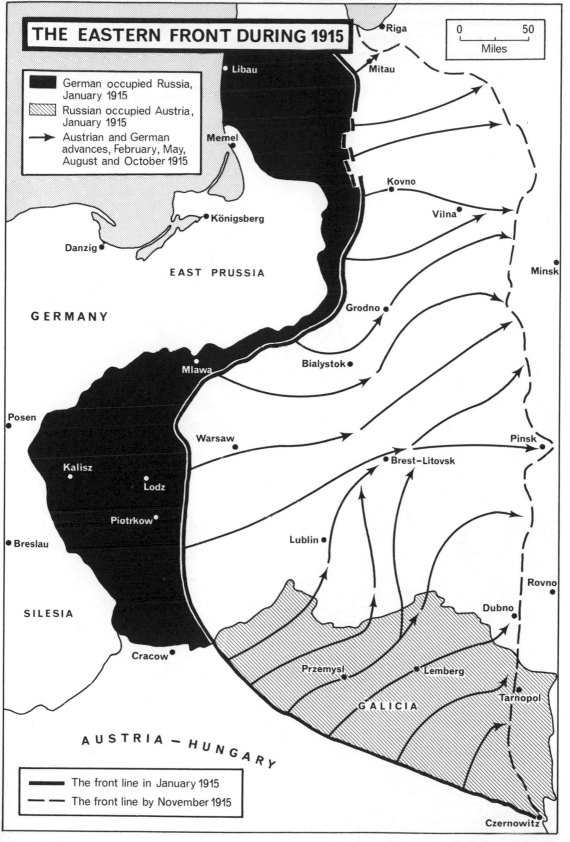

THE EASTERN FRONT DURING 1915

■ German occupied Russia, January 1915

▨ Russian occupied Austria, January 1915

→ Austrian and German advances, February, May, August and October 1915

0   50
Miles

Riga

Libau

Mitau

Memel

Königsberg

Kovno

Danzig

Vilna

EAST PRUSSIA

Minsk

GERMANY

Grodno

Mlawa

Bialystok

Posen

Warsaw

Pinsk

Kalisz

Brest–Litovsk

Lodz

Piotrkow

Breslau

Lublin

Rovno

Dubno

SILESIA

Cracow

Przemysl

Lemberg

Tarnopol

GALICIA

AUSTRIA – HUNGARY

Czernowitz

——— The front line in January 1915

‒ ‒ ‒ The front line by November 1915

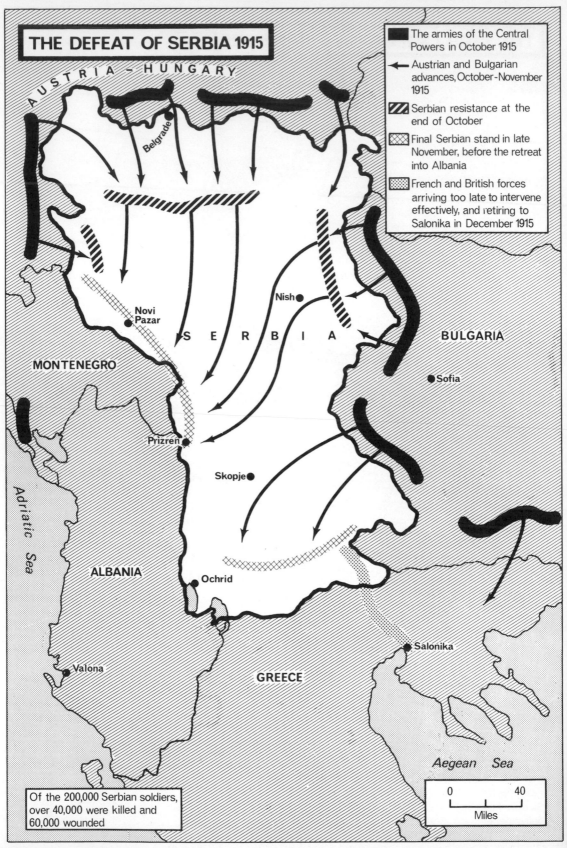

THE DEFEAT OF SERBIA 1915

Legend:
- The armies of the Central Powers in October 1915
- Austrian and Bulgarian advances, October-November 1915
- Serbian resistance at the end of October
- Final Serbian stand in late November, before the retreat into Albania
- French and British forces arriving too late to intervene effectively, and retiring to Salonika in December 1915

AUSTRIA - HUNGARY

Belgrade

S E R B I A

Novi Pazar

Nish

MONTENEGRO

BULGARIA

Sofia

Prizren

Skopje

ALBANIA

Ochrid

Adriatic Sea

Salonika

Valona

GREECE

Aegean Sea

Of the 200,000 Serbian soldiers, over 40,000 were killed and 60,000 wounded

0   40
Miles

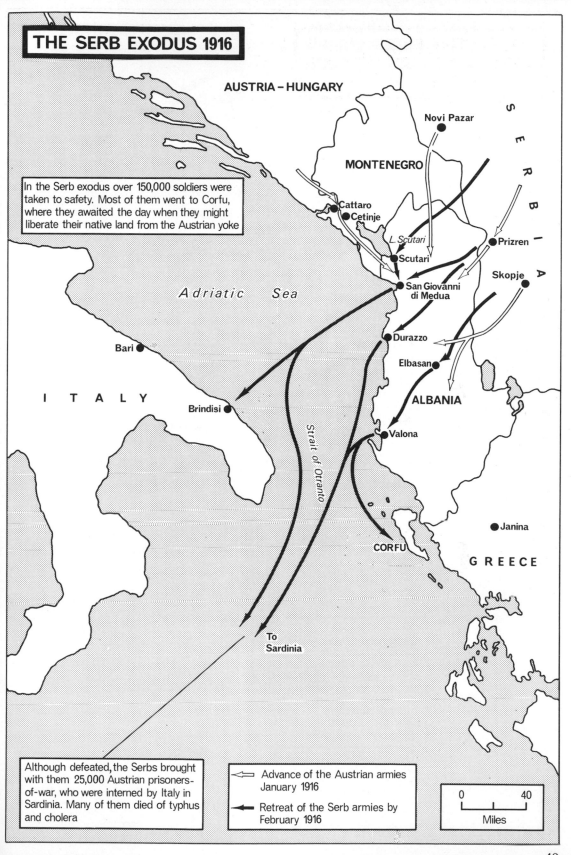

THE SERB EXODUS 1916

AUSTRIA – HUNGARY

Novi Pazar

MONTENEGRO

S E R B I A

In the Serb exodus over 150,000 soldiers were taken to safety. Most of them went to Corfu, where they awaited the day when they might liberate their native land from the Austrian yoke

Cattaro
Cetinje

L. Scutari

Scutari

Prizren

San Giovanni di Medua

Skopje

Adriatic Sea

Durazzo

Bari

Elbasan

ITALY

ALBANIA

Brindisi

Strait of Otranto

Valona

Janina

CORFU

GREECE

To Sardinia

Although defeated, the Serbs brought with them 25,000 Austrian prisoners-of-war, who were interned by Italy in Sardinia. Many of them died of typhus and cholera

⇦ Advance of the Austrian armies January 1916

◀ Retreat of the Serb armies by February 1916

0   40

Miles

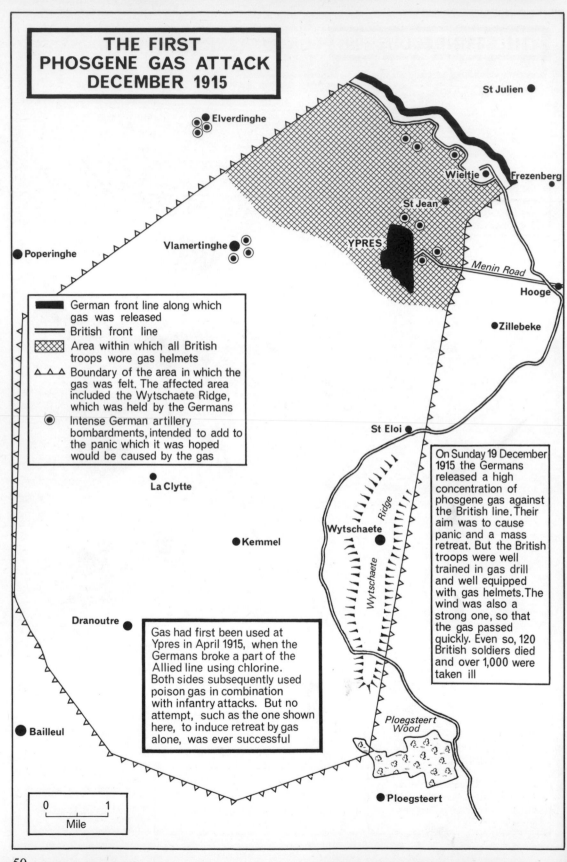

THE FIRST PHOSGENE GAS ATTACK DECEMBER 1915

St Julien

Elverdinghe

Wieltje

Frezenberg

St Jean

YPRES

Menin Road

Poperinghe

Vlamertinghe

Hooge

Zillebeke

German front line along which gas was released

British front line

Area within which all British troops wore gas helmets

Boundary of the area in which the gas was felt. The affected area included the Wytschaete Ridge, which was held by the Germans

Intense German artillery bombardments, intended to add to the panic which it was hoped would be caused by the gas

St Eloi

La Clytte

Wytschaete

Wytschaete Ridge

On Sunday 19 December 1915 the Germans released a high concentration of phosgene gas against the British line. Their aim was to cause panic and a mass retreat. But the British troops were well trained in gas drill and well equipped with gas helmets. The wind was also a strong one, so that the gas passed quickly. Even so, 120 British soldiers died and over 1,000 were taken ill

Kemmel

Dranoutre

Gas had first been used at Ypres in April 1915, when the Germans broke a part of the Allied line using chlorine. Both sides subsequently used poison gas in combination with infantry attacks. But no attempt, such as the one shown here, to induce retreat by gas alone, was ever successful

Ploegsteert Wood

Bailleul

Ploegsteert

0   1
Mile

50

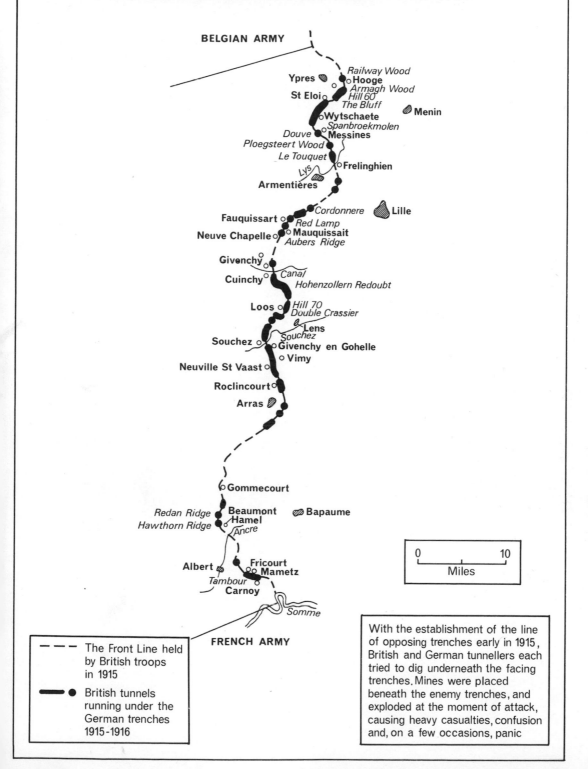

THE TUNNELLERS OF THE WESTERN FRONT
1915 – 1916

BELGIAN ARMY

Railway Wood
Ypres
Hooge
Armagh Wood
St Eloi
Hill 60
The Bluff
Menin
Wytschaete
Spanbroekmolen
Douve
Messines
Ploegsteert Wood
Le Touquet
Frelinghien
Lys
Armentières

Cordonnere
Lille
Fauquissart
Red Lamp
Neuve Chapelle
Mauquissait
Aubers Ridge

Givenchy
Cuinchy
Canal
Hohenzollern Redoubt

Loos
Hill 70
Double Crassier
Lens
Souchez
Souchez
Givenchy en Gohelle
Vimy
Neuville St Vaast
Roclincourt
Arras

Gommecourt

Redan Ridge
Beaumont
Bapaume
Hamel
Hawthorn Ridge
Ancre

Albert
Fricourt
Mametz
Tambour
Carnoy
Somme

FRENCH ARMY

0   10
Miles

- - - - The Front Line held
by British troops
in 1915

●━━━● British tunnels
running under the
German trenches
1915-1916

With the establishment of the line
of opposing trenches early in 1915,
British and German tunnellers each
tried to dig underneath the facing
trenches. Mines were placed
beneath the enemy trenches, and
exploded at the moment of attack,
causing heavy casualties, confusion
and, on a few occasions, panic

51

Section Four

1916

. . . Lines of grey, muttering faces, masked with fear,
They leave their trenches, going over the top,
While time ticks blank and busy on their wrists,
And hope, with furtive eyes and grappling fists,
Flounders in mud. O Jesus, make it stop!

SIEGFRIED SASSOON
"ATTACK"

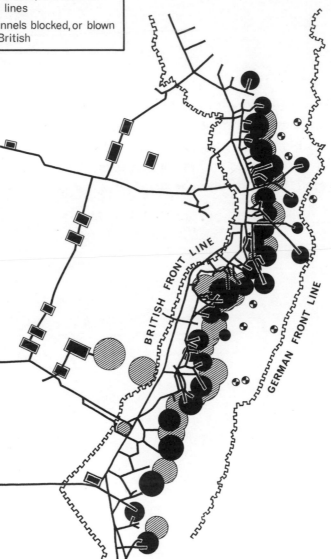

UNDERGROUND ACTIVITY ON THE WESTERN FRONT
1916

Legend:

- ⌐⌐⌐ The British and German front lines
- ▬ British dugouts, underground stores and explosive supplies
- — British tunnels below ground
- ● Craters blown by the British in no-man's-land
- ◍ Craters blown by the Germans in no-man's-land, and behind the British lines
- ⊕ German tunnels blocked, or blown in, by the British

BRITISH FRONT LINE

GERMAN FRONT LINE

0   200
Feet

Once the opposing armies had established their trench fortifications, sappers and miners began digging under no-man's-land, and even behind enemy lines. At regular intervals explosive charges were set off, destroying enemy forward positions and trench fortifications. The subsequent craters themselves became military objectives. Within a year there were over 60 craters blown in the mile long section of no-man's-land in the sector of the trenches shown here

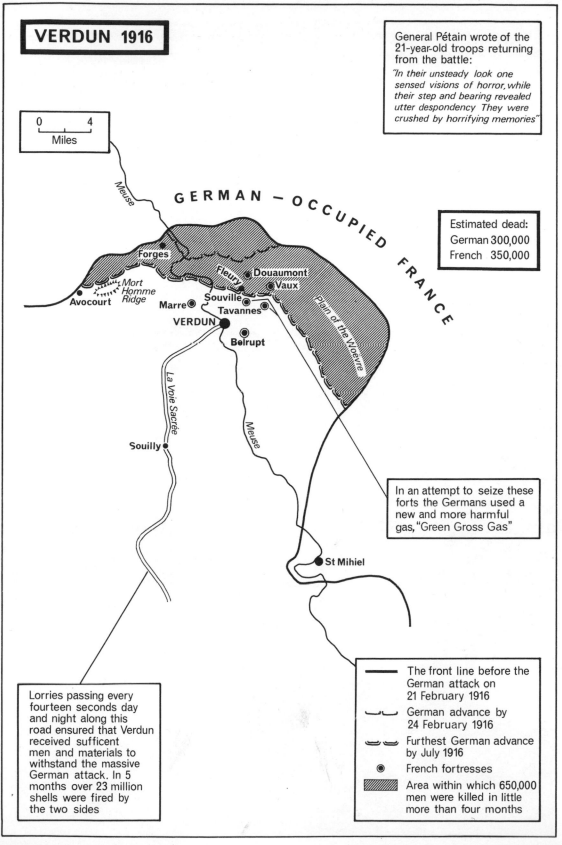

VERDUN 1916

General Pétain wrote of the 21-year-old troops returning from the battle:

"In their unsteady look one sensed visions of horror, while their step and bearing revealed utter despondency They were crushed by horrifying memories"

0   4
Miles

G E R M A N — O C C U P I E D   F R A N C E

Meuse

Estimated dead:
German 300,000
French 350,000

Forges

Fleury

Douaumont

Vaux

Mort Homme Ridge

Avocourt

Marre

Souville

Tavannes

Plain of the Woevre

VERDUN

Belrupt

La Voie Sacrée

Meuse

Souilly

In an attempt to seize these forts the Germans used a new and more harmful gas, "Green Gross Gas"

St Mihiel

Lorries passing every fourteen seconds day and night along this road ensured that Verdun received sufficent men and materials to withstand the massive German attack. In 5 months over 23 million shells were fired by the two sides

— The front line before the German attack on 21 February 1916

German advance by 24 February 1916

Furthest German advance by July 1916

● French fortresses

Area within which 650,000 men were killed in little more than four months

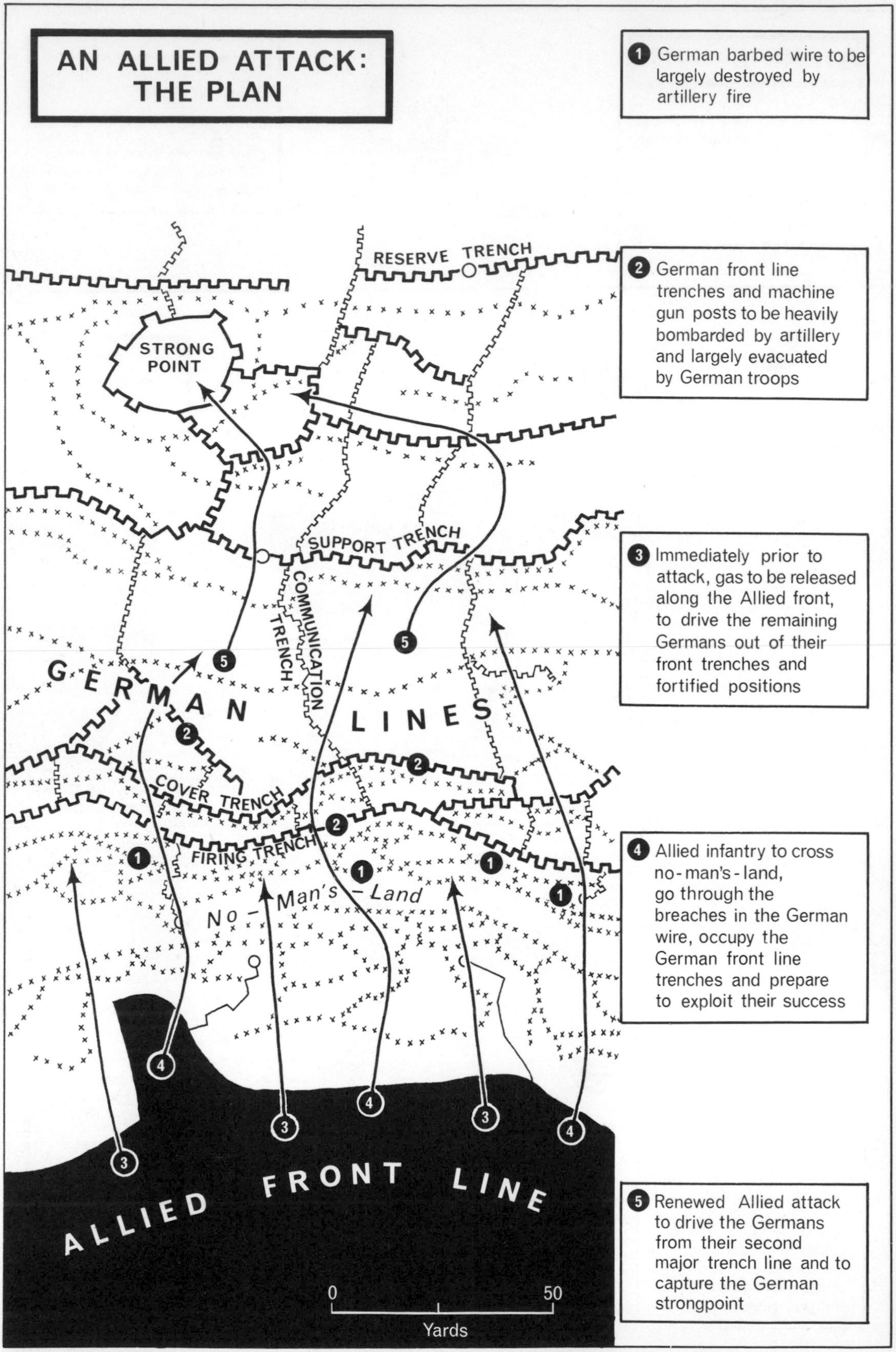

AN ALLIED ATTACK: THE PLAN

1 German barbed wire to be largely destroyed by artillery fire

2 German front line trenches and machine gun posts to be heavily bombarded by artillery and largely evacuated by German troops

3 Immediately prior to attack, gas to be released along the Allied front, to drive the remaining Germans out of their front trenches and fortified positions

4 Allied infantry to cross no-man's-land, go through the breaches in the German wire, occupy the German front line trenches and prepare to exploit their success

5 Renewed Allied attack to drive the Germans from their second major trench line and to capture the German strongpoint

RESERVE TRENCH

STRONG POINT

SUPPORT TRENCH

COMMUNICATION TRENCH

G E R M A N   L I N E S

COVER TRENCH

FIRING TRENCH

No - Man's - Land

ALLIED FRONT LINE

0   50
Yards

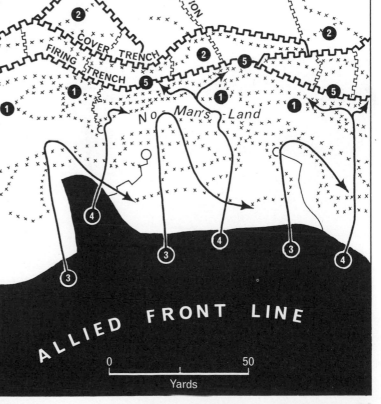

1 Insufficiently accurate or heavy artillery barrage fails to make any significant breaks in the German barbed wire

AN ALLIED ATTACK: THE RISKS

2 German concrete dugouts and well-constructed trenches not destroyed by Allied artillery, but remain occupied by German troops

3 Change of wind blows the gas back towards the Allied front line

4 The Allied troops are partly caught by their own gas, which has blown back, or has lingered in no-man's-land. Other men are trapped by the unbroken barbed wire and are then machine-gunned from German strongpoints which survived Allied artillery fire

5 A few Allied troops enter the first German trenches, but after gallant individual efforts are captured or killed. No troops reach the second German line. The Germans send up re-inforcements who rapidly repair what damage has been done. The Allied artillery, having exhausted its meagre supplies of shells, is unable to renew its heavy bombardment

RESERVE TRENCH

STRONG POINT

SUPPORT TRENCH

COMMUNICATION TRENCH

G E R M A N   L I N E S

COVER TRENCH

FIRING TRENCH

No - Man's - Land

ALLIED FRONT LINE

0 ————— 50

Yards

THE SOMME 1916

Gommecourt

Hébuterne

Miraumont

Bapaume

Beaumont Hamel

Warlencourt

0   2
Miles

Le Sars

Courcelette

Gueudecourt

le Transloy

Thiepval

Martinpuich

High wood

Delville wood

Sailly

Pozières

Longueval

Morval

Ovillers

Ginchy

Contalmaison

Mametz wood

Guillemont

Combles

Montauban

Trones wood

Albert

Fricourt

Mametz

BRITISH FRONT LINE

Maurepas

Bouchavesnes

Maricourt

Somme

Somme

Péronne

FRENCH FRONT LINE

Dompierre

Barleux

Estrées

On the first day of the battle, July 1, German machine guns, often hidden in armoured emplacements, prevented any British gains. 20,000 British troops were killed on that day: amounting to 60% of all the officers and 40% of all the men engaged. The battle continued fiercely for five months, and included the first use of tanks, by the British, in September

The British had 460, the French 850 heavy guns to maintain a continuous artillery barrage. In the preliminary bombardment alone, 1,700,000 shells were fired. By September, stocks of artillery shell were seriously low. Even on the first day, poor quality shells resulted in a general failure to destroy German dug-outs

56

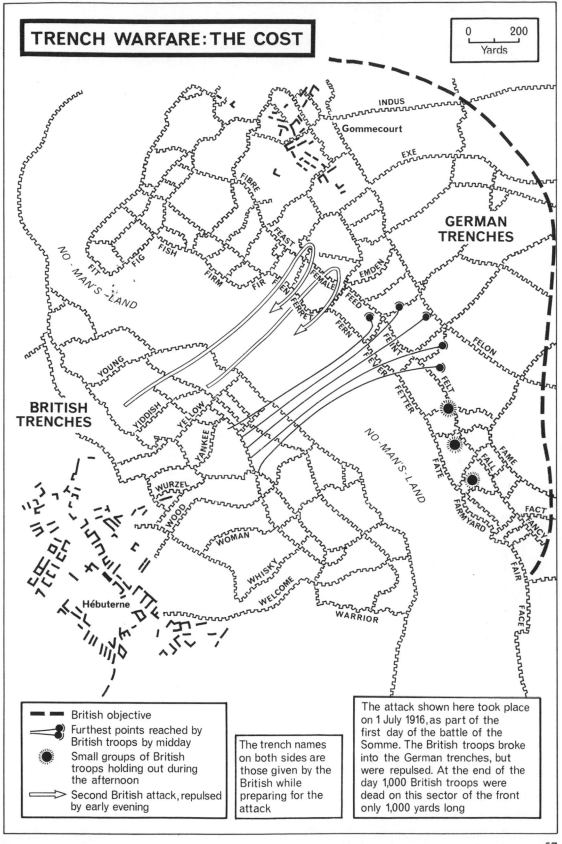

TRENCH WARFARE: THE COST

0   200
Yards

INDUS

Gommecourt

EXE

FIBRE

GERMAN
TRENCHES

FEAST

NO-MAN'S-LAND

FIT

FIG

FISH

FIRM

FIR

FIEN

FEMALE

FERRET

EMDEN

FEED

FEINT

FERN

FEVER

FELON

FETTER

FELT

FATE

FALL

FAME

YOUNG

BRITISH
TRENCHES

YIDDISH

YELLOW

YANKEE

NO-MAN'S-LAND

FARMYARD

FACT

FANCY

WURZEL

WOOD

FAIR

FACE

WOMAN

WHISKY

WELCOME

Hébuterne

WARRIOR

— — — British objective

Furthest points reached by
British troops by midday

Small groups of British
troops holding out during
the afternoon

Second British attack, repulsed
by early evening

The trench names
on both sides are
those given by the
British while
preparing for the
attack

The attack shown here took place
on 1 July 1916, as part of the
first day of the battle of the
Somme. The British troops broke
into the German trenches, but
were repulsed. At the end of the
day 1,000 British troops were
dead on this sector of the front
only 1,000 yards long

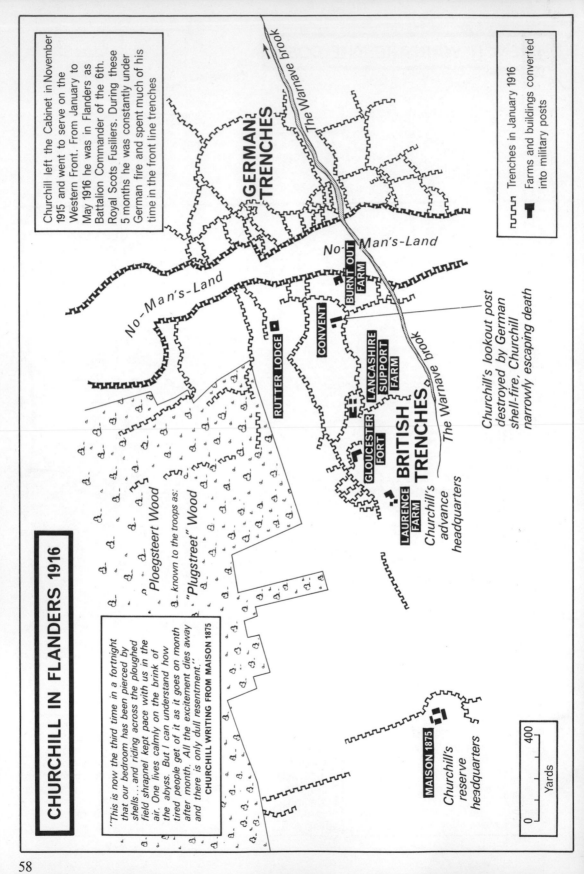

CHURCHILL IN FLANDERS 1916

Churchill left the Cabinet in November 1915 and went to serve on the Western Front. From January to May 1916 he was in Flanders as Battalion Commander of the 6th. Royal Scots Fusiliers. During these 5 months he was constantly under German fire and spent much of his time in the front line trenches

Trenches in January 1916

Farms and buildings converted into military posts

GERMAN TRENCHES

The Warnave brook

No - Man's - Land

No - Man's - Land

BURNT OUT FARM

CONVENT

RUTTER LODGE

LANCASHIRE SUPPORT FARM

Churchill's lookout post destroyed by German shell-fire, Churchill narrowly escaping death

GLOUCESTER FORT

BRITISH TRENCHES

The Warnave brook

LAURENCE FARM
Churchill's advance headquarters

Ploegsteert Wood

known to the troops as:

"Plugstreet" Wood

"This is now the third time in a fortnight that our bedroom has been pierced by shells....and riding across the ploughed field shrapnel kept pace with us in the air. One lives calmly on the brink of the abyss. But I can understand how tired people get of it as it goes on month after month. All the excitement dies away and there is only dull resentment."
CHURCHILL WRITING FROM MAISON 1875

MAISON 1875
Churchill's reserve headquarters

0   400

Yards

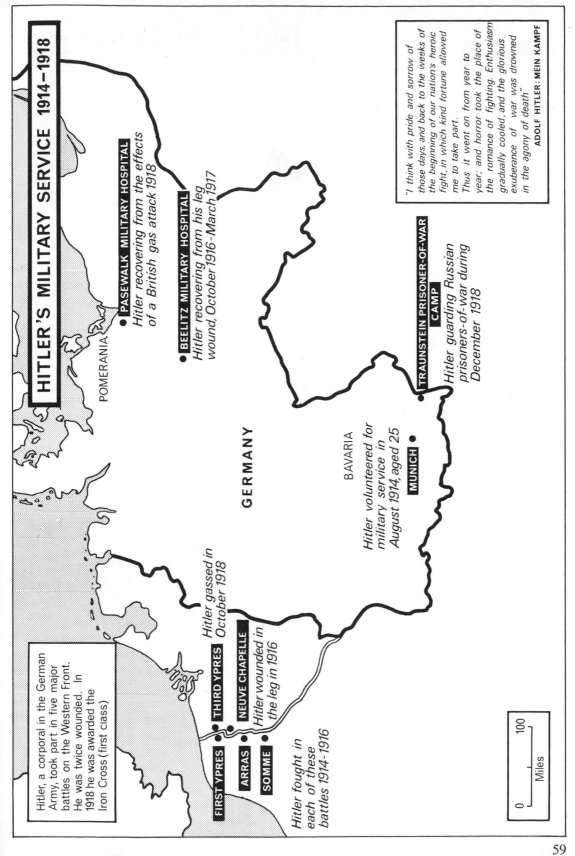

HITLER'S MILITARY SERVICE 1914–1918

"I think with pride and sorrow of those days, and back to the weeks of the beginning of our nation's heroic fight, in which kind fortune allowed me to take part.

Thus it went on from year to year; and horror took the place of the romance of fighting. Enthusiasm gradually cooled, and the glorious exuberance of war was drowned in the agony of death"

ADOLF HITLER: MEIN KAMPF

PASEWALK MILITARY HOSPITAL
Hitler recovering from the effects of a British gas attack 1918

BEELITZ MILITARY HOSPITAL
Hitler recovering from his leg wound, October 1916 - March 1917

POMERANIA

TRAUNSTEIN PRISONER-OF-WAR CAMP
Hitler guarding Russian prisoners-of-war during December 1918

GERMANY

BAVARIA

Hitler volunteered for military service in August 1914, aged 25

MUNICH

Hitler gassed in October 1918

THIRD YPRES

NEUVE CHAPELLE
Hitler wounded in the leg in 1916

FIRST YPRES

ARRAS

SOMME

Hitler fought in each of these battles 1914-1916

Hitler, a corporal in the German Army, took part in five major battles on the Western Front. He was twice wounded. In 1918 he was awarded the Iron Cross (first class)

0   100
Miles

59

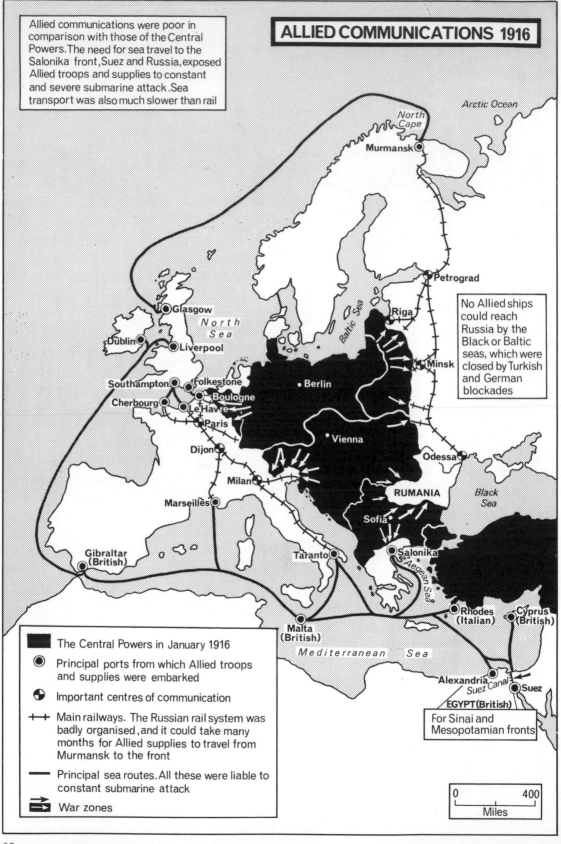

Allied communications were poor in comparison with those of the Central Powers. The need for sea travel to the Salonika front, Suez and Russia, exposed Allied troops and supplies to constant and severe submarine attack. Sea transport was also much slower than rail

ALLIED COMMUNICATIONS 1916

Arctic Ocean

North Cape

Murmansk

Petrograd

No Allied ships could reach Russia by the Black or Baltic seas, which were closed by Turkish and German blockades

Glasgow

North Sea

Riga

Baltic Sea

Dublin

Liverpool

Minsk

Southampton

Folkestone

Berlin

Cherbourg

Boulogne

Le Havre

Paris

Vienna

Dijon

Odessa

Black Sea

Milan

RUMANIA

Marseilles

Sofia

Salonika

Taranto

Aegean Sea

Gibraltar (British)

Rhodes (Italian)

Cyprus (British)

Malta (British)

Mediterranean Sea

Alexandria

Suez Canal

Suez

EGYPT (British)

For Sinai and Mesopotamian fronts

⬛ The Central Powers in January 1916

◉ Principal ports from which Allied troops and supplies were embarked

◕ Important centres of communication

+++ Main railways. The Russian rail system was badly organised, and it could take many months for Allied supplies to travel from Murmansk to the front

— Principal sea routes. All these were liable to constant submarine attack

⇉ War zones

0   400
Miles

RAIL COMMUNICATIONS OF THE CENTRAL POWERS 1916

0 200
Miles

North Sea

Baltic Sea

Libau

Memel

Vilna

Kiel

Danzig
Königsberg

Hamburg
Stettin

Berlin

Warsaw

GERMANY

Zeebrugge

Brussels

Frankfurt
Metz

AUSTRIA – HUNGARY

Vienna

Budapest

Trieste
Fiume

Adriatic Sea

RUMANIA

Nish

Sofia
BULGARIA

Varna

Black Sea

Constantinople

Aegean Sea

TURKEY

▬▬	The Central Powers in December 1915
◉	Principal ports
◔	Important railway centres
→	War zones
▨	Serbia, whose conquest in 1915 made it possible to link Turkey and Bulgaria with Austria and Germany
▨	Rumania, whose conquest in 1916 was made easier by being accessible at four different points by rail
╫╫╫	Principal railways

The Central Powers were able to make use of a pre-war railway network which was ideal for the rapid movement of troops and supplies, both from the centre to the war zones, and from zone to zone. The system was immune from Allied attack

61

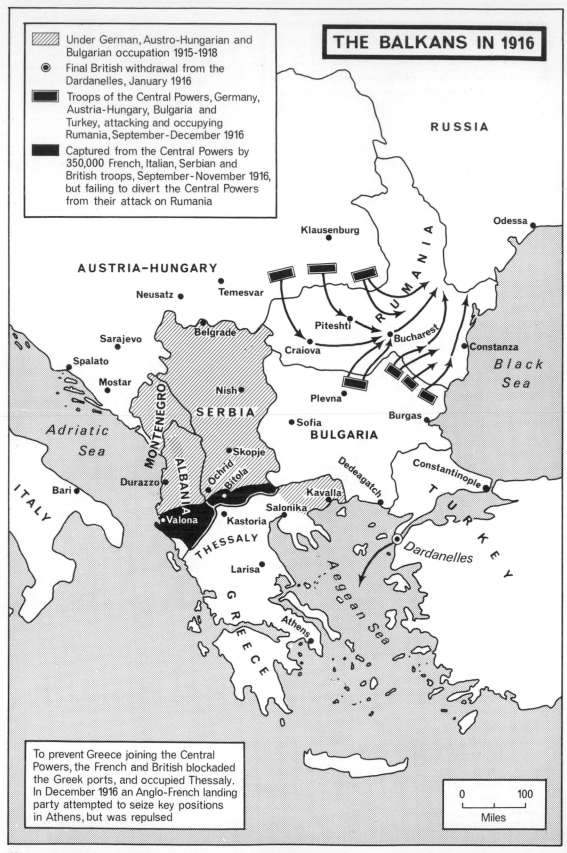

THE BALKANS IN 1916

Under German, Austro-Hungarian and Bulgarian occupation 1915-1918

Final British withdrawal from the Dardanelles, January 1916

Troops of the Central Powers, Germany, Austria-Hungary, Bulgaria and Turkey, attacking and occupying Rumania, September-December 1916

Captured from the Central Powers by 350,000 French, Italian, Serbian and British troops, September-November 1916, but failing to divert the Central Powers from their attack on Rumania

RUSSIA

AUSTRIA-HUNGARY

Klausenburg

Neusatz

Temesvar

Piteshti

RUMANIA

Bucharest

Odessa

Constanza

Black Sea

Sarajevo

Spalato

Mostar

Belgrade

Craiova

Nish

SERBIA

Plevna

Sofia

BULGARIA

Burgas

Adriatic Sea

MONTENEGRO

ALBANIA

Skopje

Ochrid

Bitola

Dedeagatch

Constantinople

ITALY

Bari

Durazzo

Valona

Kastoria

Salonika

Kavalla

THESSALY

TURKEY

Dardanelles

Larisa

GREECE

Aegean Sea

Athens

To prevent Greece joining the Central Powers, the French and British blockaded the Greek ports, and occupied Thessaly. In December 1916 an Anglo-French landing party attempted to seize key positions in Athens, but was repulsed

0   100

Miles

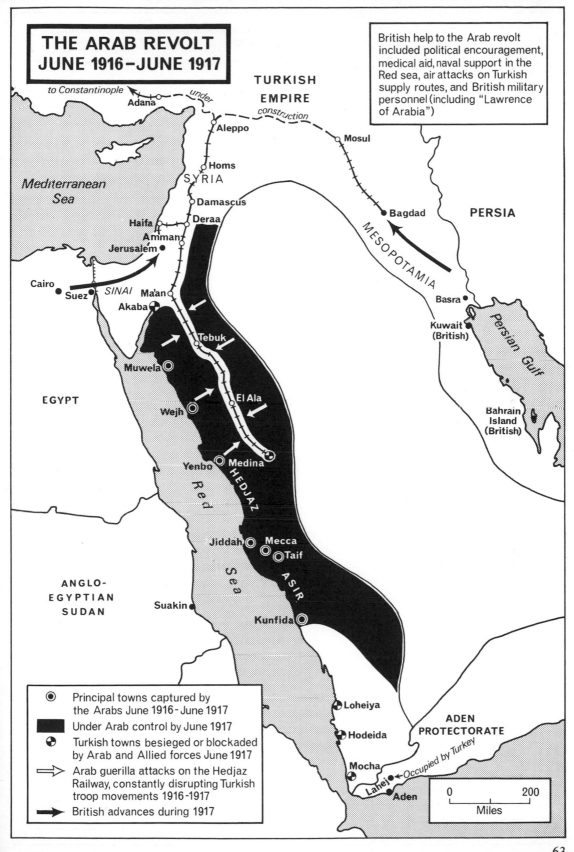

THE ARAB REVOLT
JUNE 1916 – JUNE 1917

British help to the Arab revolt
included political encouragement,
medical aid, naval support in the
Red sea, air attacks on Turkish
supply routes, and British military
personnel (including "Lawrence
of Arabia")

TURKISH
EMPIRE

to Constantinople

Adana

under

construction

Aleppo

Mosul

Homs

SYRIA

Mediterranean
Sea

Damascus

Bagdad

PERSIA

Haifa

Deraa

Amman

Jerusalem

MESOPOTAMIA

Cairo

Suez

SINAI

Ma'an

Akaba

Basra

Tebuk

Kuwait
(British)

Persian Gulf

Muwela

EGYPT

Wejh

El Ala

Bahrain
Island
(British)

Yenbo

Medina

HEDJAZ

Red

Jiddah

Mecca

Taif

Sea

ANGLO-
EGYPTIAN
SUDAN

ASIR

Suakin

Kunfida

Loheiya

ADEN
PROTECTORATE

Hodeida

Occupied by Turkey

Mocha

Lahej

Aden

	Principal towns captured by the Arabs June 1916 - June 1917
◉	Principal towns captured by the Arabs June 1916 - June 1917
▮	Under Arab control by June 1917
◓	Turkish towns besieged or blockaded by Arab and Allied forces June 1917
⇨	Arab guerilla attacks on the Hedjaz Railway, constantly disrupting Turkish troop movements 1916-1917
➡	British advances during 1917

0   200
Miles

63

Section Five

THE WAR IN THE AIR

Night shatters in mid-heaven—the bark of guns,
The roar of planes, the crash of bombs, and all
The unshackled skyey pandemonium stuns
The senses to indifference, when a fall
Of masonry nearby startles awake,
Tingling, wide-eyed, prick-eared, with bristling hair,
Each sense within the body, crouched aware
Like some sore-hunted creature in the brake. . . .

WILFRED GIBSON
"AIR-RAID"

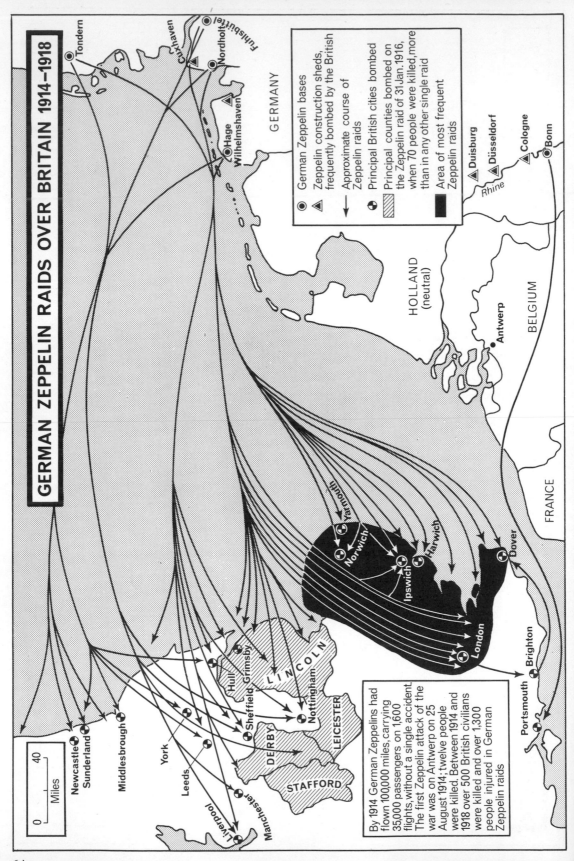

GERMAN ZEPPELIN RAIDS OVER BRITAIN 1914–1918

GERMANY

Tondern

Cuxhaven
Nordholt

Fuhlsbüttel

Hage
Wilhelmshaven

Duisburg
Düsseldorf
Cologne
Bonn

Rhine

HOLLAND
(neutral)

Antwerp

BELGIUM

FRANCE

- ⊙ German Zeppelin bases
- △ Zeppelin construction sheds, frequently bombed by the British
- ↓ Approximate course of Zeppelin raids
- ⊕ Principal British cities bombed
- ░ Principal counties bombed on the Zeppelin raid of 31 Jan.1916, when 70 people were killed, more than in any other single raid
- ■ Area of most frequent Zeppelin raids

Yarmouth
Norwich
Ipswich
Harwich
London
Dover
Brighton
Portsmouth

Newcastle
Sunderland
Middlesbrough
York
Leeds
Liverpool
Manchester
Hull
Sheffield Grimsby
LINCOLN
Nottingham
DERBY
LEICESTER
STAFFORD

By 1914 German Zeppelins had flown 100,000 miles, carrying 35,000 passengers on 1,600 flights, without a single accident. The first Zeppelin attack of the war was on Antwerp on 25 August 1914; twelve people were killed. Between 1914 and 1918 over 500 British civilians were killed and over 1,300 people injured in German Zeppelin raids.

0   40
Miles

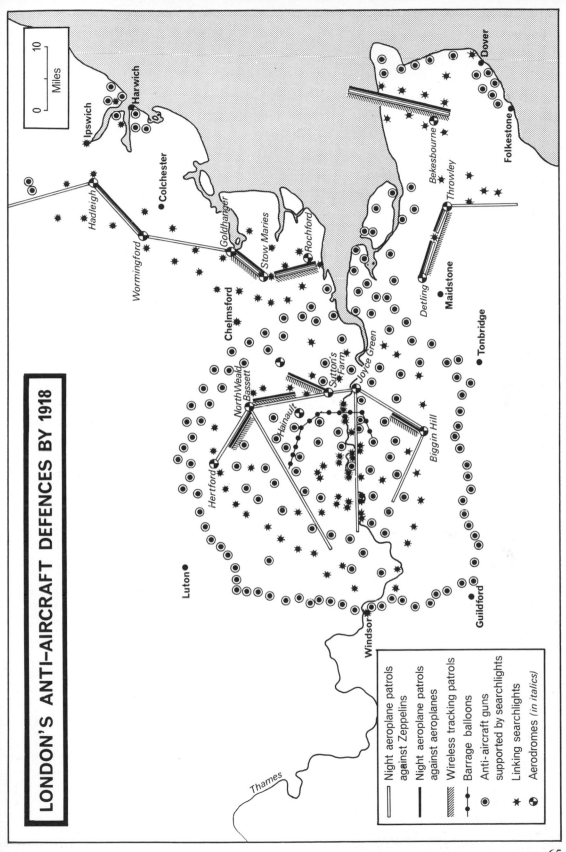

LONDON'S ANTI-AIRCRAFT DEFENCES BY 1918

10

Miles

0

Ipswich
Harwich
Colchester
Hadleigh
Wormingford
Goldhanger
Stow Maries
Rochford
Chelmsford
North Weald
Bassett
Sutton's Farm
Joyce Green
Hainault
Hertford
Biggin Hill
Luton
Windsor
Guildford
Bekesbourne
Throwley
Detling
Maidstone
Tonbridge
Dover
Folkestone
Thames

Night aeroplane patrols against Zeppelins

Night aeroplane patrols against aeroplanes

Wireless tracking patrols

Barrage balloons

Anti-aircraft guns supported by searchlights

Linking searchlights

Aerodromes *(in italics)*

65

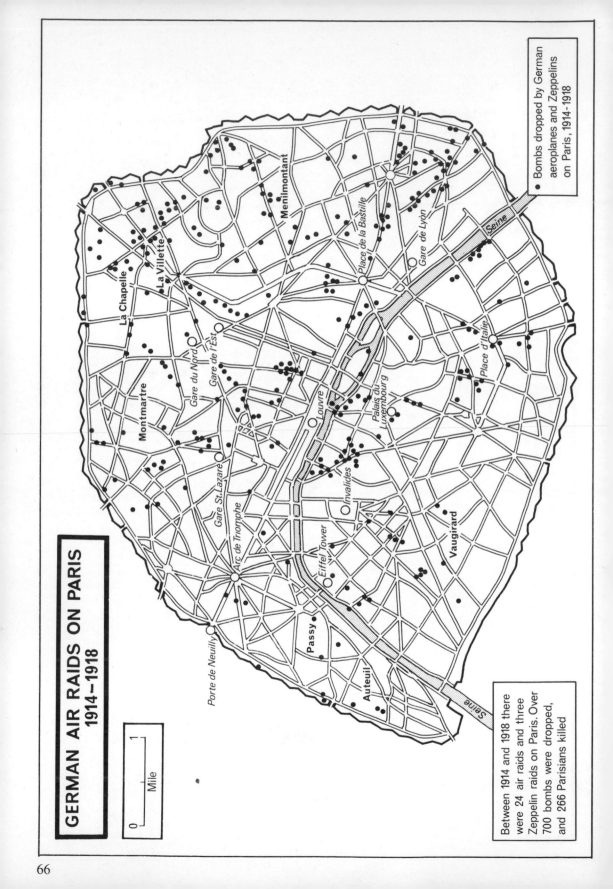

GERMAN AIR RAIDS ON PARIS
1914–1918

0 1
Mile

Porte de Neuilly

Arc de Triomphe

Gare St.Lazare

Montmartre

Gare du Nord

Gare de l'Est

La Villette

La Chapelle

Menilmontant

Place de la Bastille

Gare de Lyon

Seine

Place d'Italie

Louvre

Eiffel Tower

Invalides

Palais du Luxembourg

Vaugirard

Passy

Auteuil

Seine

• Bombs dropped by German aeroplanes and Zeppelins on Paris, 1914-1918

Between 1914 and 1918 there were 24 air raids and three Zeppelin raids on Paris. Over 700 bombs were dropped, and 266 Parisians killed

66

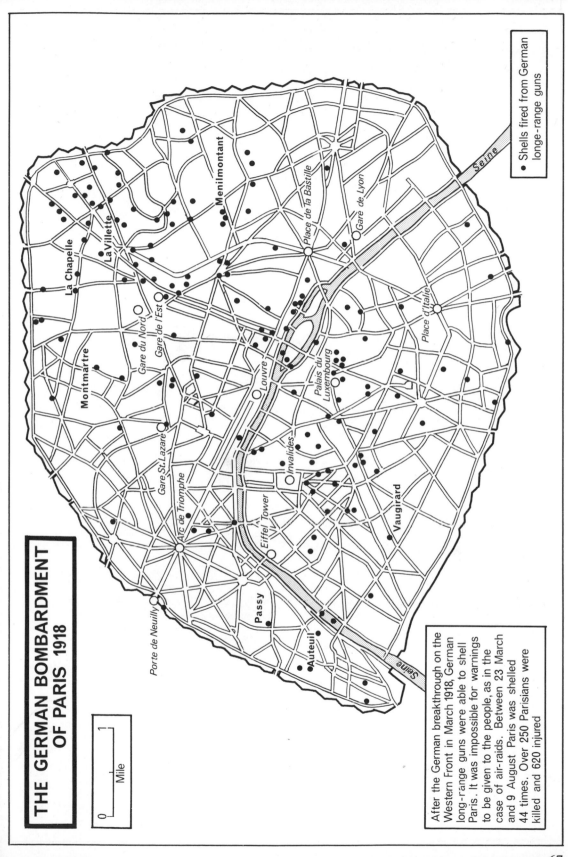

THE GERMAN BOMBARDMENT OF PARIS 1918

0 — 1
Mile

Porte de Neuilly

La Chapelle

Montmartre

Gare du Nord

Gare de l'Est

Gare St. Lazare

Arc de Triomphe

Passy

Auteuil

Eiffel Tower

Invalides

Louvre

Palais du Luxembourg

La Villette

Ménilmontant

Place de la Bastille

Gare de Lyon

Place d'Italie

Vaugirard

Seine

Seine

- Shells fired from German longe-range guns

After the German breakthrough on the Western Front in March 1918, German long-range guns were able to shell Paris. It was impossible for warnings to be given to the people, as in the case of air-raids. Between 23 March and 9 August Paris was shelled 44 times. Over 250 Parisians were killed and 620 injured

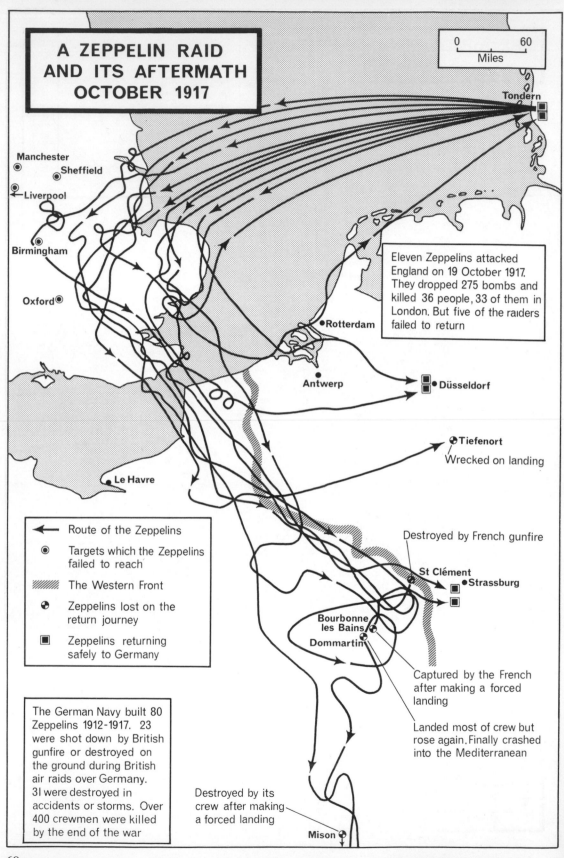

A ZEPPELIN RAID AND ITS AFTERMATH OCTOBER 1917

0 — 60
Miles

Tondern

Manchester
Sheffield
Liverpool
Birmingham
Oxford

Rotterdam

Eleven Zeppelins attacked
England on 19 October 1917.
They dropped 275 bombs and
killed 36 people, 33 of them in
London. But five of the raiders
failed to return

Antwerp

Düsseldorf

Tiefenort
Wrecked on landing

Le Havre

Destroyed by French gunfire

St Clément
Strassburg

Bourbonne
les Bains
Dommartin

Captured by the French
after making a forced
landing

Landed most of crew but
rose again. Finally crashed
into the Mediterranean

← Route of the Zeppelins

◉ Targets which the Zeppelins
failed to reach

▨ The Western Front

◕ Zeppelins lost on the
return journey

■ Zeppelins returning
safely to Germany

The German Navy built 80
Zeppelins 1912-1917. 23
were shot down by British
gunfire or destroyed on
the ground during British
air raids over Germany.
31 were destroyed in
accidents or storms. Over
400 crewmen were killed
by the end of the war

Destroyed by its
crew after making
a forced landing

Mison

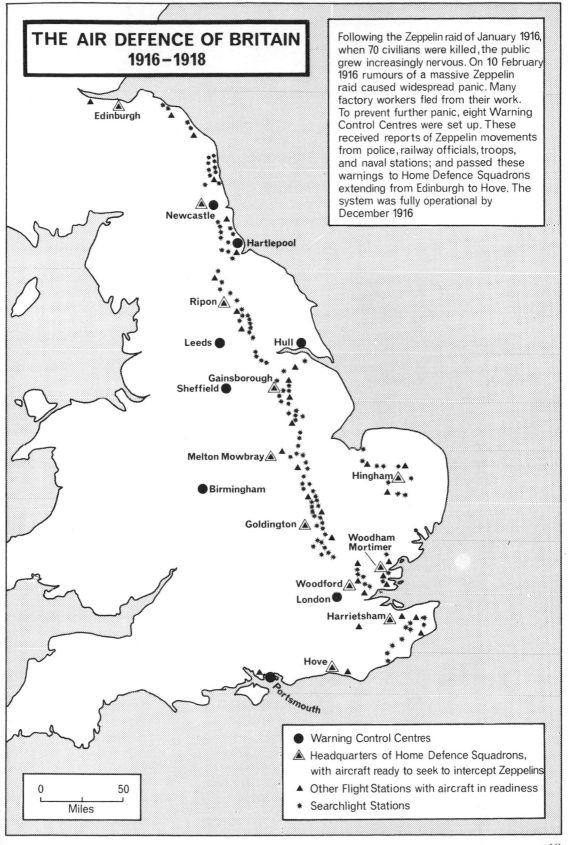

THE AIR DEFENCE OF BRITAIN 1916–1918

Following the Zeppelin raid of January 1916, when 70 civilians were killed, the public grew increasingly nervous. On 10 February 1916 rumours of a massive Zeppelin raid caused widespread panic. Many factory workers fled from their work. To prevent further panic, eight Warning Control Centres were set up. These received reports of Zeppelin movements from police, railway officials, troops, and naval stations; and passed these warnings to Home Defence Squadrons extending from Edinburgh to Hove. The system was fully operational by December 1916

Edinburgh

Newcastle

Hartlepool

Ripon

Leeds   Hull

Gainsborough
Sheffield

Melton Mowbray

Birmingham   Hingham

Goldington

Woodham
Mortimer

Woodford
London

Harrietsham

Hove

Portsmouth

● Warning Control Centres
△ Headquarters of Home Defence Squadrons, with aircraft ready to seek to intercept Zeppelins
▲ Other Flight Stations with aircraft in readiness
* Searchlight Stations

0   50
Miles

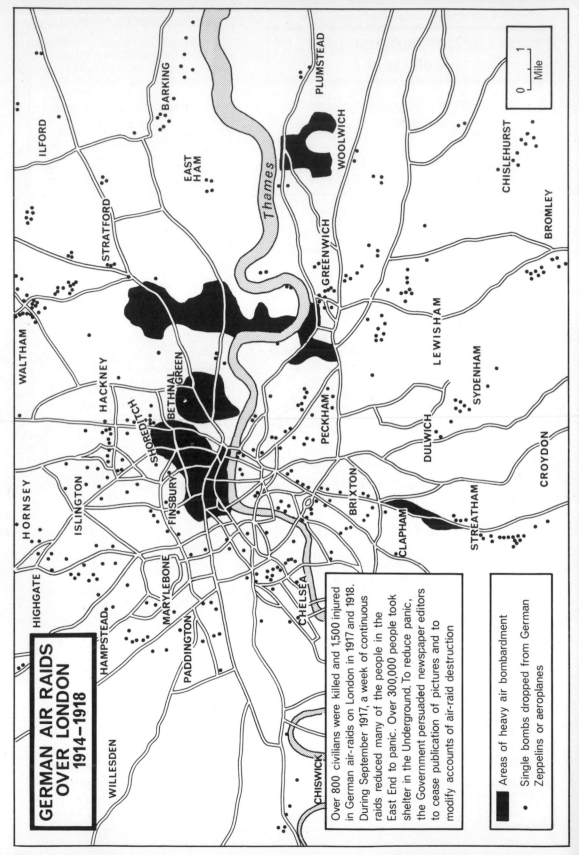

GERMAN AIR RAIDS OVER LONDON 1914–1918

Over 800 civilians were killed and 1,500 injured in German air-raids on London in 1917 and 1918. During September 1917, a week of continuous raids reduced many of the people in the East End to panic. Over 300,000 people took shelter in the Underground. To reduce panic, the Government persuaded newspaper editors to cease publication of pictures and to modify accounts of air-raid destruction

■ Areas of heavy air bombardment

• Single bombs dropped from German Zeppelins or aeroplanes

ILFORD

BARKING

PLUMSTEAD

WOOLWICH

EAST HAM

Thames

STRATFORD

CHISLEHURST

GREENWICH

BROMLEY

WALTHAM

HACKNEY

BETHNAL GREEN

LEWISHAM

SYDENHAM

SHOREDITCH

PECKHAM

HORNSEY

ISLINGTON

FINSBURY

BRIXTON

DULWICH

CROYDON

HIGHGATE

MARYLEBONE

CLAPHAM

STREATHAM

HAMPSTEAD

PADDINGTON

CHELSEA

WILLESDEN

CHISWICK

0 1
Mile

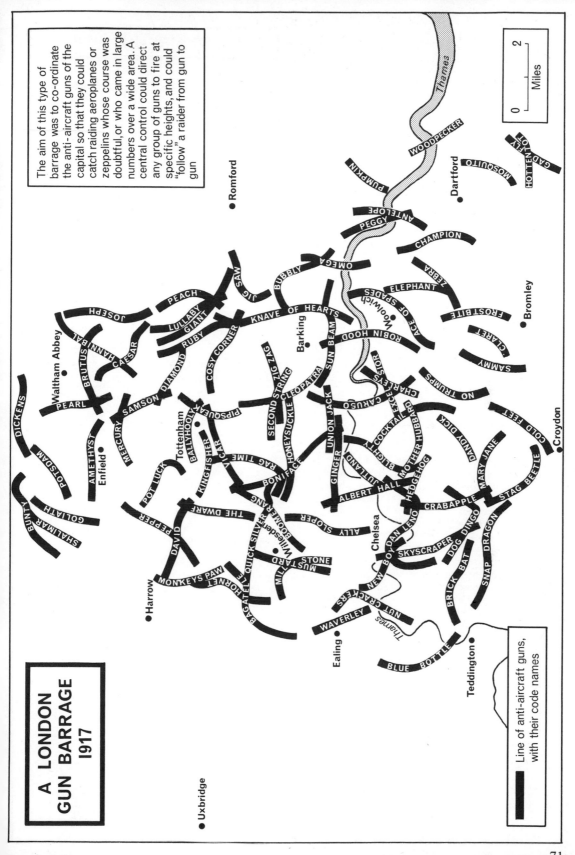

A LONDON GUN BARRAGE 1917

The aim of this type of barrage was to co-ordinate the anti-aircraft guns of the capital so that they could catch raiding aeroplanes or zeppelins whose course was doubtful, or who came in large numbers over a wide area. A central control could direct any group of guns to fire at specific heights, and could "follow" a raider from gun to gun.

Line of anti-aircraft guns, with their code names

0 2 Miles

Thames

Romford

Waltham Abbey

Enfield

Tottenham

Barking

Woolwich

Uxbridge

Harrow

Ealing

Chelsea

Teddington

Croydon

Bromley

Dartford

DICKENS
POTSDAM
SHALIMAR
GOLIATH
BUNTY
PEARL
BRUTUS
HANNIBAL
JOSEPH
PEACH
AMETHYST
MERCURY
SAMSON
CAESAR
DIAMOND
RUBY
LULLABY
GIANT
JIG SAW
BUBBLY
OMEGA
PEGGY
ANTELOPE
CHAMPION
WOODPECKER
PUMPKIN
COSY CORNER
KNAVE OF HEARTS
PIPSQUEAK
SECOND STRING
ZIG ZAG
CLEOPATRA
SUN BEAM
ROBIN HOOD
ELEPHANT
ZEBRA
FROSTBITE
CLARET
SAMMY
ACE OF SPADES
POT LUCK
BALLYHOOLY
VICAR
RAG TIME
HONEYSUCKLE
UNION JACK
CARUSO
CHARLEY
EXCELSIOR
NO TRUMPS
COLD FEET
KINGFISHER
BONIFACE
GINGER
BLIGHTY
COCKTAIL
MOTHER HUBBARD
DANDY DICK
MARY JANE
STAG BEETLE
PEPPER
DAVID
THE DWARF
BOOMERANG
ALLY SLOPER
ALBERT HALL
HEDGEHOG
CRABAPPLE
DINGO
SNAP DRAGON
MONKEYS PAW
HORNET
BAGATEL
QUICK SILVER
MUSTARD
STONE
NEW BOY
DAN LENO
SKYSCRAPER
DOG BAT
BRICK
WAVERLEY
NUT CRACKERS
BLUE BOTTLE
MILL
JUTLAND

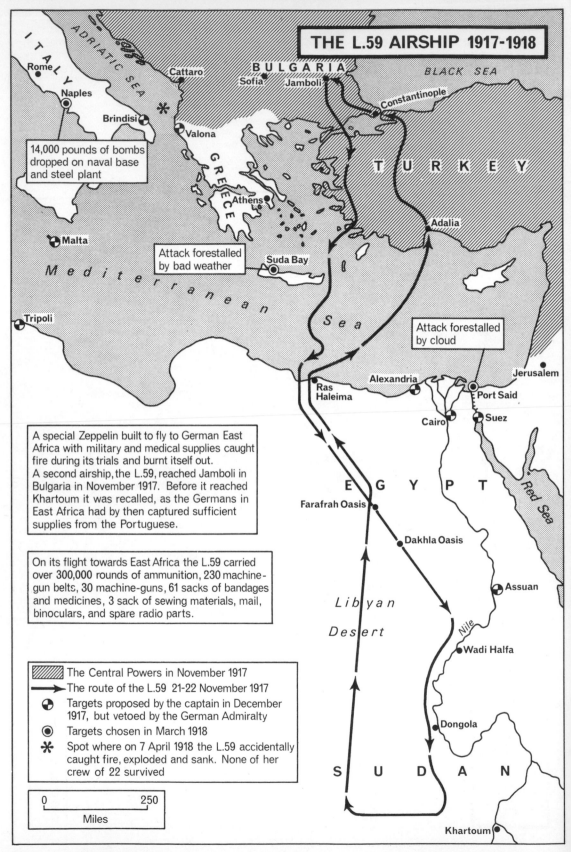

THE L.59 AIRSHIP 1917-1918

14,000 pounds of bombs dropped on naval base and steel plant

Attack forestalled by bad weather

Attack forestalled by cloud

A special Zeppelin built to fly to German East Africa with military and medical supplies caught fire during its trials and burnt itself out.
A second airship, the L.59, reached Jamboli in Bulgaria in November 1917. Before it reached Khartoum it was recalled, as the Germans in East Africa had by then captured sufficient supplies from the Portuguese.

On its flight towards East Africa the L.59 carried over 300,000 rounds of ammunition, 230 machine-gun belts, 30 machine-guns, 61 sacks of bandages and medicines, 3 sack of sewing materials, mail, binoculars, and spare radio parts.

ITALY · Rome · Naples · Brindisi

ADRIATIC SEA · Cattaro · Valona

BULGARIA · Sofia · Jamboli

BLACK SEA · Constantinople

T U R K E Y

G R E E C E · Athens

Malta

Adalia

Mediterranean

Suda Bay

Sea

Cyprus

Tripoli

Jerusalem

Ras Haleima · Alexandria · Port Said · Suez

Cairo

E G Y P T

Farafrah Oasis

Dakhla Oasis

Red Sea

Assuan

Libyan

Desert

Nile

Wadi Halfa

Dongola

S U D A N

Khartoum

The Central Powers in November 1917
The route of the L.59 21-22 November 1917
Targets proposed by the captain in December 1917, but vetoed by the German Admiralty
Targets chosen in March 1918
Spot where on 7 April 1918 the L.59 accidentally caught fire, exploded and sank. None of her crew of 22 survived

0   250
Miles

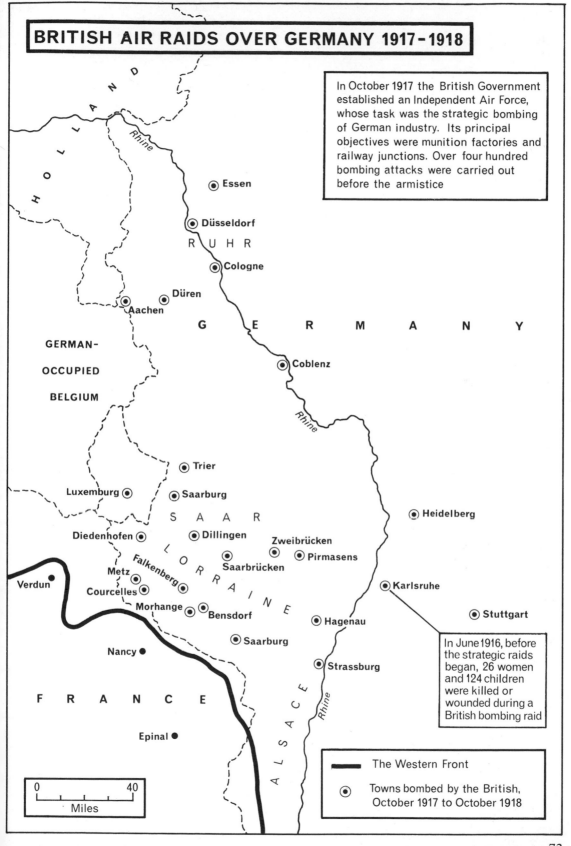

BRITISH AIR RAIDS OVER GERMANY 1917-1918

HOLLAND

Rhine

⊙ Essen

⊙ Düsseldorf

R U H R

⊙ Cologne

Düren ⊙
⊙ Aachen

G E R M A N Y

⊙ Coblenz

Rhine

GERMAN-

OCCUPIED

BELGIUM

In October 1917 the British Government established an Independent Air Force, whose task was the strategic bombing of German industry. Its principal objectives were munition factories and railway junctions. Over four hundred bombing attacks were carried out before the armistice

⊙ Trier

Luxemburg ⊙

⊙ Saarburg

S A A R

⊙ Heidelberg

Diedenhofen ⊙

⊙ Dillingen

Falkenberg
Metz ⊙
Courcelles ⊙

⊙ Saarbrücken

Zweibrücken ⊙
⊙ Pirmasens

L O R R A I N E

Morhange ⊙ ⊙ Bensdorf

⊙ Saarburg

⊙ Karlsruhe

⊙ Stuttgart

⊙ Hagenau

Verdun ●

Nancy ●

⊙ Strassburg

In June 1916, before the strategic raids began, 26 women and 124 children were killed or wounded during a British bombing raid

F R A N C E

A L S A C E

Rhine

Epinal ●

0   40

Miles

━━━ The Western Front

⊙ Towns bombed by the British, October 1917 to October 1918

Section Six

THE WAR AT SEA

We sift the drifting sea,
   and blindly grope beneath;
obscure and toilsome we,
   the fishermen of death.

E. HILTON-YOUNG
"MINE-SWEEPING TRAWLERS"

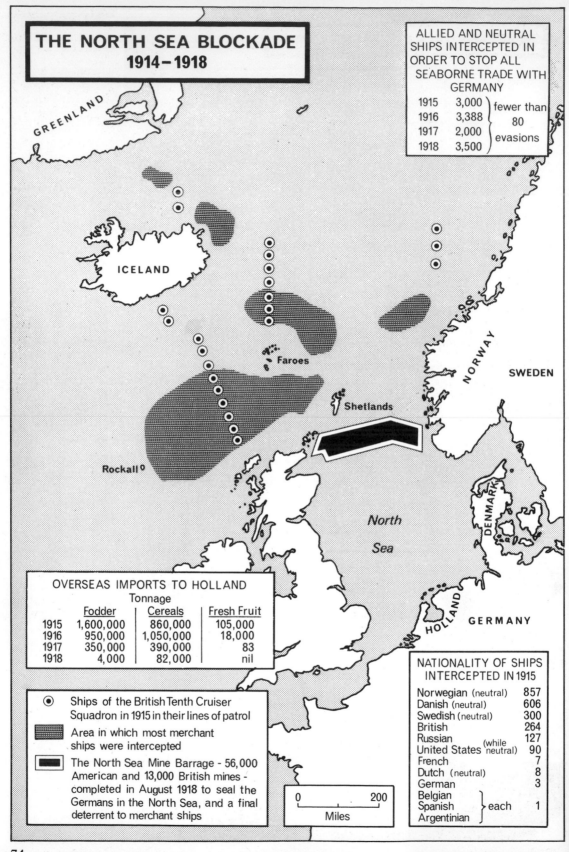

THE NORTH SEA BLOCKADE 1914–1918

GREENLAND

ICELAND

Faroes

Shetlands

Rockall

NORWAY

SWEDEN

DENMARK

North Sea

HOLLAND

GERMANY

OVERSEAS IMPORTS TO HOLLAND
Tonnage

	Fodder	Cereals	Fresh Fruit
1915	1,600,000	860,000	105,000
1916	950,000	1,050,000	18,000
1917	350,000	390,000	83
1918	4,000	82,000	nil

⊙ Ships of the British Tenth Cruiser Squadron in 1915 in their lines of patrol

▨ Area in which most merchant ships were intercepted

▬ The North Sea Mine Barrage - 56,000 American and 13,000 British mines - completed in August 1918 to seal the Germans in the North Sea, and a final deterrent to merchant ships

NATIONALITY OF SHIPS INTERCEPTED IN 1915

Norwegian (neutral)	857
Danish (neutral)	606
Swedish (neutral)	300
British	264
Russian	127
United States (while neutral)	90
French	7
Dutch (neutral)	8
German	3
Belgian	1 each
Spanish	
Argentinian	

0   200
Miles

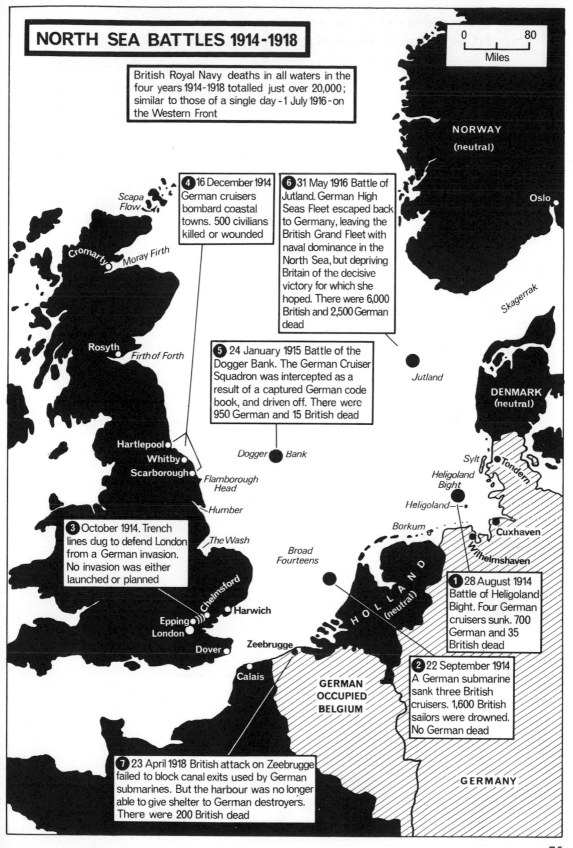

NORTH SEA BATTLES 1914-1918

0   80
Miles

British Royal Navy deaths in all waters in the four years 1914-1918 totalled just over 20,000; similar to those of a single day - 1 July 1916 - on the Western Front

NORWAY (neutral)

Oslo

Scapa Flow

Cromarty Moray Firth

4 16 December 1914 German cruisers bombard coastal towns. 500 civilians killed or wounded

6 31 May 1916 Battle of Jutland. German High Seas Fleet escaped back to Germany, leaving the British Grand Fleet with naval dominance in the North Sea, but depriving Britain of the decisive victory for which she hoped. There were 6,000 British and 2,500 German dead

Skagerrak

Rosyth   Firth of Forth

5 24 January 1915 Battle of the Dogger Bank. The German Cruiser Squadron was intercepted as a result of a captured German code book, and driven off. There were 950 German and 15 British dead

Jutland

DENMARK (neutral)

Hartlepool   Sylt   Tondern
Whitby   Heligoland Bight
Scarborough   Flamborough Head   Heligoland

Dogger Bank

Humber   Borkum   Cuxhaven
Wilhelmshaven

3 October 1914. Trench lines dug to defend London from a German invasion. No invasion was either launched or planned

The Wash

Broad Fourteens

1 28 August 1914 Battle of Heligoland Bight. Four German cruisers sunk. 700 German and 35 British dead

Chelmsford
Epping   Harwich
London

H O L L A N D (neutral)

2 22 September 1914 A German submarine sank three British cruisers. 1,600 British sailors were drowned. No German dead

Zeebrugge
Dover

Calais

GERMAN OCCUPIED BELGIUM

GERMANY

7 23 April 1918 British attack on Zeebrugge failed to block canal exits used by German submarines. But the harbour was no longer able to give shelter to German destroyers. There were 200 British dead

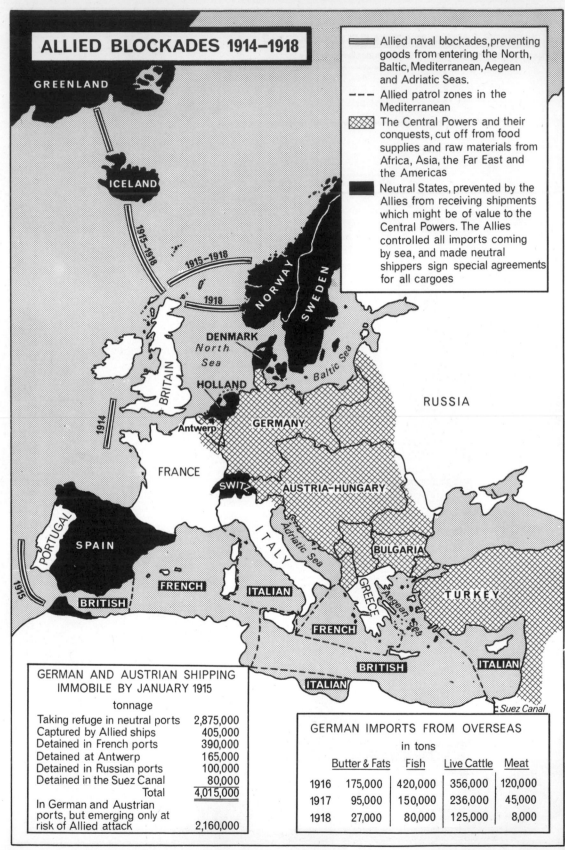

ALLIED BLOCKADES 1914–1918

GREENLAND

ICELAND

Allied naval blockades, preventing goods from entering the North, Baltic, Mediterranean, Aegean and Adriatic Seas.

- - - Allied patrol zones in the Mediterranean

The Central Powers and their conquests, cut off from food supplies and raw materials from Africa, Asia, the Far East and the Americas

Neutral States, prevented by the Allies from receiving shipments which might be of value to the Central Powers. The Allies controlled all imports coming by sea, and made neutral shippers sign special agreements for all cargoes

1915–1918

1915–1918

1918

NORWAY

SWEDEN

RUSSIA

DENMARK

North Sea

Baltic Sea

1914

BRITAIN

HOLLAND

Antwerp

GERMANY

FRANCE

SWITZ

AUSTRIA–HUNGARY

PORTUGAL

SPAIN

1915

ITALY

Adriatic Sea

BULGARIA

GREECE

TURKEY

BRITISH

FRENCH

ITALIAN

Aegean Sea

FRENCH

BRITISH

ITALIAN

ITALIAN

ITALIAN

Suez Canal

GERMAN AND AUSTRIAN SHIPPING IMMOBILE BY JANUARY 1915

tonnage

Taking refuge in neutral ports	2,875,000
Captured by Allied ships	405,000
Detained in French ports	390,000
Detained at Antwerp	165,000
Detained in Russian ports	100,000
Detained in the Suez Canal	80,000
Total	4,015,000
In German and Austrian ports, but emerging only at risk of Allied attack	2,160,000

GERMAN IMPORTS FROM OVERSEAS

in tons

	Butter & Fats	Fish	Live Cattle	Meat
1916	175,000	420,000	356,000	120,000
1917	95,000	150,000	236,000	45,000
1918	27,000	80,000	125,000	8,000

FOOD RIOTS IN GERMANY 1916

North Sea

Baltic Sea

Barnbeck
Kiel
Lübeck
Hamburg Messberg
Hammersbooch
Bremen

Charlottenburg
Hanover Brunswick Berlin
Munster Magdeburg
Posen
Duisberg
Essen
Düsseldorf Halle
Leipzig
Cologne Dresden
Aachen Jena Breslau
Coblenz Chemnitz
Frankfurt on Main

Nuremberg

Stuttgart

Colmar Munich

Number of deaths
attributed to the
blockade:
1915   88,235
1916   121,114
1917   259,627
1918   293,760

● Cities in which food riots
broke out during 1916

The British blockade led to a severe
food shortage in Germany. As a
result, riots were frequent, and
workers were often granted extra
rations to induce them to return
to work

0   100
Miles

THE WESTERN APPROACHES 1914-1918

German submarines sunk by
Britain 1914-1918: total 48

Convoy collection points, with the
number of convoys leaving every
16 days. Following the introduction
of convoys in June 1917, submarine
sinkings of merchant shipping
fell sharply

With the introduction of the convoy
system in June 1917, German submarines
attacking merchant ships were liable to
be set upon by Allied escort vessels
and even attacked from the air

SCOTLAND

2 Lamlash

ATLANTIC

OCEAN

IRELAND

Irish Sea

7 Liverpool

WALES

ENGLAND

4 Milford

Falmouth Devonport
2 4

English

Channel

FRANCE

0   100
Miles

Between 1914 and 1918 German submarines sank over
11 million tons of Allied shipping, of which nearly 8
million tons were British. Over 2,000 British naval and
merchant ships and 578 fishing boats were torpedoed,
killing 12,723 sailors, 908 civilians and 63 fishermen. The
British sank 178 U-boats, killing 515 officers and 4,849 men

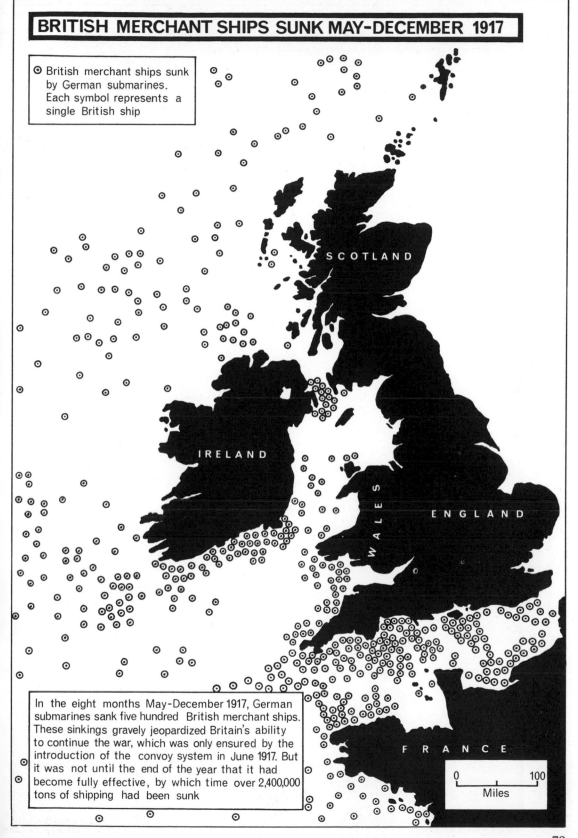

BRITISH MERCHANT SHIPS SUNK MAY–DECEMBER 1917

⊙ British merchant ships sunk by German submarines. Each symbol represents a single British ship

SCOTLAND

IRELAND

W A L E S

E N G L A N D

F R A N C E

In the eight months May–December 1917, German submarines sank five hundred British merchant ships. These sinkings gravely jeopardized Britain's ability to continue the war, which was only ensured by the introduction of the convoy system in June 1917. But it was not until the end of the year that it had become fully effective, by which time over 2,400,000 tons of shipping had been sunk

0 — 100
Miles

79

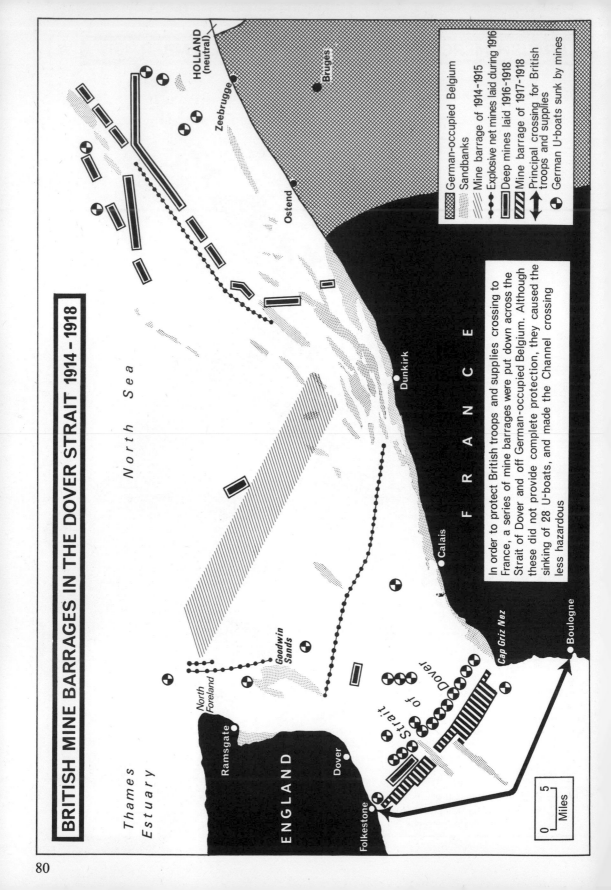

BRITISH MINE BARRAGES IN THE DOVER STRAIT 1914–1918

HOLLAND (neutral)

Bruges

Zeebrugge

Ostend

North Sea

Thames Estuary

North Foreland

Ramsgate

ENGLAND

Dover

Goodwin Sands

Folkestone

Strait of Dover

Cap Griz Nez

Calais

Dunkirk

F R A N C E

Boulogne

Legend:

- German-occupied Belgium
- Sandbanks
- Mine barrage of 1914–1915
- Explosive net mines laid during 1916
- Deep mines laid 1916–1918
- Mine barrage of 1917–1918
- Principal crossing for British troops and supplies
- German U-boats sunk by mines

In order to protect British troops and supplies crossing to France, a series of mine barrages were put down across the Strait of Dover and off German-occupied Belgium. Although these did not provide complete protection, they caused the sinking of 28 U-boats, and made the Channel crossing less hazardous

0   5
Miles

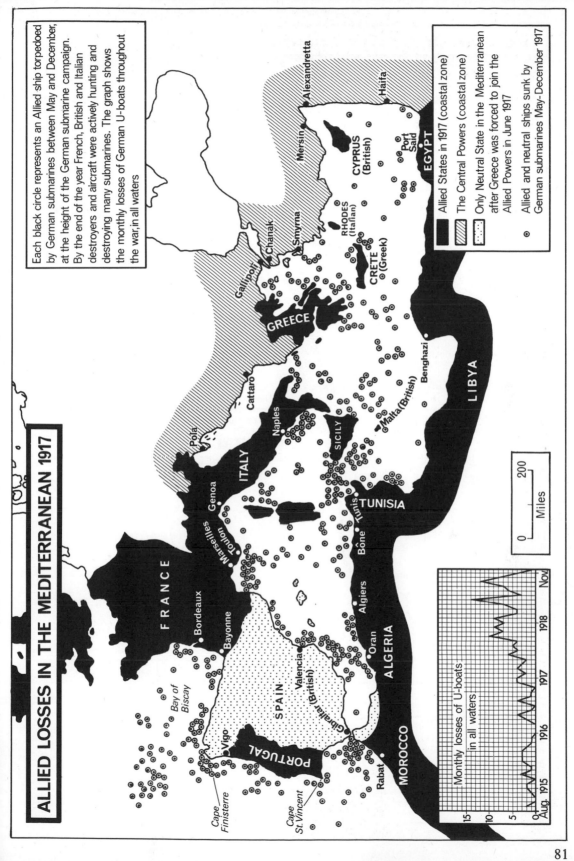

ALLIED LOSSES IN THE MEDITERRANEAN 1917

Each black circle represents an Allied ship torpedoed by German submarines between May and December, at the height of the German submarine campaign. By the end of the year French, British and Italian destroyers and aircraft were actively hunting and destroying many submarines. The graph shows the monthly losses of German U-boats throughout the war, in all waters

Allied States in 1917 (coastal zone)

The Central Powers (coastal zone)

Only Neutral State in the Mediterranean after Greece was forced to join the Allied Powers in June 1917

Allied and neutral ships sunk by German submarines May-December 1917

FRANCE

Bordeaux
Bayonne
Bay of Biscay
Cape Finisterre
Cape St. Vincent
Vigo
PORTUGAL
SPAIN
Valencia
Gibraltar (British)
Rabat
MOROCCO
ALGERIA
Oran
Algiers
Bône
Tunis
TUNISIA
LIBYA
Benghazi
EGYPT
Port Said
Haifa
Alexandretta
Mersin
CYPRUS (British)
RHODES (Italian)
CRETE (Greek)
Smyrna
Chanak
Gallipoli
GREECE
Pola
Cattaro
ITALY
Genoa
Marseilles
Toulon
Naples
SICILY
Malta (British)

0   200
Miles

Monthly losses of U-boats in all waters

15
10
5
0
Aug. 1915   1916   1917   1918   Nov

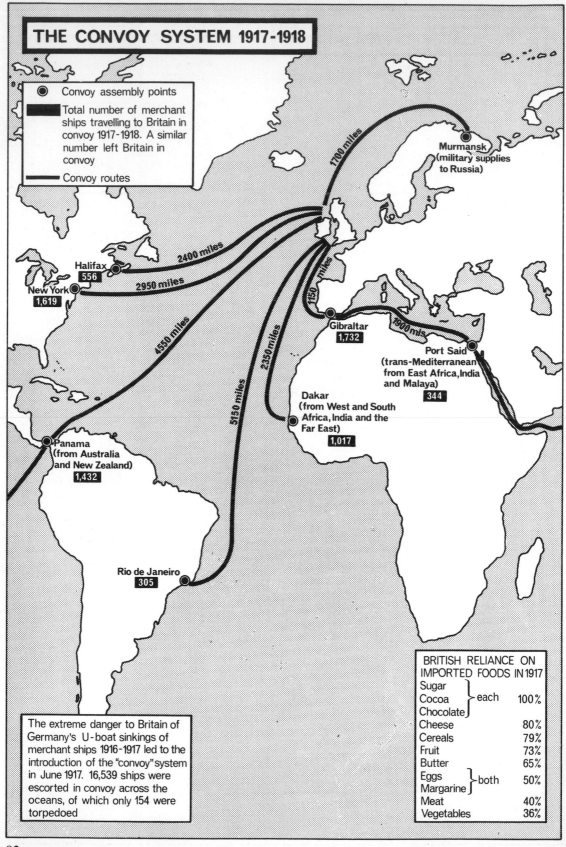

THE CONVOY SYSTEM 1917-1918

◉ Convoy assembly points

▬ Total number of merchant ships travelling to Britain in convoy 1917-1918. A similar number left Britain in convoy

━ Convoy routes

1700 miles

Murmansk
(military supplies
to Russia)

2400 miles

Halifax
556

2950 miles

New York
1,619

1150 miles

4550 miles

2350 miles

Gibraltar
1,732

1900 mls

Port Said
(trans-Mediterranean
from East Africa, India
and Malaya)
344

5150 miles

Dakar
(from West and South
Africa, India and the
Far East)
1,017

Panama
(from Australia
and New Zealand)
1,432

Rio de Janeiro
305

The extreme danger to Britain of Germany's U-boat sinkings of merchant ships 1916-1917 led to the introduction of the "convoy" system in June 1917. 16,539 ships were escorted in convoy across the oceans, of which only 154 were torpedoed

BRITISH RELIANCE ON IMPORTED FOODS IN 1917	
Sugar ⎫	
Cocoa ⎬ each	100%
Chocolate ⎭	
Cheese	80%
Cereals	79%
Fruit	73%
Butter	65%
Eggs ⎫ both	50%
Margarine ⎭	
Meat	40%
Vegetables	36%

82

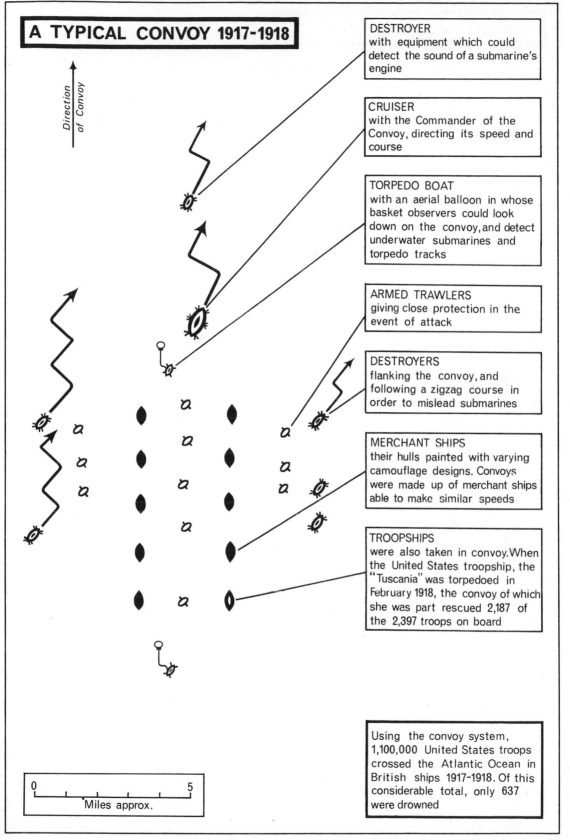

A TYPICAL CONVOY 1917-1918

Direction of Convoy

DESTROYER
with equipment which could detect the sound of a submarine's engine

CRUISER
with the Commander of the Convoy, directing its speed and course

TORPEDO BOAT
with an aerial balloon in whose basket observers could look down on the convoy, and detect underwater submarines and torpedo tracks

ARMED TRAWLERS
giving close protection in the event of attack

DESTROYERS
flanking the convoy, and following a zigzag course in order to mislead submarines

MERCHANT SHIPS
their hulls painted with varying camouflage designs. Convoys were made up of merchant ships able to make similar speeds

TROOPSHIPS
were also taken in convoy. When the United States troopship, the "Tuscania" was torpedoed in February 1918, the convoy of which she was part rescued 2,187 of the 2,397 troops on board

Using the convoy system, 1,100,000 United States troops crossed the Atlantic Ocean in British ships 1917-1918. Of this considerable total, only 637 were drowned

0   5

Miles approx.

83

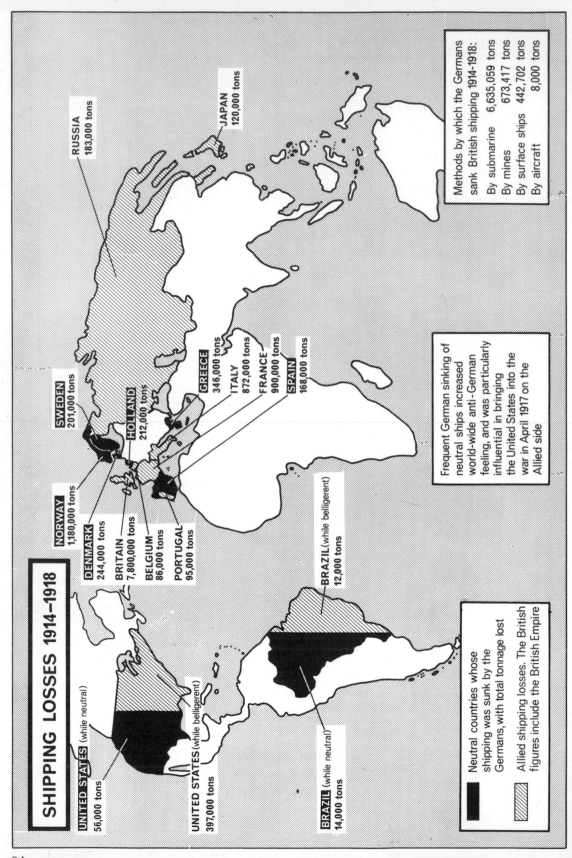

SHIPPING LOSSES 1914–1918

RUSSIA
183,000 tons

JAPAN
120,000 tons

SWEDEN
201,000 tons

HOLLAND
212,000 tons

GREECE
346,000 tons

ITALY
872,000 tons

FRANCE
900,000 tons

SPAIN
168,000 tons

NORWAY
1,180,000 tons

DENMARK
244,000 tons

BRITAIN
7,800,000 tons

BELGIUM
86,000 tons

PORTUGAL
95,000 tons

BRAZIL (while belligerent)
12,000 tons

UNITED STATES (while neutral)
56,000 tons

UNITED STATES (while belligerent)
397,000 tons

BRAZIL (while neutral)
14,000 tons

Methods by which the Germans
sank British shipping 1914-1918:

By submarine   6,635,059 tons
By mines   673,417 tons
By surface ships 442,702 tons
By aircraft   8,000 tons

Frequent German sinking of
neutral ships increased
world-wide anti-German
feeling, and was particularly
influential in bringing
the United States into the
war in April 1917 on the
Allied side

Neutral countries whose
shipping was sunk by the
Germans, with total tonnage lost

Allied shipping losses. The British
figures include the British Empire

BRITISH MERCHANT SHIP LOSSES 1917–1918

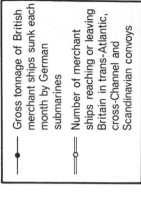

Gross tonnage of British merchant ships sunk each month by German submarines

Number of merchant ships reaching or leaving Britain in trans-Atlantic, cross-Channel and Scandinavian convoys

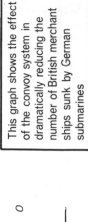

This graph shows the effect of the convoy system in dramatically reducing the number of British merchant ships sunk by German submarines

Number of ships in convoy

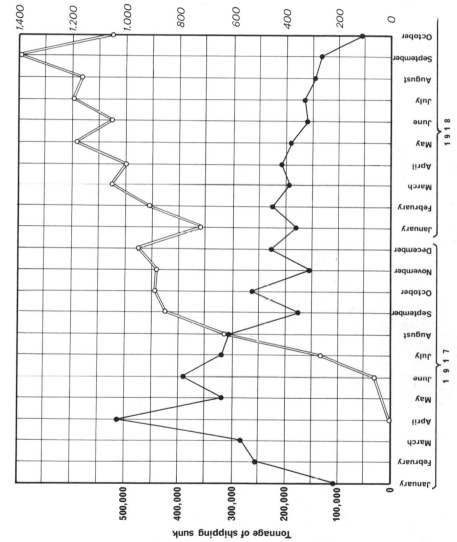

Tonnage of shipping sunk

ALLIED LOSSES OFF NORTH AMERICA 1917

On 6 April 1917 the United States declared war on Germany. This action was largely prompted because of increasingly frequent German sinkings of U.S. ships. This map shows each Allied ship sunk off North America between April and October 1917, when U-boat strength was at its peak. The graph shows the monthly strength of U-boats in all waters from 1915 to 1918

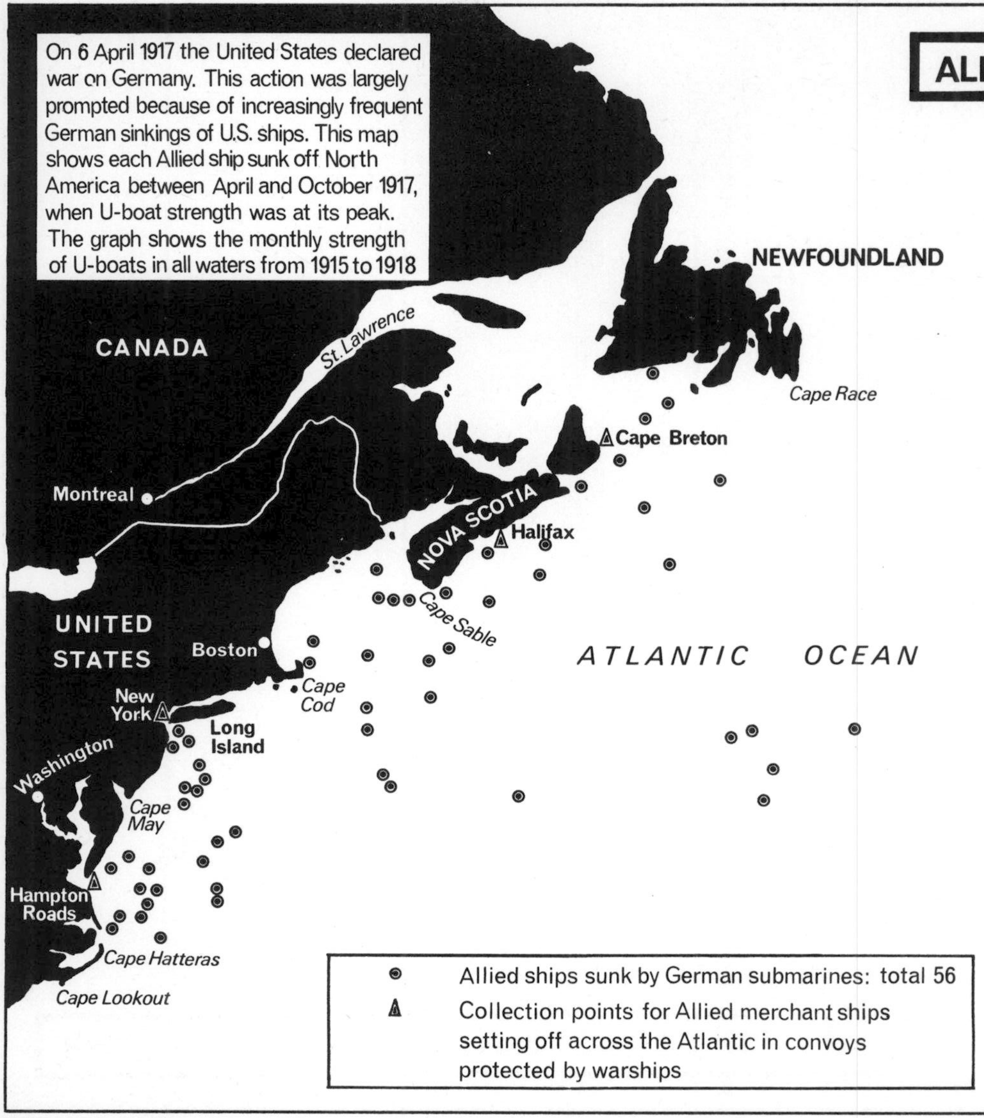

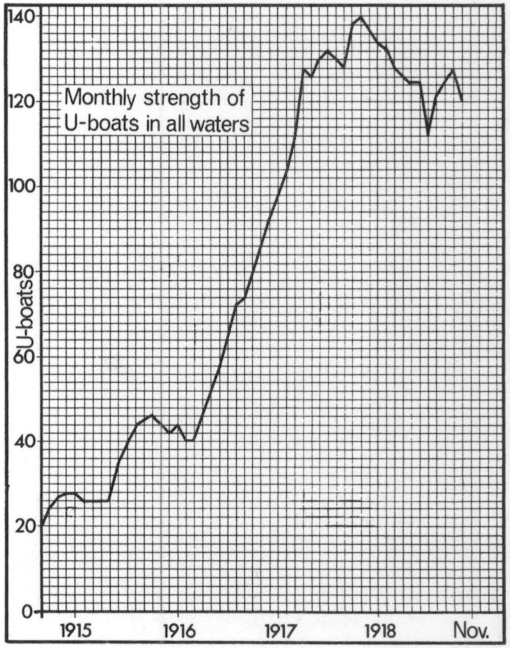

Monthly strength of U-boats in all waters

(graph axis)
U-boats: 0, 20, 40, 60, 80, 100, 120, 140
Years: 1915, 1916, 1917, 1918, Nov.

0   200
Miles

CANADA

NEWFOUNDLAND

Montreal

St. Lawrence

Cape Race

Cape Breton

NOVA SCOTIA

Halifax

Cape Sable

Boston

Long Island

New York

Cape Cod

Cape May

Washington

Hampton Roads

Cape Hatteras

Cape Lookout

UNITED STATES

ATLANTIC OCEAN

⊚   Allied ships sunk by German submarines: total 56

△   Collection points for Allied merchant ships setting off across the Atlantic in convoys protected by warships

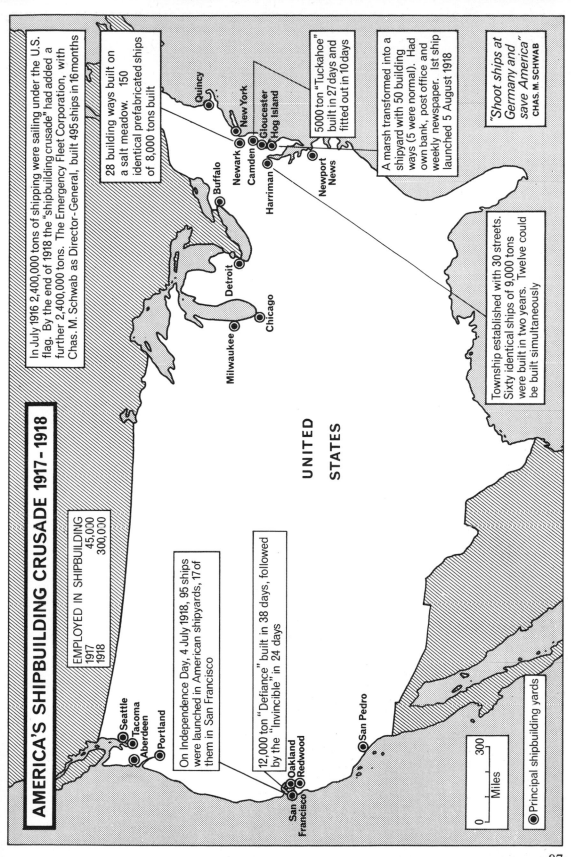

AMERICA'S SHIPBUILDING CRUSADE 1917-1918

In July 1916 2,400,000 tons of shipping were sailing under the U.S. flag. By the end of 1918 the "shipbuilding crusade" had added a further 2,400,000 tons. The Emergency Fleet Corporation, with Chas. M. Schwab as Director-General, built 495 ships in 16 months.

28 building ways built on a salt meadow. 150 identical prefabricated ships of 8,000 tons built

5000 ton "Tuckahoe" built in 27 days and fitted out in 10 days

A marsh transformed into a shipyard with 50 building ways (5 were normal). Had own bank, post office and weekly newspaper. 1st ship launched 5 August 1918

"Shoot ships at Germany and save America" **CHAS. M. SCHWAB**

EMPLOYED IN SHIPBUILDING
1917   45,000
1918   300,000

Township established with 30 streets. Sixty identical ships of 9,000 tons were built in two years. Twelve could be built simultaneously

On Independence Day, 4 July 1918, 95 ships were launched in American shipyards, 17 of them in San Francisco

12,000 ton "Defiance" built in 38 days, followed by the "Invincible" in 24 days

UNITED
STATES

Quincy
New York
Newark
Camden
Gloucester
Hog Island
Buffalo
Harriman
Newport News
Detroit
Chicago
Milwaukee

Seattle
Tacoma
Aberdeen
Portland

San Francisco
Oakland
Redwood

San Pedro

300
0
Miles

● Principal shipbuilding yards

Section Seven

1917

. . . Light many lamps and gather round his bed
Lend him your eyes, warm blood, and will to live
Speak to him; rouse him; you may save him yet.
He's young; he hated War; how should he die
When cruel old campaigners win safe through?

But death replied: "I choose him." So he went.
And there was silence in the summer night;
Silence and safety; and the veils of sleep.
Then, far away, the thudding of the guns.

SIEGFRIED SASSOON
"THE DEATH-BED"

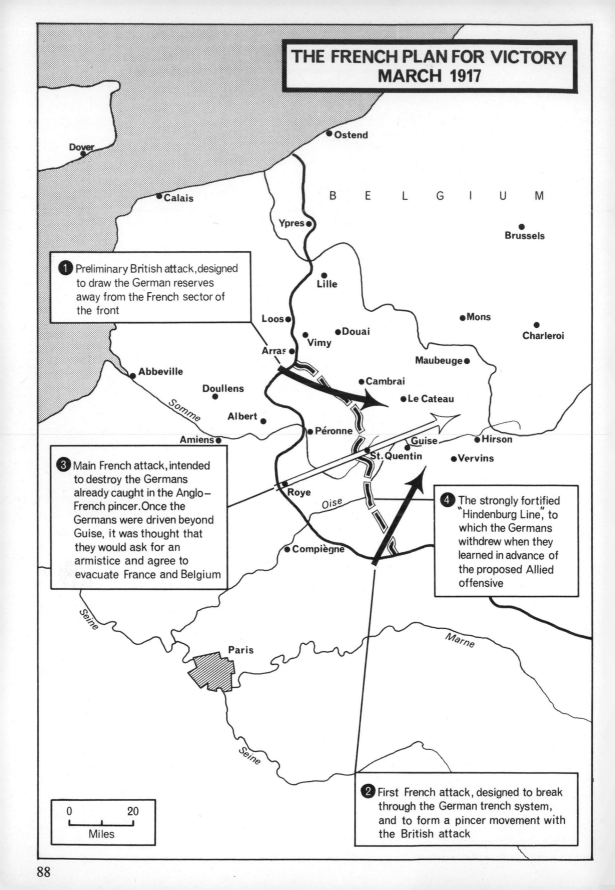

THE FRENCH PLAN FOR VICTORY MARCH 1917

Dover

Ostend

Calais

B E L G I U M

Ypres

Brussels

1 Preliminary British attack, designed to draw the German reserves away from the French sector of the front

Lille

Loos

Douai

Mons

Charleroi

Vimy

Arras

Maubeuge

Abbeville

Cambrai

Doullens

Le Cateau

Somme

Albert

Péronne

Amiens

Guise

Hirson

St. Quentin

Vervins

3 Main French attack, intended to destroy the Germans already caught in the Anglo–French pincer. Once the Germans were driven beyond Guise, it was thought that they would ask for an armistice and agree to evacuate France and Belgium

Roye

Oise

4 The strongly fortified "Hindenburg Line", to which the Germans withdrew when they learned in advance of the proposed Allied offensive

Compiègne

Seine

Marne

Paris

Seine

0   20
Miles

2 First French attack, designed to break through the German trench system, and to form a pincer movement with the British attack

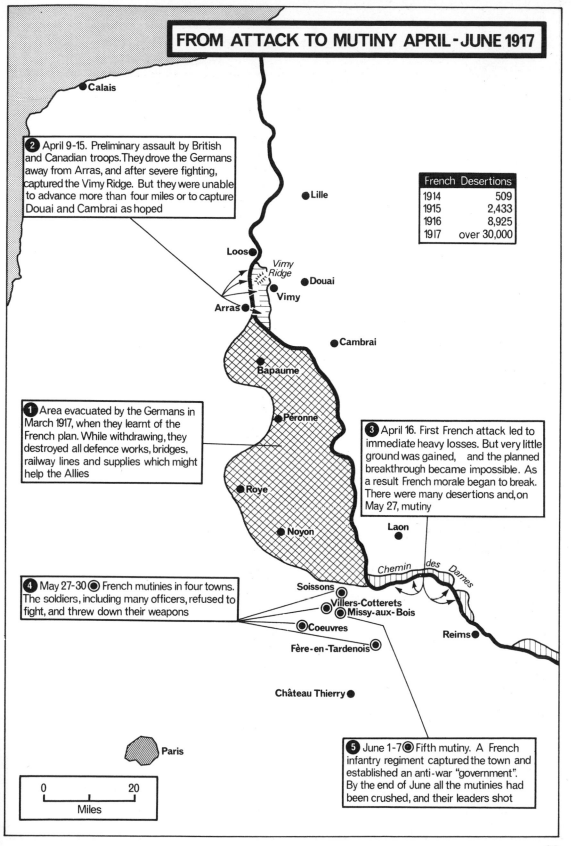

FROM ATTACK TO MUTINY APRIL - JUNE 1917

2 April 9-15. Preliminary assault by British and Canadian troops. They drove the Germans away from Arras, and after severe fighting, captured the Vimy Ridge. But they were unable to advance more than four miles or to capture Douai and Cambrai as hoped

French Desertions	
1914	509
1915	2,433
1916	8,925
1917	over 30,000

Calais

Lille

Loos

Vimy Ridge

Douai

Vimy

Arras

Cambrai

1 Area evacuated by the Germans in March 1917, when they learnt of the French plan. While withdrawing, they destroyed all defence works, bridges, railway lines and supplies which might help the Allies

Bapaume

Péronne

3 April 16. First French attack led to immediate heavy losses. But very little ground was gained, and the planned breakthrough became impossible. As a result French morale began to break. There were many desertions and, on May 27, mutiny

Roye

Noyon

Laon

Chemin des Dames

4 May 27-30 ◉ French mutinies in four towns. The soldiers, including many officers, refused to fight, and threw down their weapons

Soissons

Villers-Cotterets

Missy-aux-Bois

Coeuvres

Fère-en-Tardenois

Reims

Château Thierry

Paris

0	20

Miles

5 June 1-7 ◉ Fifth mutiny. A French infantry regiment captured the town and established an anti-war "government". By the end of June all the mutinies had been crushed, and their leaders shot

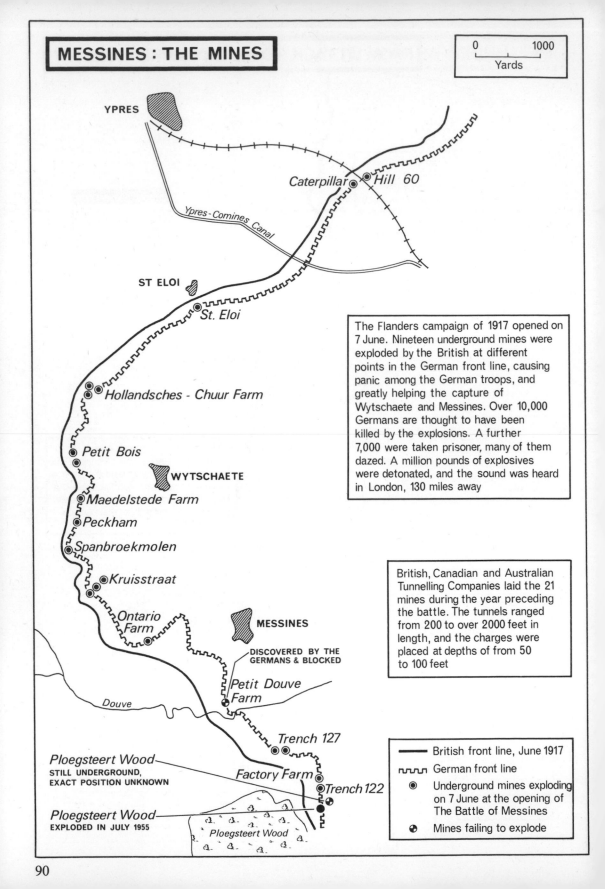

MESSINES : THE MINES

0   1000
Yards

YPRES

Caterpillar ● Hill 60

Ypres - Comines Canal

ST ELOI

St. Eloi

Hollandsches - Chuur Farm

Petit Bois

WYTSCHAETE

Maedelstede Farm

Peckham

Spanbroekmolen

Kruisstraat

Ontario Farm

MESSINES

DISCOVERED BY THE
GERMANS & BLOCKED

Petit Douve Farm

Douve

Trench 127

Ploegsteert Wood
STILL UNDERGROUND,
EXACT POSITION UNKNOWN

Factory Farm

Trench 122

Ploegsteert Wood
EXPLODED IN JULY 1955

Ploegsteert Wood

The Flanders campaign of 1917 opened on
7 June. Nineteen underground mines were
exploded by the British at different
points in the German front line, causing
panic among the German troops, and
greatly helping the capture of
Wytschaete and Messines. Over 10,000
Germans are thought to have been
killed by the explosions. A further
7,000 were taken prisoner, many of them
dazed. A million pounds of explosives
were detonated, and the sound was heard
in London, 130 miles away

British, Canadian and Australian
Tunnelling Companies laid the 21
mines during the year preceding
the battle. The tunnels ranged
from 200 to over 2000 feet in
length, and the charges were
placed at depths of from 50
to 100 feet

─────── British front line, June 1917

ⅢⅢⅢ German front line

● Underground mines exploding
on 7 June at the opening of
The Battle of Messines

◉ Mines failing to explode

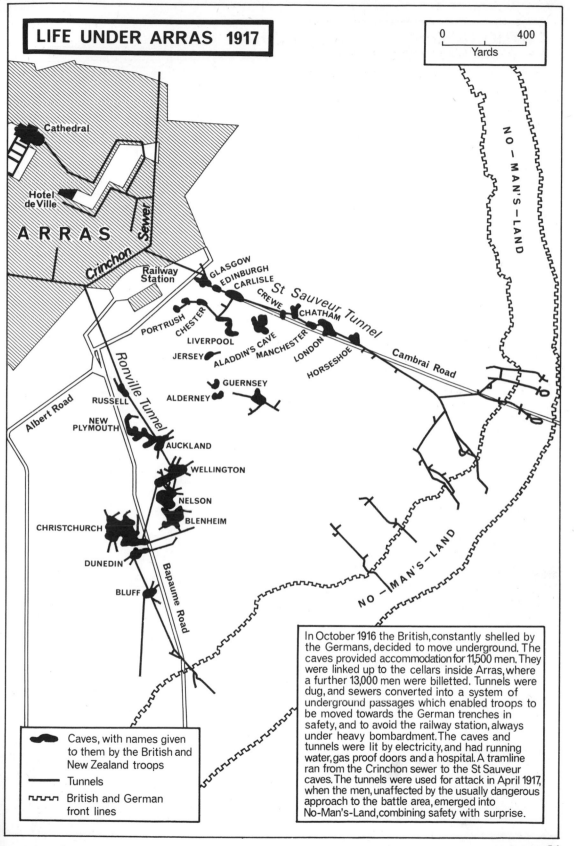

LIFE UNDER ARRAS 1917

0   400
Yards

Cathedral

Hotel de Ville

A R R A S

Crinchon Sewer

Railway Station

GLASGOW
EDINBURGH
CARLISLE
St Sauveur Tunnel
CREWE
CHATHAM
PORTRUSH
CHESTER
LIVERPOOL
ALADDIN'S CAVE
MANCHESTER
LONDON
HORSESHOE
Cambrai Road
JERSEY

GUERNSEY
ALDERNEY

RUSSELL
Ronville Tunnel
NEW PLYMOUTH
AUCKLAND
WELLINGTON
NELSON
BLENHEIM
CHRISTCHURCH
DUNEDIN
BLUFF
Bapaume Road

Albert Road

N O – M A N ' S – L A N D

N O – M A N ' S – L A N D

Caves, with names given to them by the British and New Zealand troops

Tunnels

British and German front lines

In October 1916 the British, constantly shelled by the Germans, decided to move underground. The caves provided accommodation for 11,500 men. They were linked up to the cellars inside Arras, where a further 13,000 men were billetted. Tunnels were dug, and sewers converted into a system of underground passages which enabled troops to be moved towards the German trenches in safety, and to avoid the railway station, always under heavy bombardment. The caves and tunnels were lit by electricity, and had running water, gas proof doors and a hospital. A tramline ran from the Crinchon sewer to the St Sauveur caves. The tunnels were used for attack in April 1917, when the men, unaffected by the usually dangerous approach to the battle area, emerged into No-Man's-Land, combining safety with surprise.

91

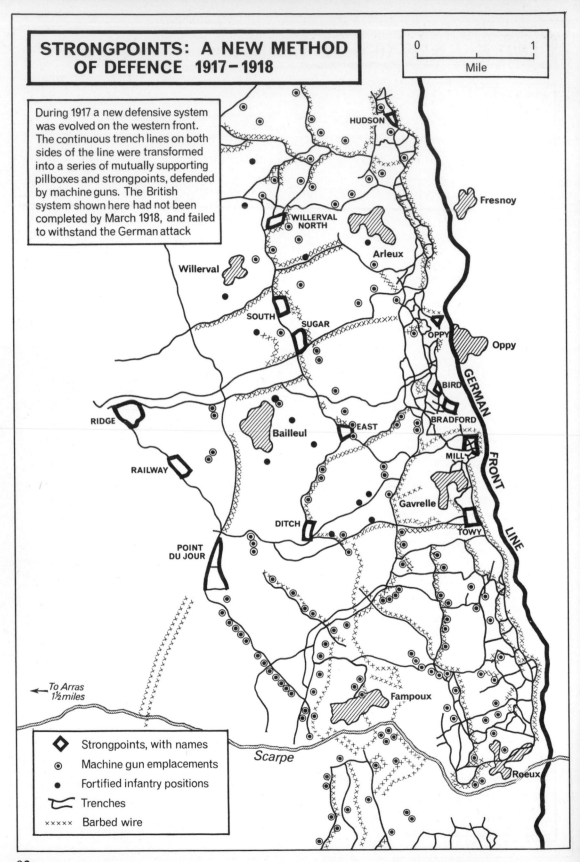

STRONGPOINTS: A NEW METHOD OF DEFENCE 1917–1918

0   1
Mile

During 1917 a new defensive system was evolved on the western front. The continuous trench lines on both sides of the line were transformed into a series of mutually supporting pillboxes and strongpoints, defended by machine guns. The British system shown here had not been completed by March 1918, and failed to withstand the German attack

HUDSON

Fresnoy

WILLERVAL NORTH

Arleux

Willerval

SOUTH

SUGAR

OPPY

Oppy

BIRD

GERMAN

RIDGE

BRADFORD

Bailleul

EAST

MILL

RAILWAY

Gavrelle

FRONT

DITCH

TOWY

POINT DU JOUR

LINE

← To Arras
1½ miles

Fampoux

Scarpe

Roeux

◆   Strongpoints, with names

◉   Machine gun emplacements

●   Fortified infantry positions

〰   Trenches

××××   Barbed wire

TANKS: A NEW METHOD OF ATTACK 1917-1918

Legend:
- ▬▬▬ The front line on November 19
- ◀▬▬ Main direction of Tank advance
- ▬ ▬ ▬ Furthest British advance, November 29
- ◁═══ German counter attacks
- ••••• Final front line, December 7

"Accusing as I do without exception all the great ally offensives of 1915, 1916, and 1917, as needless and wrongly conceived operations of infinite cost, I am bound to reply to the question, What else could be done? And I answer it, pointing to the Battle of Cambrai, 'This could have been done.' This in many variants, this in larger and better forms ought to have been done, and would have been done if only the Generals had not been content to fight machine-gun bullets with the breasts of gallant men, and think that that was waging war."

CHURCHILL "WORLD CRISIS" Vol. 4 p.348

Bourlon

Bourlon Wood

CAMBRAI

Fontaine Notre Dame

Anneux

Canal de l'Escaut

Flesquières

Marcoing

Masnières

Havrincourt

Ribécourt

Crevecœur

Canal du Nord

Lateau Wood

Villers Plouich

Gonnelieu

Banteux

Gouzeaucourt

Villers Guislain

The Tank was a British invention of the First World War. On 20 November 1917, at Cambrai, 381 Tanks lumbered towards the German trenches, heralding a new era of warfare. But their initial success was countered by the tenacity of the German infantry, and two weeks later the British had lost almost as much ground as they had gained. As a result the Germans failed to appreciate the the significance of the Tank, and its role in 1918 was decisive in the final Allied advance

0	1	2	3

Miles

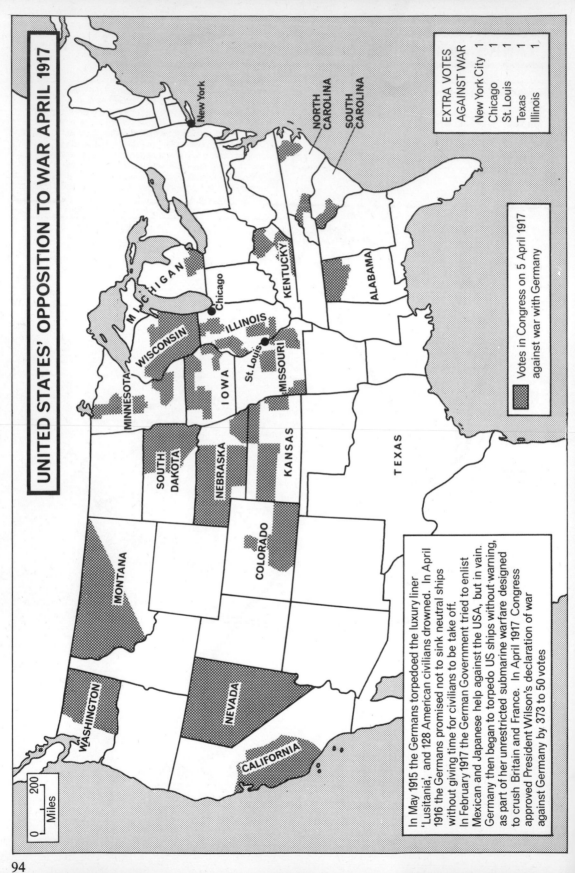

UNITED STATES' OPPOSITION TO WAR APRIL 1917

New York

NORTH
CAROLINA

SOUTH
CAROLINA

EXTRA VOTES
AGAINST WAR

New York City	1
Chicago	1
St. Louis	1
Texas	1
Illinois	1

MICHIGAN

Chicago

WISCONSIN

ILLINOIS

MINNESOTA

IOWA

St. Louis

MISSOURI

KENTUCKY

ALABAMA

SOUTH
DAKOTA

NEBRASKA

KANSAS

TEXAS

COLORADO

MONTANA

NEVADA

WASHINGTON

CALIFORNIA

Votes in Congress on 5 April 1917
against war with Germany

In May 1915 the Germans torpedoed the luxury liner
'Lusitania', and 128 American civilians drowned. In April
1916 the Germans promised not to sink neutral ships
without giving time for civilians to be take off.
In February 1917 the German Government tried to enlist
Mexican and Japanese help against the USA, but in vain.
Germany then began to torpedo US ships without warning,
as part of her unrestricted submarine warfare designed
to crush Britain and France. In April 1917 Congress
approved President Wilson's declaration of war
against Germany by 373 to 50 votes

200
Miles
0

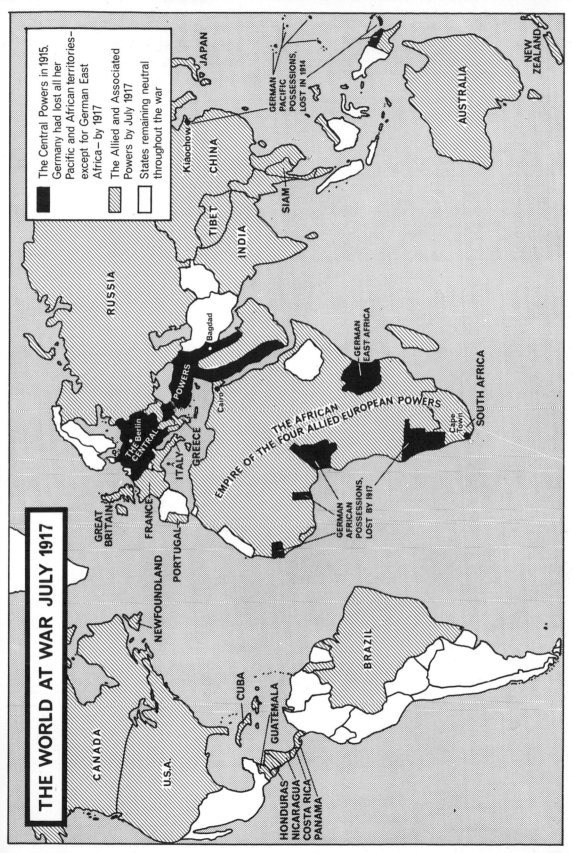

THE WORLD AT WAR JULY 1917

The Central Powers in 1915. Germany had lost all her Pacific and African territories—except for German East Africa—by 1917

The Allied and Associated Powers by July 1917

States remaining neutral throughout the war

CANADA

U.S.A.

NEWFOUNDLAND

CUBA

GUATEMALA

HONDURAS
NICARAGUA
COSTA RICA
PANAMA

BRAZIL

GREAT BRITAIN

FRANCE

PORTUGAL

THE CENTRAL POWERS

Berlin

ITALY

GREECE

RUSSIA

Bagdad

Cairo

EMPIRE OF THE FOUR ALLIED EUROPEAN POWERS

THE AFRICAN

GERMAN AFRICAN POSSESSIONS, LOST BY 1917

GERMAN EAST AFRICA

SOUTH AFRICA

Cape Town

TIBET

INDIA

SIAM

CHINA

Kiaochow

JAPAN

GERMAN PACIFIC POSSESSIONS, LOST IN 1914

AUSTRALIA

NEW ZEALAND

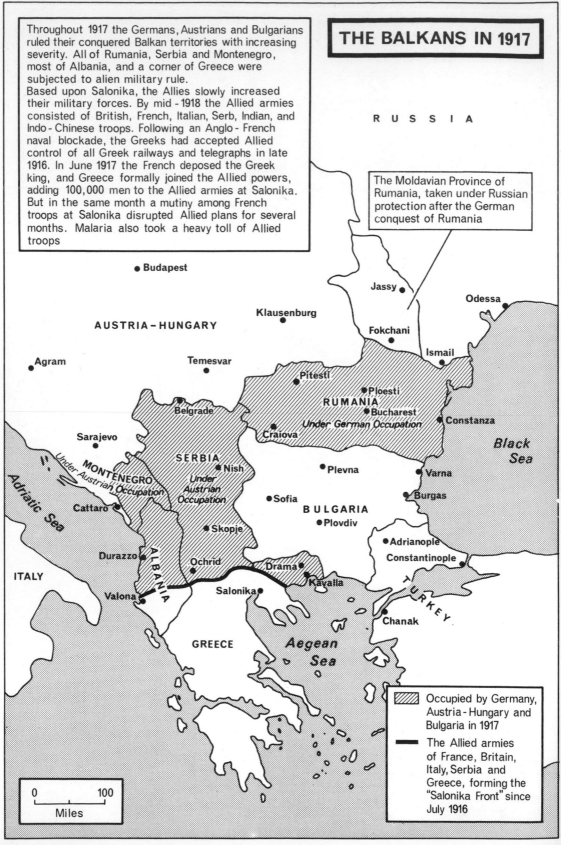

THE BALKANS IN 1917

Throughout 1917 the Germans, Austrians and Bulgarians ruled their conquered Balkan territories with increasing severity. All of Rumania, Serbia and Montenegro, most of Albania, and a corner of Greece were subjected to alien military rule.
Based upon Salonika, the Allies slowly increased their military forces. By mid-1918 the Allied armies consisted of British, French, Italian, Serb, Indian, and Indo-Chinese troops. Following an Anglo-French naval blockade, the Greeks had accepted Allied control of all Greek railways and telegraphs in late 1916. In June 1917 the French deposed the Greek king, and Greece formally joined the Allied powers, adding 100,000 men to the Allied armies at Salonika. But in the same month a mutiny among French troops at Salonika disrupted Allied plans for several months. Malaria also took a heavy toll of Allied troops

The Moldavian Province of Rumania, taken under Russian protection after the German conquest of Rumania

RUSSIA

• Budapest

Jassy •

Odessa •

Klausenburg •

AUSTRIA-HUNGARY

Fokchani •

Ismail •

• Agram

Temesvar •

Pitesti •

Ploesti •

RUMANIA
• Bucharest
Under German Occupation

Constanza •

Belgrade •

Craiova •

Sarajevo •

SERBIA

Nish •

Plevna •

Varna •

Black
Sea

MONTENEGRO
Under Austrian Occupation

Under Austrian Occupation

• Sofia

BULGARIA

Burgas •

Cattaro •

Adriatic
Sea

Skopje •

• Plovdiv

ITALY

Durazzo •

ALBANIA

Ochrid •

Drama •

• Adrianople

Constantinople

Kavalla •

TURKEY

Valona •

Salonika •

Chanak •

GREECE

Aegean
Sea

/// Occupied by Germany, Austria-Hungary and Bulgaria in 1917

━━ The Allied armies of France, Britain, Italy, Serbia and Greece, forming the "Salonika Front" since July 1916

0   100
Miles

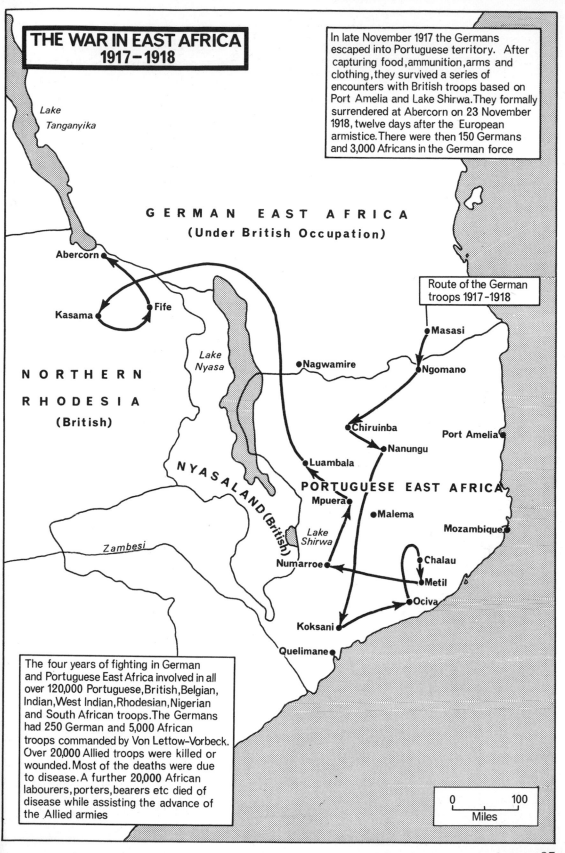

THE WAR IN EAST AFRICA 1917–1918

In late November 1917 the Germans escaped into Portuguese territory. After capturing food, ammunition, arms and clothing, they survived a series of encounters with British troops based on Port Amelia and Lake Shirwa. They formally surrendered at Abercorn on 23 November 1918, twelve days after the European armistice. There were then 150 Germans and 3,000 Africans in the German force

Lake Tanganyika

GERMAN EAST AFRICA
(Under British Occupation)

Abercorn

Kasama ● ●Fife

Route of the German troops 1917–1918

N O R T H E R N

R H O D E S I A

(British)

Lake Nyasa

●Nagwamire

●Masasi

●Ngomano

●Chiruinba

Port Amelia●

●Nanungu

Luambala●

N Y A S A L A N D (British)

PORTUGUESE EAST AFRICA

Mpuera●

●Malema

Mozambique●

Lake Shirwa

Zambesi

Numarroe●

●Chalau

●Metil

●Ociva

Koksani●

Quelimane●

The four years of fighting in German and Portuguese East Africa involved in all over 120,000 Portuguese, British, Belgian, Indian, West Indian, Rhodesian, Nigerian and South African troops. The Germans had 250 German and 5,000 African troops commanded by Von Lettow–Vorbeck. Over 20,000 Allied troops were killed or wounded. Most of the deaths were due to disease. A further 20,000 African labourers, porters, bearers etc died of disease while assisting the advance of the Allied armies

0   100
Miles

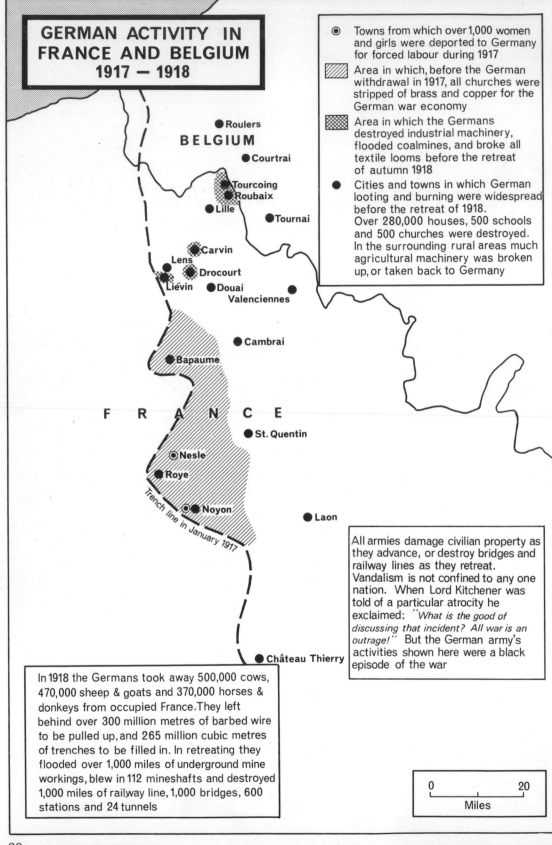

GERMAN ACTIVITY IN FRANCE AND BELGIUM 1917 — 1918

◉ Towns from which over 1,000 women and girls were deported to Germany for forced labour during 1917

▨ Area in which, before the German withdrawal in 1917, all churches were stripped of brass and copper for the German war economy

▨ Area in which the Germans destroyed industrial machinery, flooded coalmines, and broke all textile looms before the retreat of autumn 1918

● Cities and towns in which German looting and burning were widespread before the retreat of 1918.
Over 280,000 houses, 500 schools and 500 churches were destroyed. In the surrounding rural areas much agricultural machinery was broken up, or taken back to Germany

BELGIUM

● Roulers

● Courtrai

● Tourcoing
● Roubaix
● Lille
● Tournai

● Carvin
● Lens
● Drocourt
● Liévin
● Douai
Valenciennes

F R A N C E

● Cambrai

● Bapaume

● St. Quentin

◉ Nesle

● Roye

◉ Noyon

● Laon

Trench line in January 1917

● Château Thierry

All armies damage civilian property as they advance, or destroy bridges and railway lines as they retreat. Vandalism is not confined to any one nation. When Lord Kitchener was told of a particular atrocity he exclaimed: *"What is the good of discussing that incident? All war is an outrage!"* But the German army's activities shown here were a black episode of the war

In 1918 the Germans took away 500,000 cows, 470,000 sheep & goats and 370,000 horses & donkeys from occupied France. They left behind over 300 million metres of barbed wire to be pulled up, and 265 million cubic metres of trenches to be filled in. In retreating they flooded over 1,000 miles of underground mine workings, blew in 112 mineshafts and destroyed 1,000 miles of railway line, 1,000 bridges, 600 stations and 24 tunnels

0   20
Miles

GERMAN SOCIAL UNREST 1917–1918

North Sea

Baltic Sea

SCHLESWIG-HOLSTEIN

Danzig●

Kiel●

◉●Hamburg

●Bremen

P R U S S I A

◉●Berlin

◉●Magdeburg

Duisberg●
Essen●

RHINELAND

Halle●
◉●Leipzig

S A X O N Y
Chemnitz●
●Dresden

●Nuremburg

B A V A R I A

●Munich

Throughout 1917 there was growing industrial
unrest in Germany. The Allied blockade forced
the German Government to introduce
increasingly severe food rationing. Early in 1918
"meatless weeks" were decreed. These heightened
the discontent, and led to growing hatred of the
rich, who could still afford contraband food.
Added to social unrest was a mounting war-
weariness, stimulated by the Russian Bolshevik
decision in November 1917, to leave the war
altogether. Bolshevik ideas and propaganda
inside Germany were also gaining significant
successes

◉ Strikes in April 1917, against
   reduction in the bread ration.
● Strikes in January 1918, against
   the continuation of the war

0   90
Miles

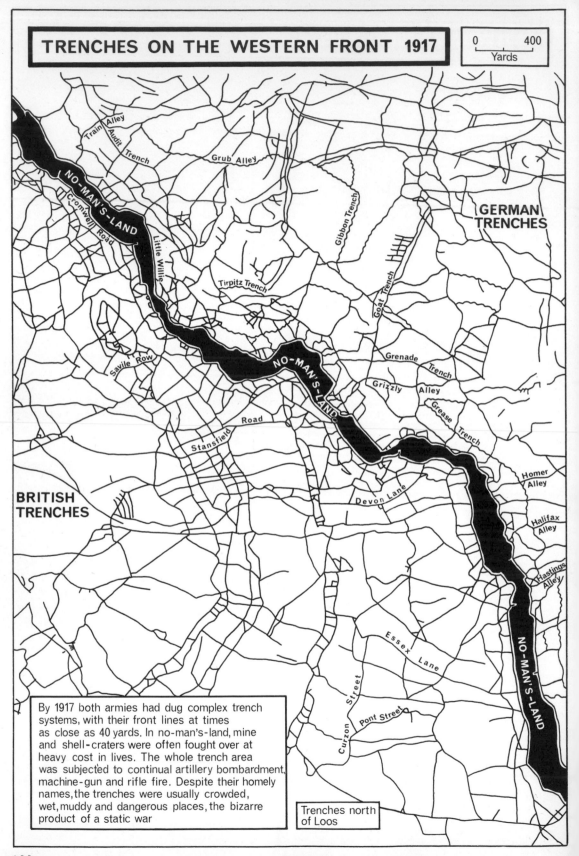

TRENCHES ON THE WESTERN FRONT 1917

0   400
Yards

NO-MAN'S-LAND

Train Alley
Audit Trench
Grub Alley
Cromwell Road
Little Willie
Tirpitz Trench
Gibbon Trench

GERMAN TRENCHES

Goat Trench
Grenade Trench
Grizzly Alley
Grease Trench

Savile Row

NO-MAN'S-LAND

Road
Stansfield
Devon Lane

BRITISH TRENCHES

Homer Alley
Halifax Alley
Hastings Alley

NO-MAN'S-LAND

Essex Lane

Curzon Street
Pont Street

By 1917 both armies had dug complex trench
systems, with their front lines at times
as close as 40 yards. In no-man's-land, mine
and shell-craters were often fought over at
heavy cost in lives. The whole trench area
was subjected to continual artillery bombardment,
machine-gun and rifle fire. Despite their homely
names, the trenches were usually crowded,
wet, muddy and dangerous places, the bizarre
product of a static war

Trenches north
of Loos

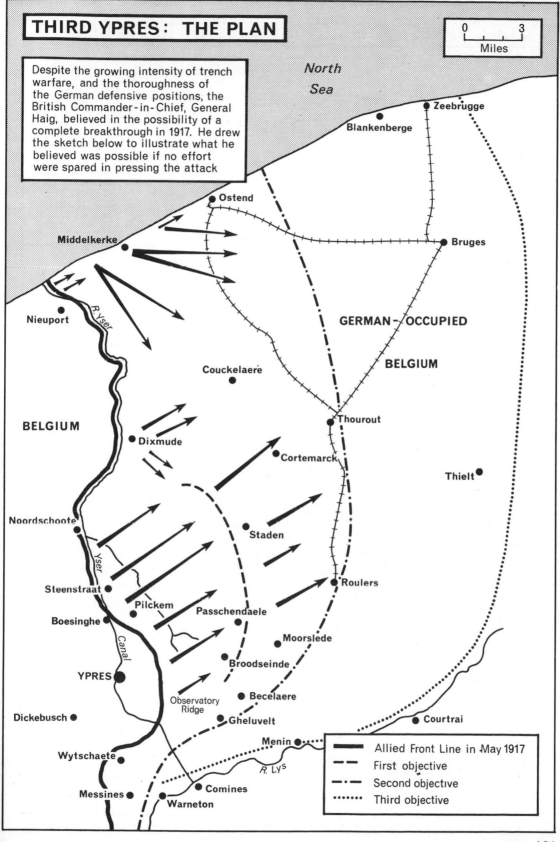

THIRD YPRES: THE PLAN

Despite the growing intensity of trench warfare, and the thoroughness of the German defensive positions, the British Commander-in-Chief, General Haig, believed in the possibility of a complete breakthrough in 1917. He drew the sketch below to illustrate what he believed was possible if no effort were spared in pressing the attack

0   3
Miles

North Sea

Zeebrugge

Blankenberge

Ostend

Middelkerke

Bruges

Nieuport

R. Yser

GERMAN — OCCUPIED

BELGIUM

Couckelaere

BELGIUM

Dixmude

Thourout

Cortemarck

Thielt

Noordschoote

Yser

Staden

Steenstraat

Pilckem

Roulers

Boesinghe

Passchendaele

Canal

Moorslede

YPRES

Broodseinde

Observatory Ridge

Becelaere

Dickebusch

Gheluvelt

Courtrai

Menin

Allied Front Line in May 1917

Wytschaete

R. Lys

First objective

Second objective

Messines

Comines

Third objective

Warneton

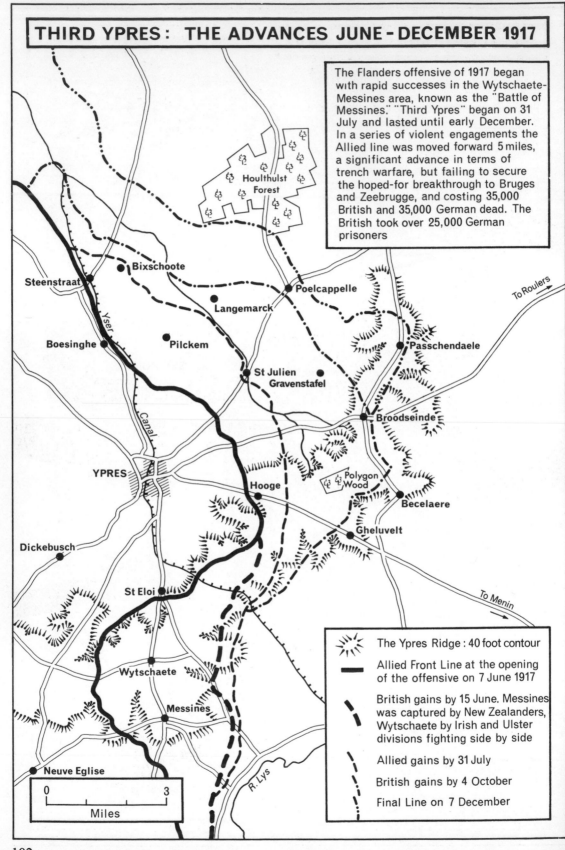

THIRD YPRES: THE ADVANCES JUNE - DECEMBER 1917

The Flanders offensive of 1917 began with rapid successes in the Wytschaete-Messines area, known as the "Battle of Messines." "Third Ypres" began on 31 July and lasted until early December. In a series of violent engagements the Allied line was moved forward 5 miles, a significant advance in terms of trench warfare, but failing to secure the hoped-for breakthrough to Bruges and Zeebrugge, and costing 35,000 British and 35,000 German dead. The British took over 25,000 German prisoners

Houlthulst Forest

Bixschoote

Steenstraat

To Roulers

Poelcappelle

Langemarck

Boesinghe

Pilckem

Passchendaele

St Julien
Gravenstafel

Broodseinde

YPRES

Hooge

Polygon Wood

Becelaere

Dickebusch

Gheluvelt

To Menin

St Eloi

Wytschaete

Messines

Neuve Eglise

R. Lys

Yser

Canal

The Ypres Ridge : 40 foot contour

Allied Front Line at the opening of the offensive on 7 June 1917

British gains by 15 June. Messines was captured by New Zealanders, Wytschaete by Irish and Ulster divisions fighting side by side

Allied gains by 31 July

British gains by 4 October

Final Line on 7 December

0   3
Miles

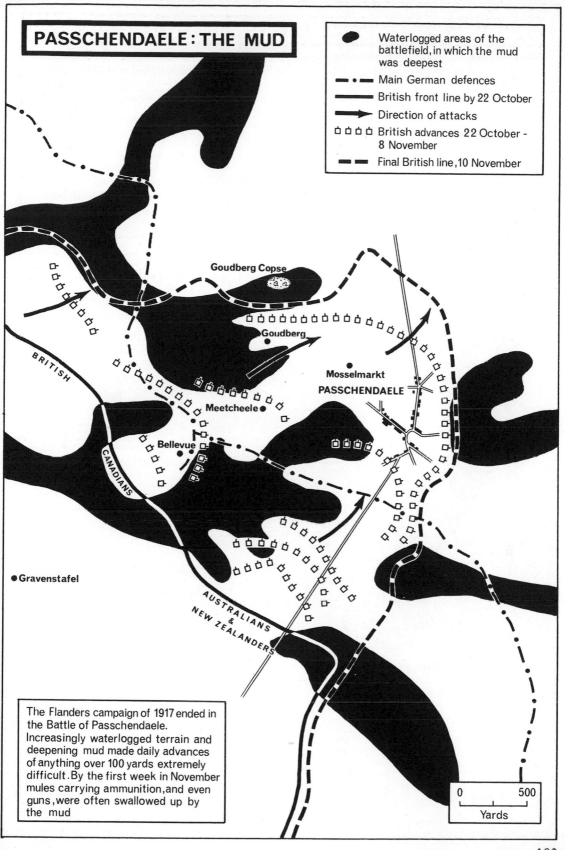

PASSCHENDAELE: THE MUD

Legend:
- Waterlogged areas of the battlefield, in which the mud was deepest
- Main German defences
- British front line by 22 October
- Direction of attacks
- British advances 22 October – 8 November
- Final British line, 10 November

Goudberg Copse

Goudberg

Mosselmarkt

PASSCHENDAELE

Meetcheele

Bellevue

BRITISH

CANADIANS

AUSTRALIANS & NEW ZEALANDERS

● Gravenstafel

The Flanders campaign of 1917 ended in the Battle of Passchendaele. Increasingly waterlogged terrain and deepening mud made daily advances of anything over 100 yards extremely difficult. By the first week in November mules carrying ammunition, and even guns, were often swallowed up by the mud

0   500
Yards

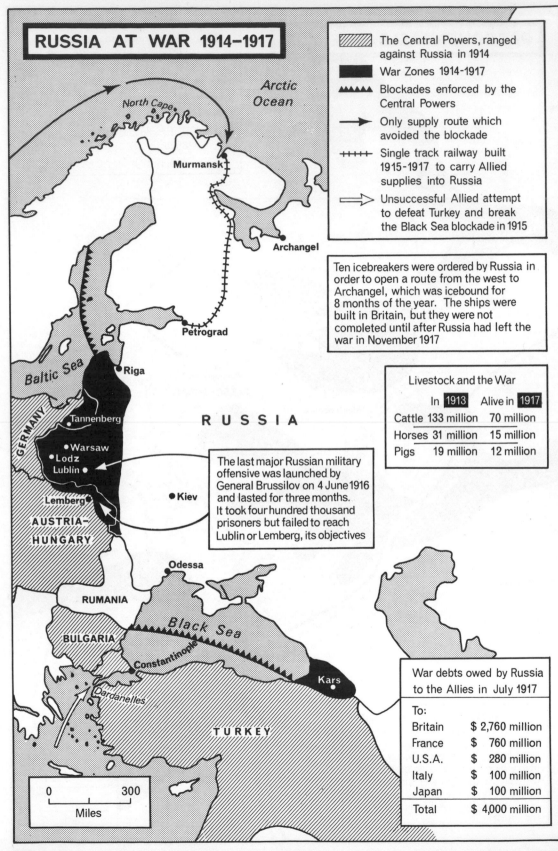

RUSSIA AT WAR 1914–1917

The Central Powers, ranged against Russia in 1914

War Zones 1914-1917

Blockades enforced by the Central Powers

Only supply route which avoided the blockade

Single track railway built 1915-1917 to carry Allied supplies into Russia

Unsuccessful Allied attempt to defeat Turkey and break the Black Sea blockade in 1915

Arctic Ocean

North Cape

Murmansk

Archangel

Petrograd

Baltic Sea

Riga

Tannenberg

Warsaw

Lodz

Lublin

Lemberg

AUSTRIA-HUNGARY

GERMANY

RUSSIA

Kiev

Odessa

RUMANIA

BULGARIA

Black Sea

Constantinople

Dardanelles

Kars

TURKEY

Ten icebreakers were ordered by Russia in order to open a route from the west to Archangel, which was icebound for 8 months of the year. The ships were built in Britain, but they were not completed until after Russia had left the war in November 1917

The last major Russian military offensive was launched by General Brussilov on 4 June 1916 and lasted for three months. It took four hundred thousand prisoners but failed to reach Lublin or Lemberg, its objectives

Livestock and the War		
In 1913	Alive in 1917	
Cattle	133 million	70 million
Horses	31 million	15 million
Pigs	19 million	12 million

War debts owed by Russia to the Allies in July 1917	
To:	
Britain	$ 2,760 million
France	$ 760 million
U.S.A.	$ 280 million
Italy	$ 100 million
Japan	$ 100 million
Total	$ 4,000 million

0   300
Miles

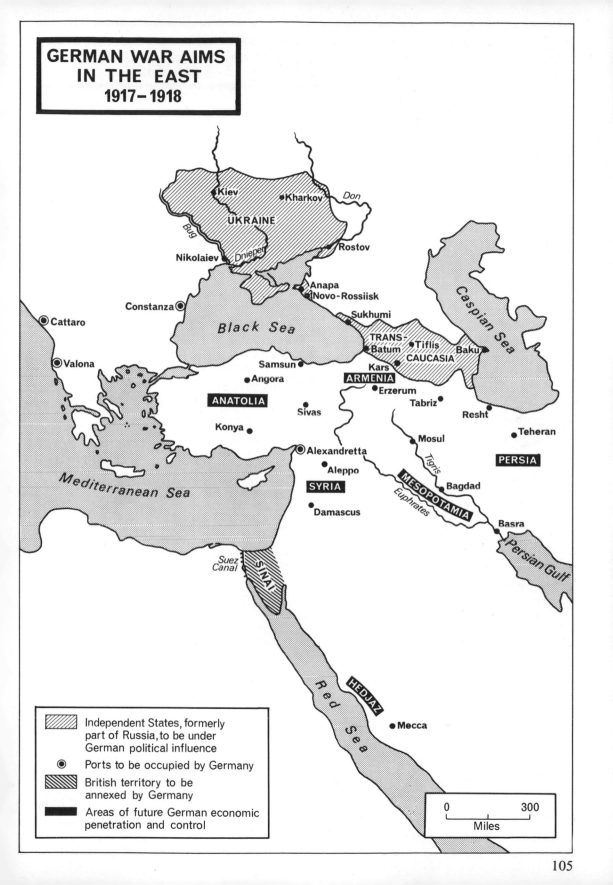

GERMAN WAR AIMS IN THE EAST 1917–1918

Kiev

Kharkov

Don

UKRAINE

Bug

Rostov

Dnieper

Nikolaiev

Anapa

Novo-Rossiisk

Constanza

Sukhumi

Black Sea

Caspian Sea

Cattaro

TRANS-

Batum

Tiflis

Baku

Valona

CAUCASIA

Samsun

Kars

ARMENIA

Angora

Erzerum

Tabriz

Resht

ANATOLIA

Sivas

Mosul

Teheran

Konya

PERSIA

Alexandretta

Tigris

Mediterranean Sea

Aleppo

MESOPOTAMIA

Bagdad

SYRIA

Euphrates

Damascus

Basra

Persian Gulf

Suez
Canal

SINAI

Red Sea

HEDJAZ

Mecca

Independent States, formerly
part of Russia, to be under
German political influence

Ports to be occupied by Germany

British territory to be
annexed by Germany

Areas of future German economic
penetration and control

0   300

Miles

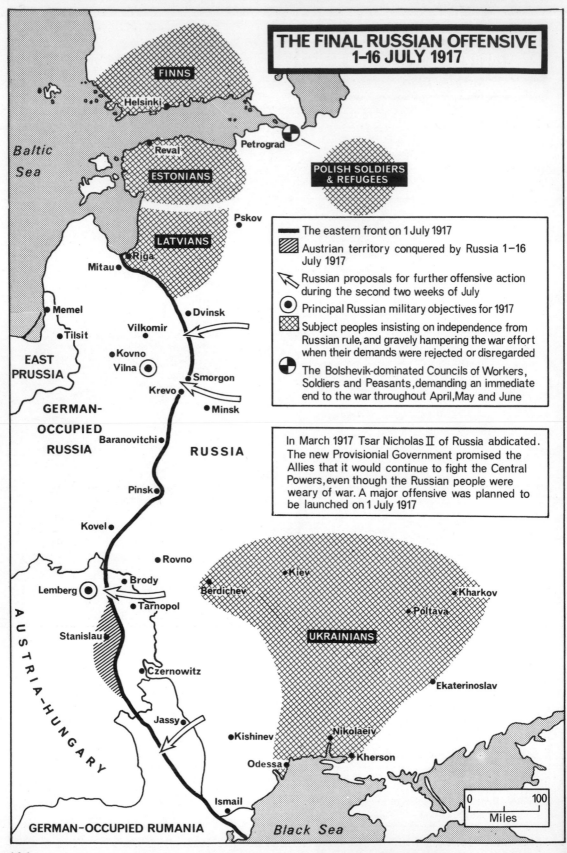

THE FINAL RUSSIAN OFFENSIVE
1–16 JULY 1917

FINNS

Helsinki

Baltic
Sea

Reval

Petrograd

ESTONIANS

POLISH SOLDIERS
& REFUGEES

Pskov

LATVIANS

Riga

Mitau

Memel

Tilsit

Dvinsk

Vilkomir

Kovno
Vilna

EAST
PRUSSIA

Smorgon

Krevo

GERMAN-

Minsk

OCCUPIED

Baranovitchi

RUSSIA

RUSSIA

Pinsk

Kovel

Rovno

Brody

Lemberg

Kiev

Tarnopol

Berdichev

Kharkov

Stanislau

Poltava

Czernowitz

UKRAINIANS

AUSTRIA-HUNGARY

Ekaterinoslav

Jassy

Kishinev

Nikolaeiv

Odessa

Kherson

Ismail

GERMAN-OCCUPIED RUMANIA

Black Sea

The eastern front on 1 July 1917

Austrian territory conquered by Russia 1–16 July 1917

Russian proposals for further offensive action during the second two weeks of July

Principal Russian military objectives for 1917

Subject peoples insisting on independence from Russian rule, and gravely hampering the war effort when their demands were rejected or disregarded

The Bolshevik-dominated Councils of Workers, Soldiers and Peasants, demanding an immediate end to the war throughout April, May and June

---

In March 1917 Tsar Nicholas II of Russia abdicated. The new Provisional Government promised the Allies that it would continue to fight the Central Powers, even though the Russian people were weary of war. A major offensive was planned to be launched on 1 July 1917

0   100
Miles

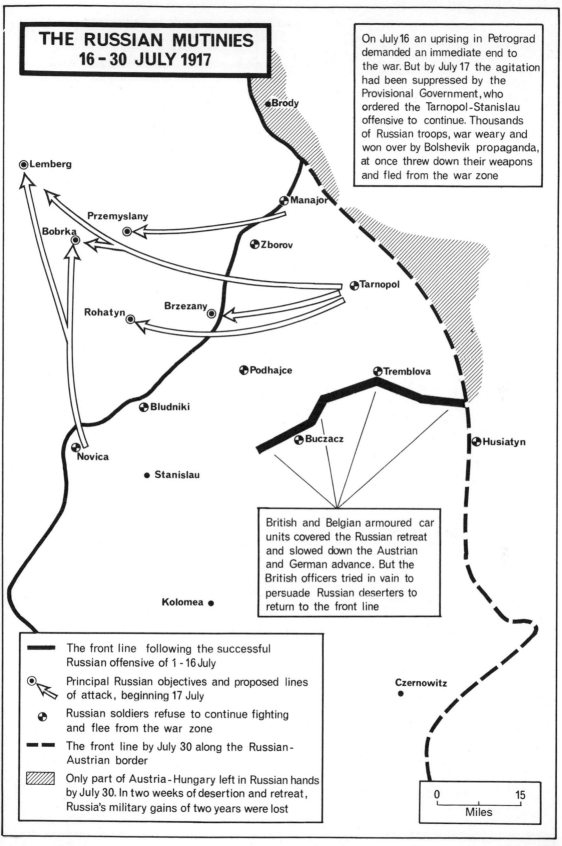

THE RUSSIAN MUTINIES
16 - 30 JULY 1917

On July 16 an uprising in Petrograd demanded an immediate end to the war. But by July 17 the agitation had been suppressed by the Provisional Government, who ordered the Tarnopol-Stanislau offensive to continue. Thousands of Russian troops, war weary and won over by Bolshevik propaganda, at once threw down their weapons and fled from the war zone

Brody

Lemberg

Manajor

Przemyslany

Bobrka

Zborov

Rohatyn

Brzezany

Tarnopol

Podhajce

Tremblova

Bludniki

Buczacz

Husiatyn

Novica

Stanislau

British and Belgian armoured car units covered the Russian retreat and slowed down the Austrian and German advance. But the British officers tried in vain to persuade Russian deserters to return to the front line

Kolomea

Czernowitz

The front line following the successful Russian offensive of 1 - 16 July

Principal Russian objectives and proposed lines of attack, beginning 17 July

Russian soldiers refuse to continue fighting and flee from the war zone

The front line by July 30 along the Russian-Austrian border

Only part of Austria-Hungary left in Russian hands by July 30. In two weeks of desertion and retreat, Russia's military gains of two years were lost

0   15
Miles

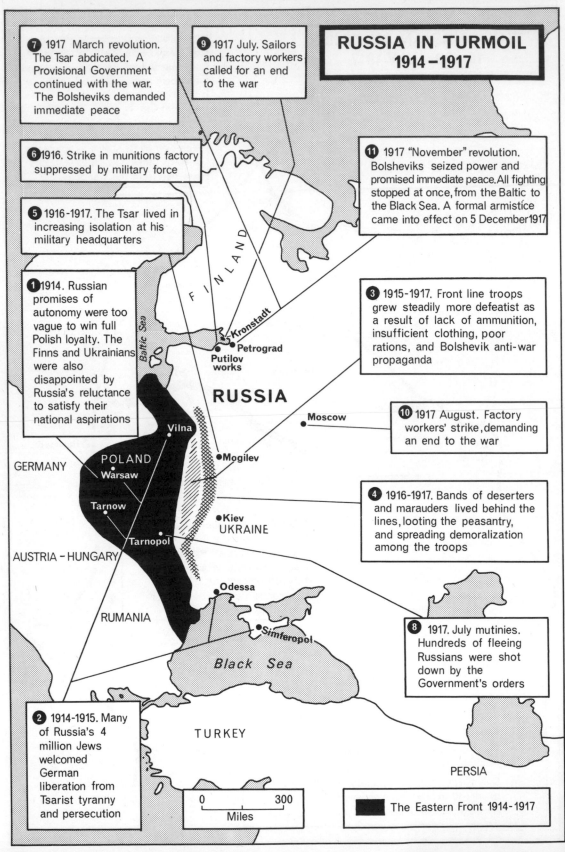

RUSSIA IN TURMOIL 1914-1917

7 1917 March revolution. The Tsar abdicated. A Provisional Government continued with the war. The Bolsheviks demanded immediate peace

9 1917 July. Sailors and factory workers called for an end to the war

6 1916. Strike in munitions factory suppressed by military force

5 1916-1917. The Tsar lived in increasing isolation at his military headquarters

11 1917 "November" revolution. Bolsheviks seized power and promised immediate peace. All fighting stopped at once, from the Baltic to the Black Sea. A formal armistice came into effect on 5 December 1917

1 1914. Russian promises of autonomy were too vague to win full Polish loyalty. The Finns and Ukrainians were also disappointed by Russia's reluctance to satisfy their national aspirations

3 1915-1917. Front line troops grew steadily more defeatist as a result of lack of ammunition, insufficient clothing, poor rations, and Bolshevik anti-war propaganda

10 1917 August. Factory workers' strike, demanding an end to the war

4 1916-1917. Bands of deserters and marauders lived behind the lines, looting the peasantry, and spreading demoralization among the troops

8 1917. July mutinies. Hundreds of fleeing Russians were shot down by the Government's orders

2 1914-1915. Many of Russia's 4 million Jews welcomed German liberation from Tsarist tyranny and persecution

FINLAND

Baltic Sea

Kronstadt

Petrograd

Putilov works

RUSSIA

Moscow

Vilna

POLAND

Warsaw

Mogilev

GERMANY

Tarnow

Kiev

UKRAINE

Tarnopol

AUSTRIA – HUNGARY

Odessa

RUMANIA

Simferopol

Black Sea

TURKEY

PERSIA

0   300
Miles

■ The Eastern Front 1914-1917

108

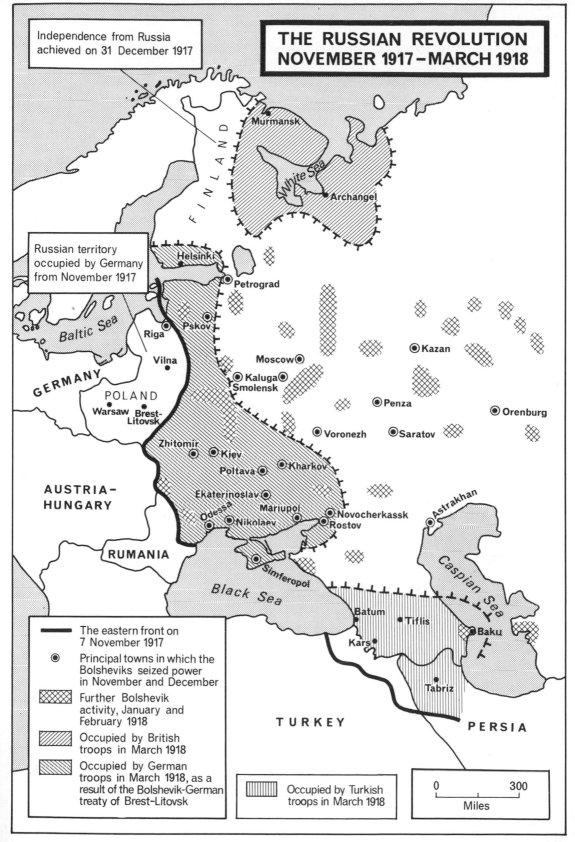

Independence from Russia
achieved on 31 December 1917

THE RUSSIAN REVOLUTION
NOVEMBER 1917 – MARCH 1918

Murmansk

White Sea

Archangel

Russian territory
occupied by Germany
from November 1917

FINLAND

Helsinki

Petrograd

Baltic Sea

Ösel

Riga

Pskov

Vilna

Moscow

Kazan

GERMANY

POLAND

Kaluga

Smolensk

Warsaw

Brest-
Litovsk

Penza

Orenburg

Zhitomir

Kiev

Voronezh

Saratov

AUSTRIA-
HUNGARY

Poltava

Kharkov

Ekaterinoslav

Odessa

Mariupol

Nikolaev

Novocherkassk

Rostov

Astrakhan

RUMANIA

Simferopol

Black Sea

Caspian Sea

Batum

Tiflis

Baku

Kars

Tabriz

TURKEY

PERSIA

The eastern front on
7 November 1917

Principal towns in which the
Bolsheviks seized power
in November and December

Further Bolshevik
activity, January and
February 1918

Occupied by British
troops in March 1918

Occupied by German
troops in March 1918, as a
result of the Bolshevik-German
treaty of Brest-Litovsk

Occupied by Turkish
troops in March 1918

0   300

Miles

109

Section Eight

1918

. . . You smug-faced crowds with kindling eye
Who cheer when soldier lads march by,
Sneak home and pray you'll never know
The hell where youth and laughter go.

SIEGFRIED SASSOON
"SUICIDE IN THE TRENCHES"

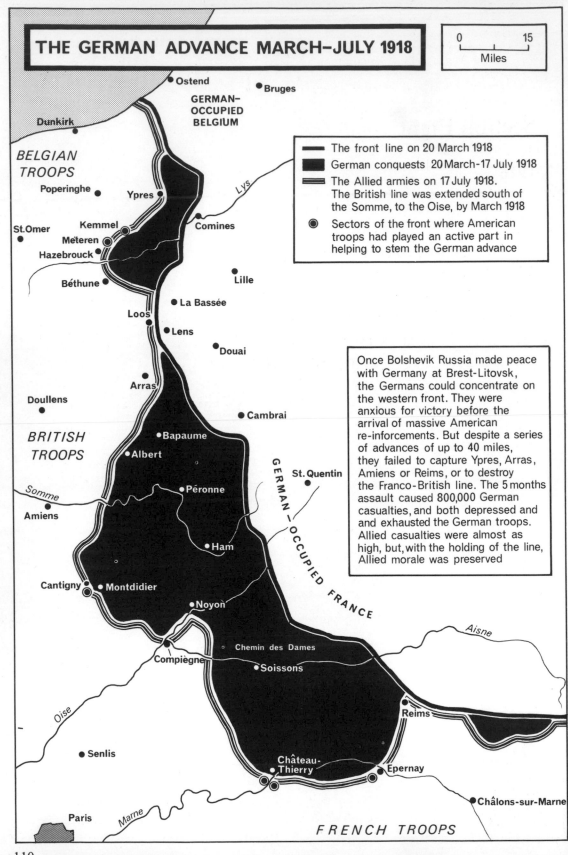

THE GERMAN ADVANCE MARCH–JULY 1918

0   15
Miles

Ostend
Bruges
GERMAN–
OCCUPIED
BELGIUM
Dunkirk

BELGIAN
TROOPS
Poperinghe
Ypres
Lys
Comines
St.Omer
Kemmel
Méteren
Hazebrouck
Béthune
Lille
La Bassée
Loos
Lens
Douai
Arras
Doullens
Cambrai
BRITISH
TROOPS
Bapaume
Albert
St. Quentin
Somme
Péronne
Amiens
Ham
GERMAN – OCCUPIED FRANCE
Cantigny
Montdidier
Noyon
Aisne
Compiègne
Chemin des Dames
Soissons
Oise
Reims
Senlis
Château-
Thierry
Epernay
Châlons-sur-Marne
Paris
Marne
FRENCH TROOPS

— The front line on 20 March 1918
▆ German conquests 20 March–17 July 1918
☰ The Allied armies on 17 July 1918.
The British line was extended south of
the Somme, to the Oise, by March 1918
◉ Sectors of the front where American
troops had played an active part in
helping to stem the German advance

Once Bolshevik Russia made peace
with Germany at Brest-Litovsk,
the Germans could concentrate on
the western front. They were
anxious for victory before the
arrival of massive American
re-inforcements. But despite a series
of advances of up to 40 miles,
they failed to capture Ypres, Arras,
Amiens or Reims, or to destroy
the Franco-British line. The 5 months
assault caused 800,000 German
casualties, and both depressed and
and exhausted the German troops.
Allied casualties were almost as
high, but, with the holding of the line,
Allied morale was preserved

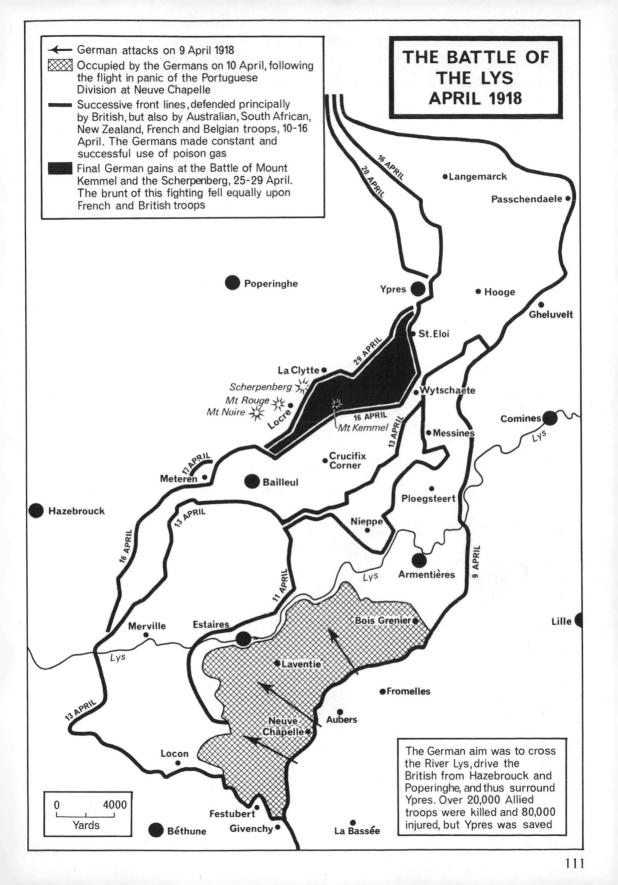

THE BATTLE OF THE LYS APRIL 1918

Legend:

→ German attacks on 9 April 1918

▨ Occupied by the Germans on 10 April, following the flight in panic of the Portuguese Division at Neuve Chapelle

▬ Successive front lines, defended principally by British, but also by Australian, South African, New Zealand, French and Belgian troops, 10-16 April. The Germans made constant and successful use of poison gas

■ Final German gains at the Battle of Mount Kemmel and the Scherpenberg, 25-29 April. The brunt of this fighting fell equally upon French and British troops

Map labels:

16 APRIL
20 APRIL
29 APRIL
16 APRIL
13 APRIL
17 APRIL
13 APRIL
16 APRIL
11 APRIL
13 APRIL
9 APRIL

Langemarck
Passchendaele
Poperinghe
Ypres
Hooge
Gheluvelt
St. Eloi
La Clytte
Scherpenberg
Mt Rouge
Mt Noire
Locre
Wytschaete
Comines
Lys
Messines
Mt Kemmel
Crucifix Corner
Meteren
Bailleul
Ploegsteert
Hazebrouck
Nieppe
Lys
Armentières
Lille
Merville
Estaires
Bois Grenier
Lys
Laventie
Fromelles
Neuve Chapelle
Aubers
Locon
Festubert
Givenchy
La Bassée
Béthune

Scale: 0 — 4000 Yards

The German aim was to cross the River Lys, drive the British from Hazebrouck and Poperinghe, and thus surround Ypres. Over 20,000 Allied troops were killed and 80,000 injured, but Ypres was saved

THE AMERICAN EXPEDITIONARY FORCE 1918

GERMANY

BELGIUM

LUXEMBURG

FRANCE

Scale: 0 — 50 Miles

Brussels

Ghent

Ypres
Kemmel
Armentières

Calais

Somme

Meuse

Meuse

Sedan

11 NOVEMBER

ARMISTICE LINE

Cambrai

Péronne

Montdidier

Noyon

Amiens
Cantigny

Belleau
Wood

Seine

Seine

Paris

Le Havre

Marne

Château
Thierry

FRENCH LINE APRIL 1918

St. Mihiel

Toul
(General
Pershing's
Headquarters)

Key:
- Initial U.S. military activity
- Major U.S. advances
- ↑ U.S. troop support for allied attacks

9 26 September–11 November. 1,200,000 U.S. troops in major advance. 120,000 U.S. dead and wounded. Over 16,000 Germans and 468 guns captured

8 12-16 September. 550,000 U.S. troops advance. 16,000 Germans and 443 guns captured

U.S. DEAD
In battle   48,909
Of influenza   62,000

5 18 July–6 August. 270,000 U.S. troops play major part in first Allied advance of 1918

3 27 May–5 June. U.S. troops help French to stem German advance

7 19 August. 108,000 U.S. troops with British advance

2 9-29 April. 500 U.S. troops with British defence

6 8 August. 54,000 U.S. troops join British in Somme advance

1 6 April. Over 2,000 U.S. troops join British Army in the defence of Amiens

4 9-15 June. 27,500 U.S. troops engaged in repulsing German advance and retaking Belleau Wood

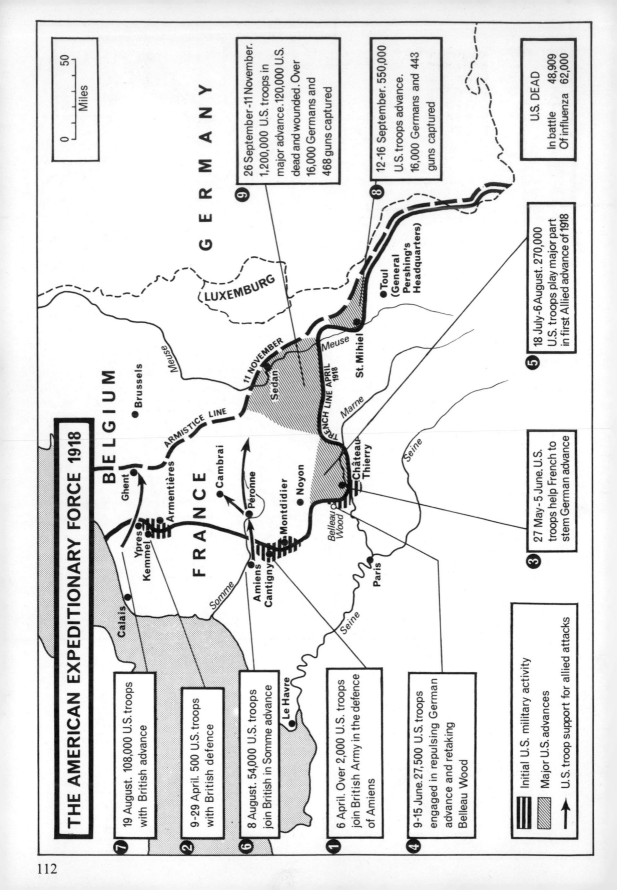

112

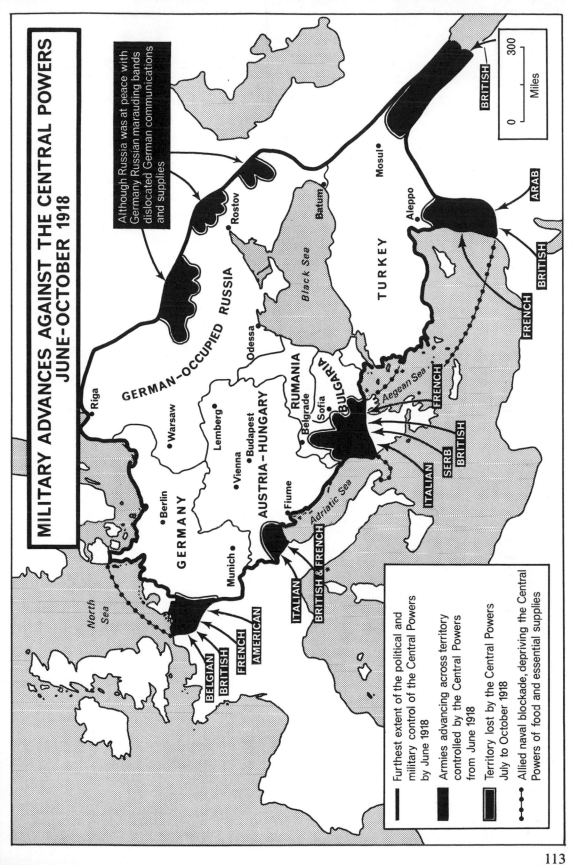

MILITARY ADVANCES AGAINST THE CENTRAL POWERS
JUNE–OCTOBER 1918

Although Russia was at peace with Germany Russian marauding bands dislocated German communications and supplies

BRITISH

0   300
Miles

ARAB

BRITISH

FRENCH

Mosul

Aleppo

Batum

Rostov

GERMAN-OCCUPIED RUSSIA

Black Sea

TURKEY

Odessa

Riga

Warsaw

Lemberg

Budapest

RUMANIA

BULGARIA

Belgrade

Sofia

Aegean Sea

FRENCH

Vienna

AUSTRIA–HUNGARY

SERB

BRITISH

GERMANY

Berlin

Fiume

ITALIAN

Adriatic Sea

Munich

BRITISH & FRENCH

ITALIAN

North
Sea

BELGIAN
BRITISH
FRENCH
AMERICAN

Furthest extent of the political and military control of the Central Powers by June 1918

Armies advancing across territory controlled by the Central Powers from June 1918

Territory lost by the Central Powers July to October 1918

Allied naval blockade, depriving the Central Powers of food and essential supplies

113

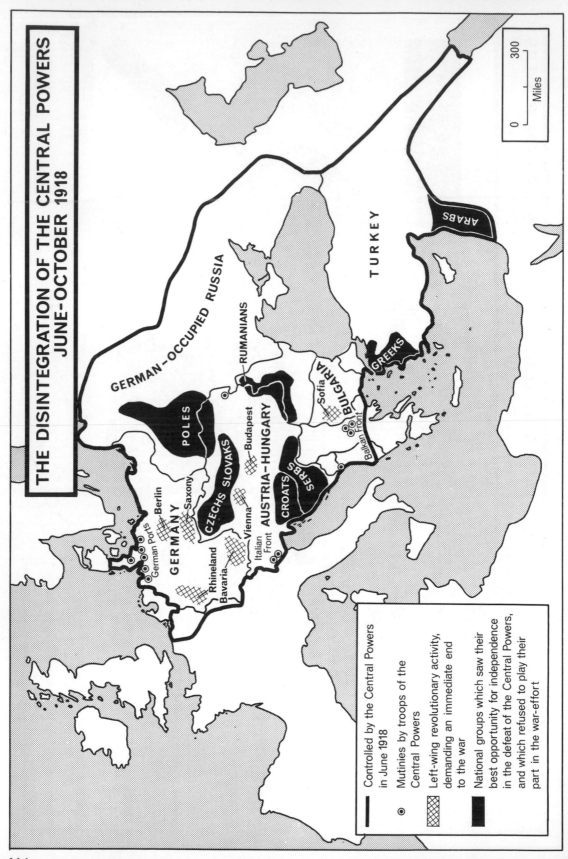

THE DISINTEGRATION OF THE CENTRAL POWERS
JUNE–OCTOBER 1918

GERMAN-OCCUPIED RUSSIA

RUMANIANS

POLES

Saxony

Berlin

German Ports

GERMANY

Rhineland

Bavaria

Budapest

CZECHS SLOVAKS

Vienna

AUSTRIA–HUNGARY

Italian
Front

CROATS

SERBS

Sofia

BULGARIA

Balkan Front

GREEKS

TURKEY

ARABS

Miles

0   300

Controlled by the Central Powers
in June 1918

Mutinies by troops of the
Central Powers

Left-wing revolutionary activity,
demanding an immediate end
to the war

National groups which saw their
best opportunity for independence
in the defeat of the Central Powers,
and which refused to play their
part in the war-effort

114

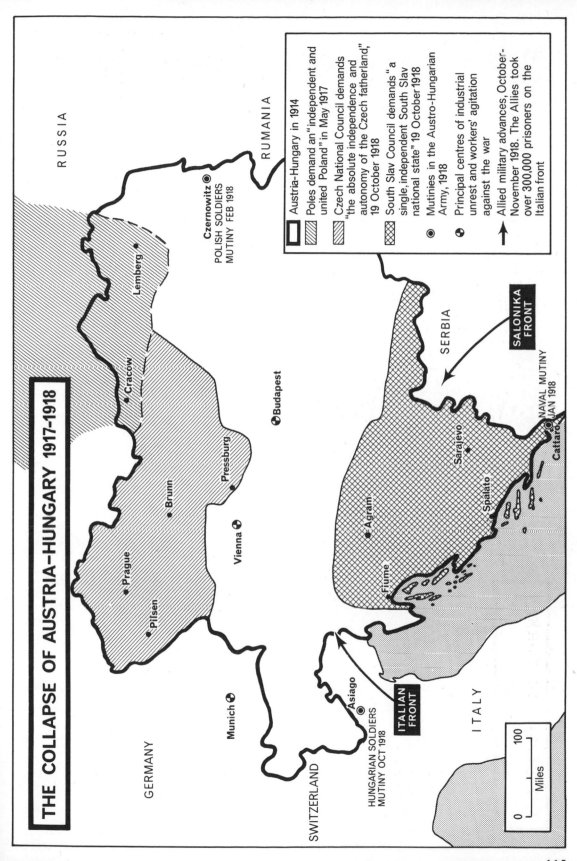

THE COLLAPSE OF AUSTRIA–HUNGARY 1917–1918

RUSSIA

RUMANIA

Czernowitz
POLISH SOLDIERS MUTINY FEB 1918

Lemberg

Cracow

Budapest

Pressburg

Brunn

Prague

Pilsen

Vienna

GERMANY

Munich

SWITZERLAND

Asiago
HUNGARIAN SOLDIERS MUTINY OCT 1918

ITALIAN FRONT

ITALY

Fiume

Spalato

Agram

Sarajevo

SERBIA

SALONIKA FRONT

NAVAL MUTINY JAN 1918
Cattaro

Austria-Hungary in 1914

Poles demand an "independent and united Poland" in May 1917

Czech National Council demands "the absolute independence and autonomy of the Czech fatherland", 19 October 1918

South Slav Council demands "a single, independent South Slav national state" 19 October 1918

Mutinies in the Austro-Hungarian Army, 1918

Principal centres of industrial unrest and workers' agitation against the war

Allied military advances, October-November 1918. The Allies took over 300,000 prisoners on the Italian front

0   100
Miles

115

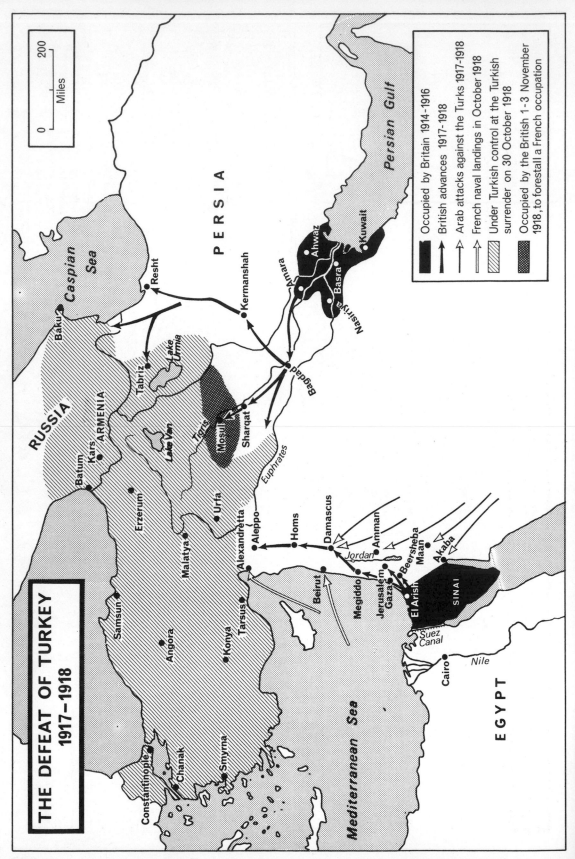

THE DEFEAT OF TURKEY 1917–1918

200
0 — Miles

Caspian Sea

Persian Gulf

PERSIA

RUSSIA

ARMENIA

Baku

Resht

Kermanshah

Tabriz

Lake Urmia

Kars

Batum

Erzerum

Lake Van

Mosul

Sharqat

Tigris

Euphrates

Amara

Baghdad

Ahwaz

Basra

Nasiriya

Kuwait

Urfa

Malatya

Samsun

Angora

Konya

Tarsus

Alexandretta

Aleppo

Homs

Damascus

Jordan

Amman

Beersheba

Maan

Akaba

Megiddo

Beirut

Jerusalem

Gaza

El Arish

SINAI

Suez Canal

Cairo

Nile

EGYPT

Mediterranean Sea

Constantinople

Chanak

Smyrna

Legend:
- ▮ Occupied by Britain 1914–1916
- ➤ British advances 1917–1918
- ▷ Arab attacks against the Turks 1917–1918
- ▷ French naval landings in October 1918
- ▨ Under Turkish control at the Turkish surrender on 30 October 1918
- ▓ Occupied by the British 1–3 November 1918, to forestall a French occupation

116

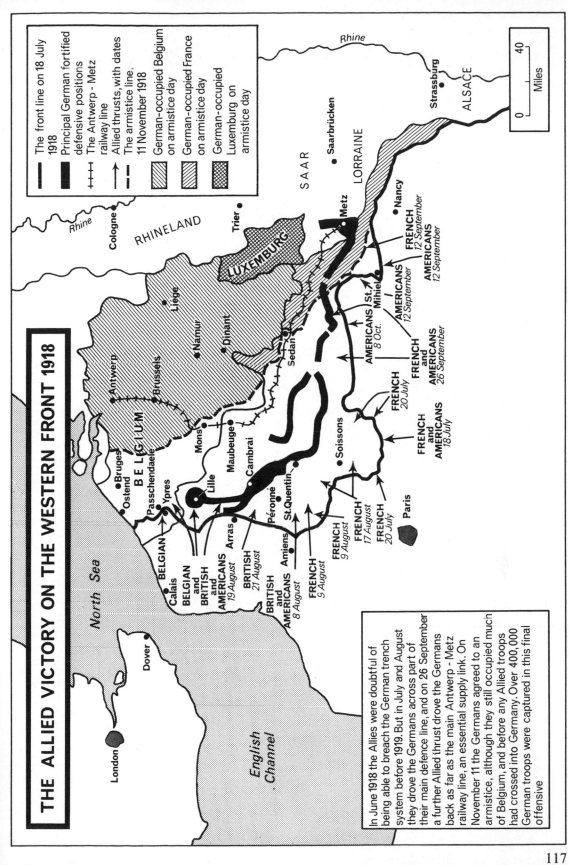

THE ALLIED VICTORY ON THE WESTERN FRONT 1918

Legend:
- The front line on 18 July 1918
- Principal German fortified defensive positions
- The Antwerp - Metz railway line
- Allied thrusts, with dates
- The armistice line, 11 November 1918
- German-occupied Belgium on armistice day
- German-occupied France on armistice day
- German-occupied Luxemburg on armistice day

North Sea

English Channel

Rhine

London

Dover

Calais

Ostend
Bruges
Passchendaele
Ypres
Lille

Cologne
RHINELAND
Trier

LUXEMBURG

Antwerp
Brussels
B E L G I U M
Liège
Namur
Dinant
Mons
Maubeuge
Cambrai
Sedan

SAAR
Saarbrücken
LORRAINE
Metz
Nancy
ALSACE
Strassburg
Rhine

Arras
Péronne
St.Quentin
Amiens
Soissons
Paris

BELGIAN
BELGIAN and BRITISH and AMERICANS *19 August*
BRITISH and AMERICANS *8 August*
BRITISH *21 August*
FRENCH *5 August*
FRENCH *9 August*
FRENCH *17 August*
FRENCH *20 July*
FRENCH *20 July*
FRENCH and AMERICANS *18 July*
FRENCH and AMERICANS *20 July*
FRENCH and AMERICANS *26 September*
AMERICANS *12 September*
AMERICANS *12 September*
AMERICANS *12 September*
AMERICANS *8 Oct.*
FRENCH *12 September*
St. Mihiel

0   40
Miles

In June 1918 the Allies were doubtful of being able to breach the German trench system before 1919. But in July and August they drove the Germans across part of their main defence line, and on 26 September a further Allied thrust drove the Germans back as far as the main Antwerp - Metz railway line, an essential supply link. On November 11 the Germans agreed to an armistice, although they still occupied much of Belgium, and before any Allied troops had crossed into Germany. Over 400,000 German troops were captured in this final offensive

117

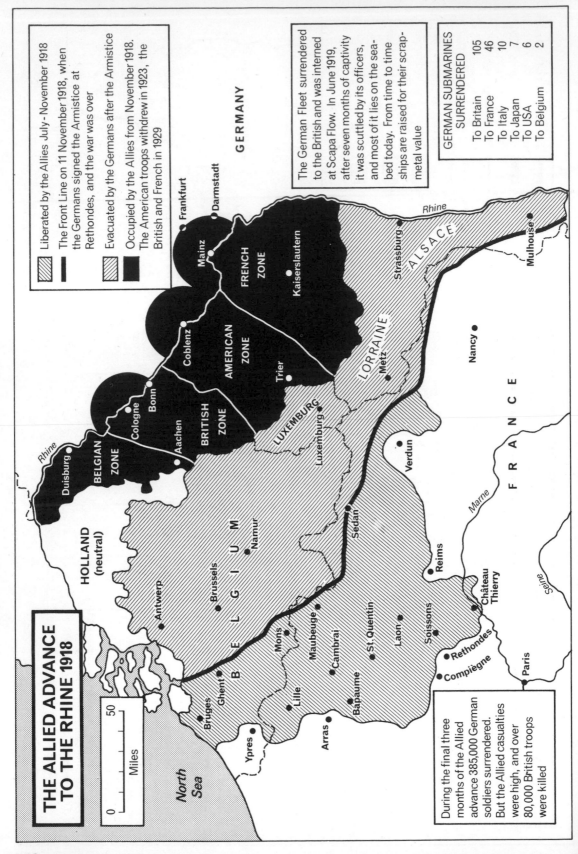

THE ALLIED ADVANCE TO THE RHINE 1918

North Sea

0 — 50

Miles

HOLLAND (neutral)

Duisburg
Rhine

BELGIAN ZONE

Cologne
Bonn
Aachen

BRITISH ZONE

Coblenz

AMERICAN ZONE

Trier

Frankfurt
Darmstadt

Mainz

FRENCH ZONE

Kaiserslautern

GERMANY

Rhine

Strassburg

ALSACE

Mulhouse

Metz

LORRAINE

LUXEMBURG
Luxemburg

Nancy

Verdun

Antwerp

Bruges
Ghent
Ypres
Arras
Lille

B E L G I U M

Brussels

Namur

Sedan

Mons
Maubeuge
Cambrai
Bapaume
St. Quentin
Laon
Soissons
Reims

Château Thierry

Rethondes
Compiegne

Marne

F R A N C E

Paris

Seine

Liberated by the Allies July - November 1918

The Front Line on 11 November 1918, when the Germans signed the Armistice at Rethondes, and the war was over

Evacuated by the Germans after the Armistice

Occupied by the Allies from November 1918. The American troops withdrew in 1923, the British and French in 1929

The German Fleet surrendered to the British and was interned at Scapa Flow. In June 1919, after seven months of captivity it was scuttled by its officers, and most of it lies on the sea-bed today. From time to time ships are raised for their scrap-metal value

GERMAN SUBMARINES SURRENDERED

To Britain	105
To France	46
To Italy	10
To Japan	7
To USA	6
To Belgium	2

During the final three months of the Allied advance 385,000 German soldiers surrendered. But the Allied casualties were high, and over 80,000 British troops were killed

118

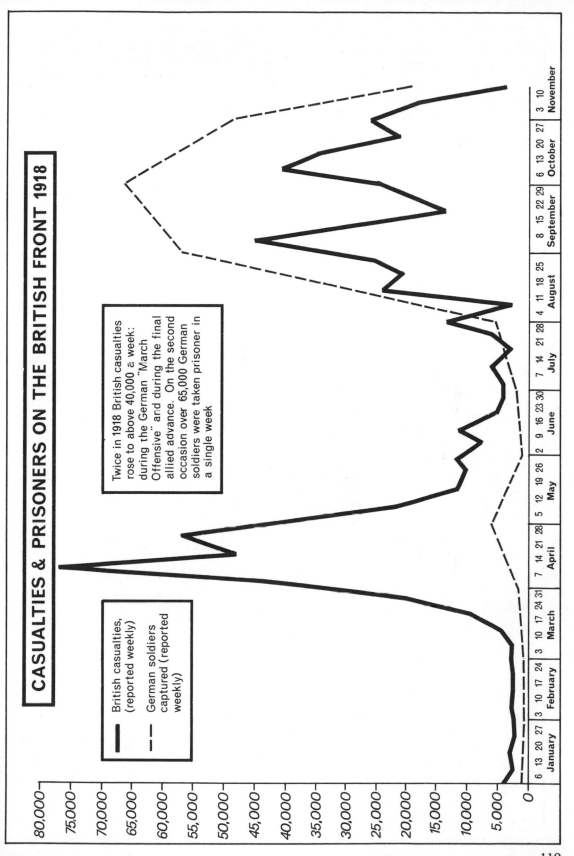

CASUALTIES & PRISONERS ON THE BRITISH FRONT 1918

British casualties,
(reported weekly)

German soldiers
captured (reported
weekly)

Twice in 1918 British casualties
rose to above 40,000 a week:
during the German "March
Offensive" and during the final
allied advance. On the second
occasion over 65,000 German
soldiers were taken prisoner in
a single week

80,000
75,000
70,000
65,000
60,000
55,000
50,000
45,000
40,000
35,000
30,000
25,000
20,000
15,000
10,000
5,000
0

January	February	March	April	May	June	July	August	September	October	November
6 13 20 27	3 10 17 24	3 10 17 24 31	7 14 21 28	5 12 19 26	2 9 16 23 30	7 14 21 28	4 11 18 25	8 15 22 29	6 13 20 27	3 10

THE WAR IN THE BALKANS SEPTEMBER – OCTOBER 1918

In 1917 the Bulgarians, having conquered Serbia Macedonia and the Dobruja, began secret negotiations with the Allies to end the war, but without success. In June 1918 Germany ended her annual 50 million francs subsidy, and stopped sending munitions. The Bulgars resented the way in which the Germans treated them increasingly as a conquered people, requisitioning food and supplies. On 20 September troop mutinies began. On 29 September Bulgaria surrendered unconditionally to the Allies

0   60
Miles

RUSSIA
(Under German Control)

Vienna

Budapest

Lake Balaton

A U S T R I A — H U N G A R Y

Arad

Pécs

Temesvar

Zadar

Belgrade

RUMANIA
(Under German Occupation)

DOBRUJA

(Under Bulgarian Occupation)

Sarajevo

BOSNIA

S E R B I A

Vidin

Nish

Plevna

Mostar

MONTENEGRO

Cattaro

Sofia

B U L G A R I A

ITALY

Skopje

MACEDONIA

Ochrid

Adrianople

Constantinople

Salonika

T U R K E Y

Allied Fleet 10 November 1918

Chanak
Dardanelles

GREECE

The Allied armies on 14 September 1918

Liberated by the Allies, 14–29 September

Serbs, Bosnians and Montenegrins rising against their Austrian overlords in the last two weeks of September

Area in which 30,000 Bulgarian troops mutinied, refused to continue the war and marched on Sofia, 20–29 September

Allied advances 29 September to 30 October

BALKAN DEAD IN 1918	
Bulgarians	63,000
Serbs	45,000
French	20,000
British	10,000
Greeks	5,000
Italians	3,000

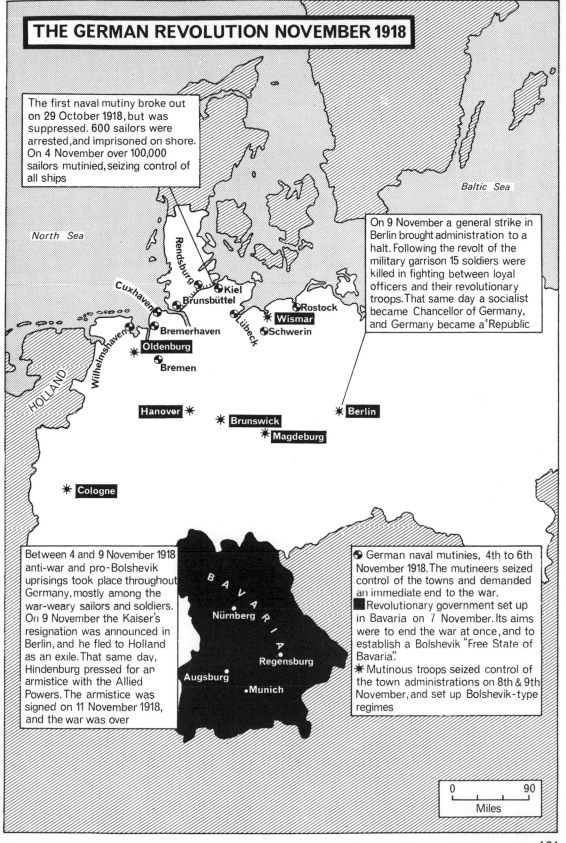

THE GERMAN REVOLUTION NOVEMBER 1918

The first naval mutiny broke out on 29 October 1918, but was suppressed. 600 sailors were arrested, and imprisoned on shore. On 4 November over 100,000 sailors mutinied, seizing control of all ships

Baltic Sea

North Sea

On 9 November a general strike in Berlin brought administration to a halt. Following the revolt of the military garrison 15 soldiers were killed in fighting between loyal officers and their revolutionary troops. That same day a socialist became Chancellor of Germany, and Germany became a 'Republic'

Rendsburg

Cuxhaven

Kiel

Brunsbüttel

Rostock

Wismar

Lübeck

Schwerin

Bremerhaven

Wilhelmshaven

HOLLAND

Oldenburg

Bremen

Hanover

Brunswick

Berlin

Magdeburg

Cologne

Between 4 and 9 November 1918 anti-war and pro-Bolshevik uprisings took place throughout Germany, mostly among the war-weary sailors and soldiers. On 9 November the Kaiser's resignation was announced in Berlin, and he fled to Holland as an exile. That same day, Hindenburg pressed for an armistice with the Allied Powers. The armistice was signed on 11 November 1918, and the war was over

B A V A R I A

Nürnberg

Regensburg

Augsburg

Munich

⊕ German naval mutinies, 4th to 6th November 1918. The mutineers seized control of the towns and demanded an immediate end to the war.

■ Revolutionary government set up in Bavaria on 7 November. Its aims were to end the war at once, and to establish a Bolshevik "Free State of Bavaria".

✳ Mutinous troops seized control of the town administrations on 8th & 9th November, and set up Bolshevik-type regimes

0   90
Miles

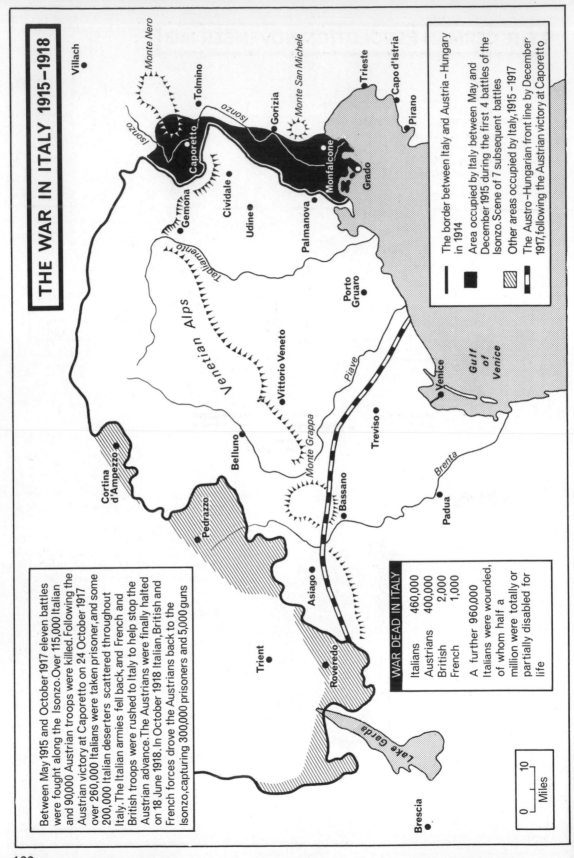

THE WAR IN ITALY 1915–1918

Monte Nero

Villach

Isonzo

Tolmino

Caporetto

Monte San Michele

Trieste

Capo d'Istria

Gorizia

Pirano

Isonzo

Monfalcone

Grado

Gemona

Cividale

Palmanova

Udine

Venetian Alps

Porto Gruaro

Tagliamento

Vittorio Veneto

Gulf of Venice

Piave

Venice

Monte Grappa

Treviso

Belluno

Brenta

Cortina d'Ampezzo

Bassano

Padua

Pedrazzo

Asiago

Trient

Roveredo

Lake Garda

Brescia

The border between Italy and Austria–Hungary in 1914

Area occupied by Italy between May and December 1915 during the first 4 battles of the Isonzo. Scene of 7 subsequent battles

Other areas occupied by Italy, 1915–1917

The Austro–Hungarian front line by December 1917, following the Austrian victory at Caporetto

Between May 1915 and October 1917 eleven battles were fought along the Isonzo. Over 115,000 Italian and 90,000 Austrian troops were killed. Following the Austrian victory at Caporetto on 24 October 1917 over 260,000 Italians were taken prisoner, and some 200,000 Italian deserters scattered throughout Italy. The Italian armies fell back, and French and British troops were rushed to Italy to help stop the Austrian advance. The Austrians were finally halted on 18 June 1918. In October 1918 Italian, British and French forces drove the Austrians back to the Isonzo, capturing 300,000 prisoners and 5,000 guns

WAR DEAD IN ITALY	
Italians	460,000
Austrians	400,000
British	2,000
French	1,000

A further 960,000 Italians were wounded, of whom half a million were totally or partially disabled for life

0   10
Miles

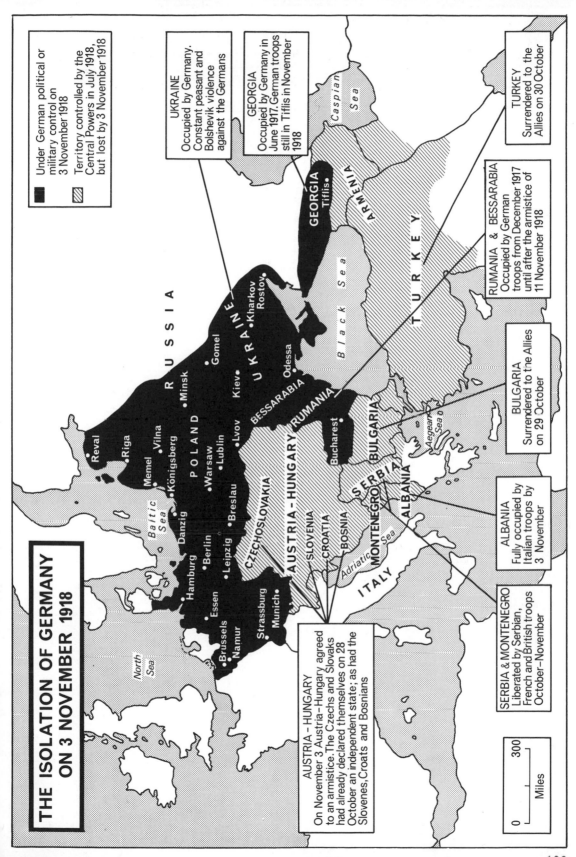

THE ISOLATION OF GERMANY ON 3 NOVEMBER 1918

■ Under German political or military control on 3 November 1918

▨ Territory controlled by the Central Powers in July 1918, but lost by 3 November 1918

UKRAINE
Occupied by Germany. Constant peasant and Bolshevik violence against the Germans

GEORGIA
Occupied by Germany in June 1917. German troops still in Tiflis in November 1918

TURKEY
Surrendered to the Allies on 30 October

RUMANIA & BESSARABIA
Occupied by German troops from December 1917 until after the armistice of 11 November 1918

BULGARIA
Surrendered to the Allies on 29 October

ALBANIA
Fully occupied by Italian troops by 3 November

SERBIA & MONTENEGRO
Liberated by Serbian, French and British troops October–November

AUSTRIA – HUNGARY
On November 3 Austria–Hungary agreed to an armistice. The Czechs and Slovaks had already declared themselves on 28 October an independent state; as had the Slovenes, Croats and Bosnians

RUSSIA

UKRAINE

POLAND

AUSTRIA – HUNGARY

RUMANIA

BESSARABIA

CZECHOSLOVAKIA

SLOVENIA

CROATIA

BOSNIA

SERBIA

MONTENEGRO

ALBANIA

BULGARIA

TURKEY

ARMENIA

GEORGIA

ITALY

Caspian Sea

Black Sea

Baltic Sea

North Sea

Aegean Sea

Adriatic Sea

Reval
Riga
Vilna
Memel
Königsberg
Danzig
Hamburg
Berlin
Essen
Leipzig
Breslau
Brussels
Namur
Strassburg
Munich
Warsaw
Lublin
Lvov
Kiev
Minsk
Gomel
Kharkov
Rostov
Odessa
Bucharest
Tiflis

0   300
Miles

123

Section Nine

THE WORLD AT WAR

Oh Oh Oh it's a lovely war
Who wouldn't be a soldier, eh?
Oh it's a shame to take the pay.
As soon as reveille has gone
We feel just as heavy as lead
But we never get up till the Sergeant
Brings our breakfast up to bed.
Oh Oh Oh it's a lovely war. . . .

Who wouldn't join the army
That's what we all inquire
Don't we pity the poor civilians
Sitting beside the fire.
Oh Oh Oh it's a lovely war. . . .

POPULAR SONG

GERMAN WAR AIMS IN THE WEST 1914–1918

0   50
Miles

North Sea

BRITAIN

HOLLAND

Amsterdam
The Hague
Rotterdam
Arnhem

Rhine

Düsseldorf

Cologne

Zeebrugge
Ostend
Bruges
Dunkirk
Calais
Boulogne
Montreuil

Antwerp

Scheldt

Ypres
Lille
Arras
Cambrai

Brussels

BELGIUM
Liege
Namur

GERMANY

Dover

Somme

Sedan

LUXEMBURG

Trier

FRANCE

Speyer

Verdun

Saarbrücken

Paris

Nancy
Toul

ALSACE – LORRAINE

Strassburg

Epinal

Mulhouse

Belfort

Territory to be annexed outright
in the event of a German victory

Future possible annexations to be
obtained at the Peace Conference

The "Tributary State" of Flanders-
Wallonia, to be under German political
and economic supervision

"Strongpoints", or fortified towns
to be under German control

Area to come within the German
Customs Union, and to subordinate its
economic life to that of Germany

— — Western boundary of German strategic
control, within which the existing French
fortresses were to be dismantled

124

FRENCH WAR AIMS IN THE WEST 1914–1918

0   50
Miles

HOLLAND

Rhine

RUHR

•Düsseldorf

•Ostend

•Antwerp

Calais•

•Ypres

Cologne•

•Brussels

Aachen•

BELGIUM

Liége•

GERMANY

•Namur

•Coblenz

•Arras

•Cambrai

LUXEMBURG

FRANCE

•Trier

•Sedan

SAAR

•Speyer

•Soissons

•Reims

•Verdun

•Metz

ALSACE – LORRAINE

•Paris

•Strassburg

Rhine

•Mulhouse

Belfort•

SWITZERLAND

Belgian neutrality to be guaranteed and secured

To be detached from the German Customs Union and brought into the French economic orbit

To become part of France (having been annexed by Germany in 1871)

German coalfields to be under French economic and political control

A Rhineland-Palatinate State, to be separated from Germany, and under French political influence

— — War zone, within which Germany was to pay financial reparations for all war damage

Principal German industrial zone, to be occupied by France in the event of Germany refusing to pay reparations for war damage

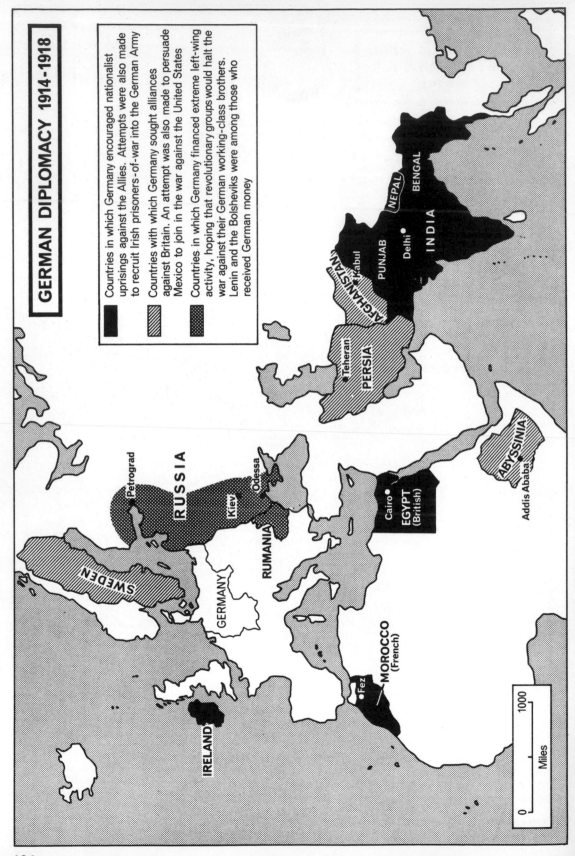

GERMAN DIPLOMACY 1914-1918

Countries in which Germany encouraged nationalist uprisings against the Allies. Attempts were also made to recruit Irish prisoners-of-war into the German Army

Countries with which Germany sought alliances against Britain. An attempt was also made to persuade Mexico to join in the war against the United States

Countries in which Germany financed extreme left-wing activity, hoping that revolutionary groups would halt the war against their German working-class brothers. Lenin and the Bolsheviks were among those who received German money

IRELAND

SWEDEN

GERMANY

RUMANIA

Petrograd

RUSSIA

Kiev

Odessa

MOROCCO
(French)

Fez

Cairo

EGYPT
(British)

ABYSSINIA

Addis Ababa

PERSIA

Teheran

AFGHANISTAN

Kabul

NEPAL

PUNJAB

Delhi

INDIA

BENGAL

0   1000

Miles

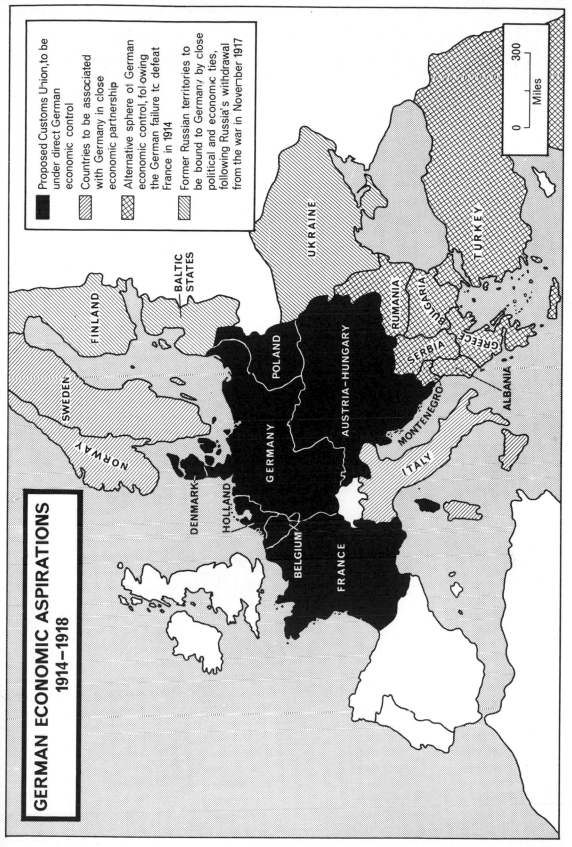

GERMAN ECONOMIC ASPIRATIONS 1914–1918

Legend:

- Proposed Customs Union, to be under direct German economic control
- Countries to be associated with Germany in close economic partnership
- Alternative sphere of German economic control, following the German failure to defeat France in 1914
- Former Russian territories to be bound to Germany by close political and economic ties, following Russia's withdrawal from the war in November 1917

Scale: 0 — 300 Miles

FINLAND

BALTIC STATES

SWEDEN

NORWAY

UKRAINE

POLAND

GERMANY

AUSTRIA-HUNGARY

RUMANIA

BULGARIA

SERBIA

GREECE

TURKEY

MONTENEGRO

ALBANIA

ITALY

DENMARK

HOLLAND

BELGIUM

FRANCE

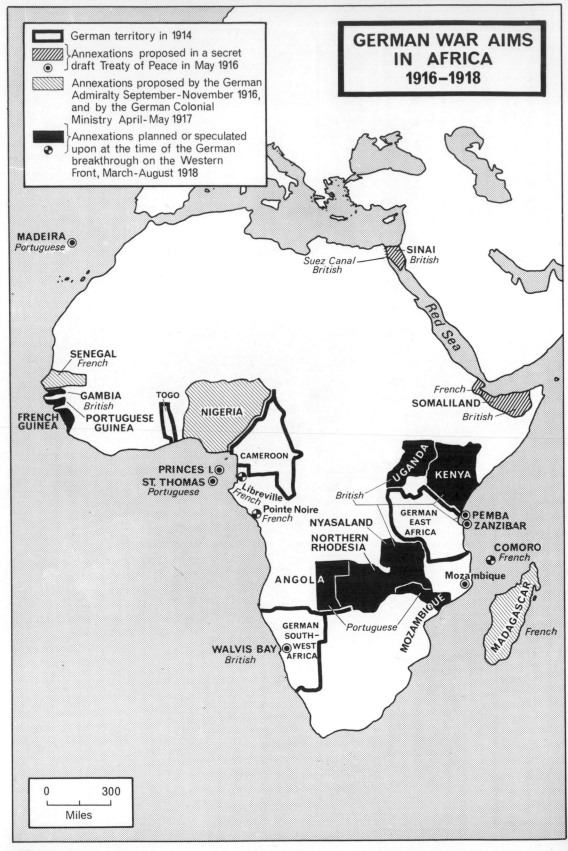

GERMAN WAR AIMS
IN AFRICA
1916–1918

German territory in 1914

Annexations proposed in a secret draft Treaty of Peace in May 1916

Annexations proposed by the German Admiralty September–November 1916, and by the German Colonial Ministry April–May 1917

Annexations planned or speculated upon at the time of the German breakthrough on the Western Front, March–August 1918

MADEIRA
Portuguese

SINAI
British

Suez Canal
British

Red Sea

SENEGAL
French

GAMBIA
British

FRENCH GUINEA

PORTUGUESE GUINEA

TOGO

NIGERIA

French
SOMALILAND
British

CAMEROON

PRINCES I.
ST. THOMAS
Portuguese

Libreville
French

Pointe Noire
French

British

UGANDA

KENYA

GERMAN EAST AFRICA

PEMBA
ZANZIBAR

NYASALAND

NORTHERN RHODESIA

COMORO
French

ANGOLA

Mozambique

Portuguese

MOZAMBIQUE

MADAGASCAR

French

GERMAN SOUTH-WEST AFRICA

WALVIS BAY
British

0   300
Miles

128

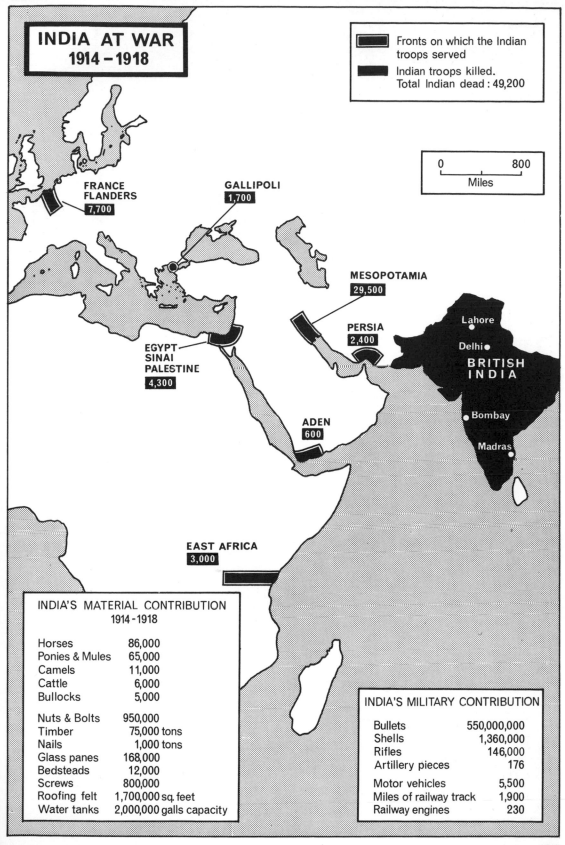

INDIA AT WAR
1914 – 1918

Fronts on which the Indian troops served

Indian troops killed.
Total Indian dead : 49,200

0   800
Miles

FRANCE
FLANDERS
7,700

GALLIPOLI
1,700

MESOPOTAMIA
29,500

PERSIA
2,400

EGYPT
SINAI
PALESTINE
4,300

ADEN
600

EAST AFRICA
3,000

Lahore

Delhi

BRITISH
INDIA

Bombay

Madras

INDIA'S MATERIAL CONTRIBUTION
1914 - 1918

Horses	86,000
Ponies & Mules	65,000
Camels	11,000
Cattle	6,000
Bullocks	5,000
Nuts & Bolts	950,000
Timber	75,000 tons
Nails	1,000 tons
Glass panes	168,000
Bedsteads	12,000
Screws	800,000
Roofing felt	1,700,000 sq. feet
Water tanks	2,000,000 galls capacity

INDIA'S MILITARY CONTRIBUTION

Bullets	550,000,000
Shells	1,360,000
Rifles	146,000
Artillery pieces	176
Motor vehicles	5,500
Miles of railway track	1,900
Railway engines	230

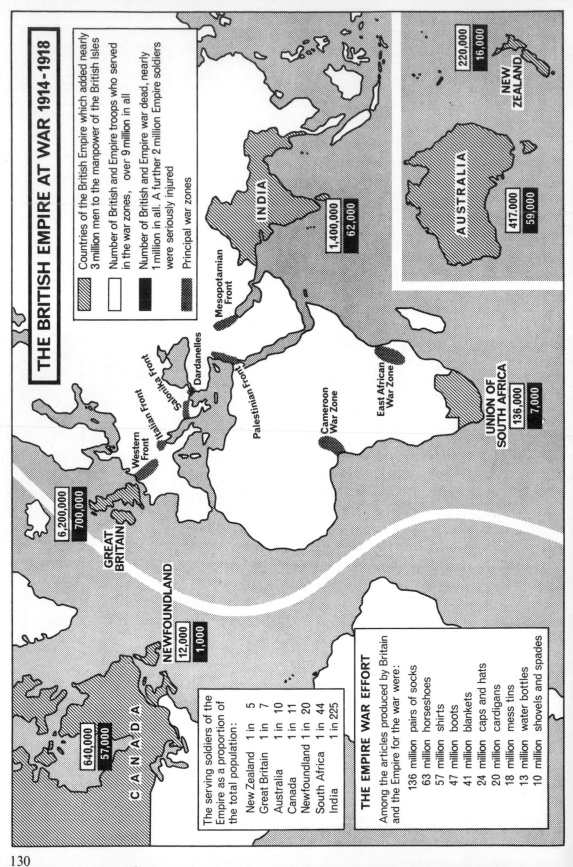

THE BRITISH EMPIRE AT WAR 1914-1918

Countries of the British Empire which added nearly 3 million men to the manpower of the British Isles

Number of British and Empire troops who served in the war zones, over 9 million in all

Number of British and Empire war dead, nearly 1 million in all. A further 2 million Empire soldiers were seriously injured

Principal war zones

NEW ZEALAND 220,000 16,000

AUSTRALIA 417,000 59,000

INDIA 1,400,000 62,000

Mesopotamian Front

Dardanelles

Salonika Front

Italian Front

Palestinian Front

Western Front

Cameroon War Zone

East African War Zone

UNION OF SOUTH AFRICA 136,000 7,000

GREAT BRITAIN 6,200,000 700,000

NEWFOUNDLAND 12,000 1,000

CANADA 640,000 57,000

The serving soldiers of the Empire as a proportion of the total population:

New Zealand	1 in	5
Great Britain	1 in	7
Australia	1 in	10
Canada	1 in	11
Newfoundland	1 in	20
South Africa	1 in	44
India	1 in	225

THE EMPIRE WAR EFFORT

Among the articles produced by Britain and the Empire for the war were:

136 million	pairs of socks
63 million	horseshoes
57 million	shirts
47 million	boots
41 million	blankets
24 million	caps and hats
20 million	cardigans
18 million	mess tins
13 million	water bottles
10 million	shovels and spades

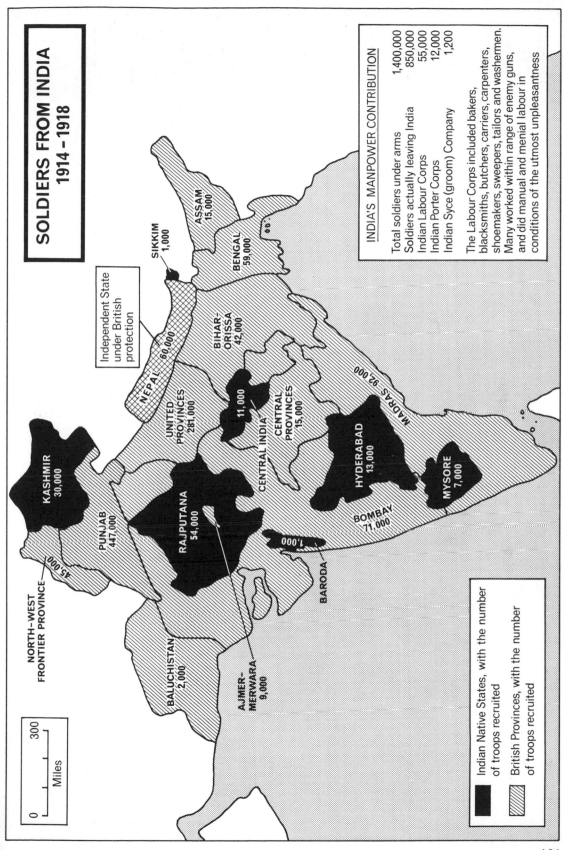

SOLDIERS FROM INDIA
1914 – 1918

INDIA'S MANPOWER CONTRIBUTION

Total soldiers under arms	1,400,000
Soldiers actually leaving India	850,000
Indian Labour Corps	55,000
Indian Porter Corps	12,000
Indian Syce (groom) Company	1,200

The Labour Corps included bakers, blacksmiths, butchers, carriers, carpenters, shoemakers, sweepers, tailors and washermen. Many worked within range of enemy guns, and did manual and menial labour in conditions of the utmost unpleasantness

Independent State under British protection

SIKKIM 1,000

ASSAM 15,000

BENGAL 59,000

NEPAL 60,000

BIHAR-ORISSA 42,000

UNITED PROVINCES 261,000

CENTRAL INDIA 11,000

CENTRAL PROVINCES 15,000

MADRAS 92,000

KASHMIR 30,000

PUNJAB 447,000

RAJPUTANA 54,000

HYDERABAD 13,000

MYSORE 7,000

BOMBAY 71,000

BARODA 1,000

NORTH-WEST FRONTIER PROVINCE 45,000

BALUCHISTAN 2,000

AJMER-MERWARA 9,000

Indian Native States, with the number of troops recruited

British Provinces, with the number of troops recruited

300

Miles

0

131

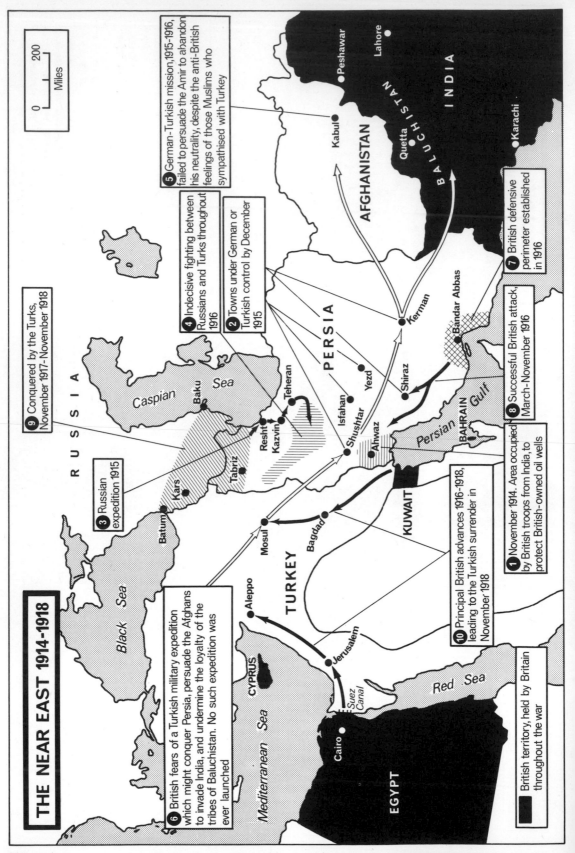

THE NEAR EAST 1914-1918

0 200 Miles

5 German-Turkish mission,1915-1916, failed to persuade the Amir to abandon his neutrality, despite the anti-British feelings of those Muslims who sympathised with Turkey

4 Indecisive fighting between Russians and Turks throughout 1916

2 Towns under German or Turkish control by December 1915

7 British defensive perimeter established in 1916

9 Conquered by the Turks, November 1917- November 1918

3 Russian expedition 1915

8 Successful British attack, March-November 1916

6 British fears of a Turkish military expedition which might conquer Persia, persuade the Afghans to invade India, and undermine the loyalty of the tribes of Baluchistan. No such expedition was ever launched

1 November 1914. Area occupied by British troops from India, to protect British-owned oil wells

10 Principal British advances 1916-1918, leading to the Turkish surrender in November 1918

INDIA

Peshawar

Lahore

Kabul

AFGHANISTAN

Quetta

BALUCHISTAN

Karachi

PERSIA

Kerman

Bandar Abbas

Yezd

Shiraz

Isfahan

Shushtar

Ahwaz

Persian Gulf

BAHRAIN

Teheran

Kazvin

Resht

Baku

Caspian Sea

Tabriz

Kars

Batum

RUSSIA

Black Sea

Mosul

Bagdad

KUWAIT

TURKEY

Aleppo

Jerusalem

CYPRUS

Mediterranean Sea

Suez Canal

Cairo

EGYPT

Red Sea

■ British territory, held by Britain throughout the war

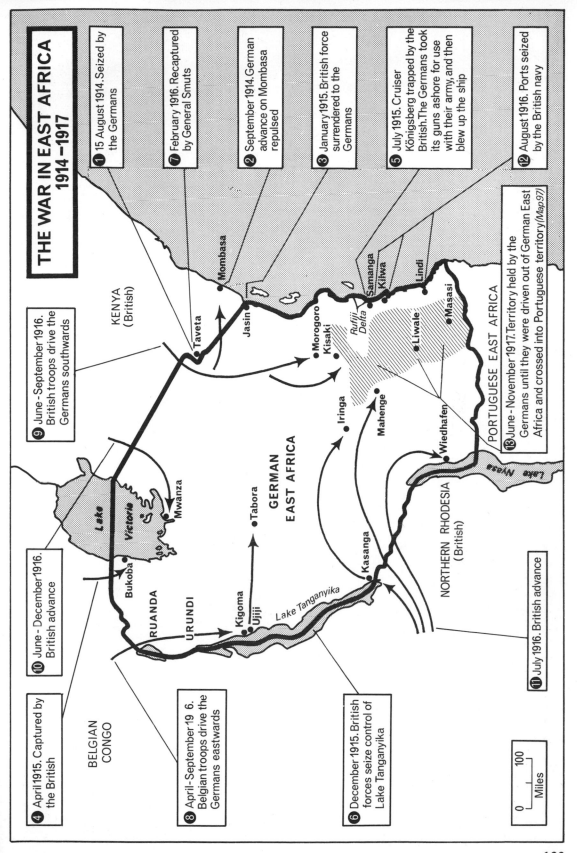

THE WAR IN EAST AFRICA 1914–1917

1 15 August 1914. Seized by the Germans

7 February 1916. Recaptured by General Smuts

2 September 1914. German advance on Mombasa repulsed

3 January 1915. British force surrendered to the Germans

5 July 1915. Cruiser Königsberg trapped by the British. The Germans took its guns ashore for use with their army, and then blew up the ship

12 August 1916. Ports seized by the British navy

13 June–November 1917. Territory held by the Germans until they were driven out of German East Africa and crossed into Portuguese territory *(Map 97)*

9 June–September 1916. British troops drive the Germans southwards

4 April 1915. Captured by the British

10 June–December 1916. British advance

8 April–September 1916. Belgian troops drive the Germans eastwards

6 December 1915. British forces seize control of Lake Tanganyika

11 July 1916. British advance

KENYA (British)

Mombasa

Taveta

Jasin

GERMAN EAST AFRICA

Morogoro
Kisaki

Rufiji Delta

Samanga
Kilwa
Lindi

Masasi

Liwale

Iringa

Mahenge

Wiedhafen

PORTUGUESE EAST AFRICA

NORTHERN RHODESIA (British)

Lake Nyasa

Kasanga

Lake Tanganyika

Kigoma
Ujiji

Tabora

Lake Victoria

Mwanza

Bukoba

RUANDA

URUNDI

BELGIAN CONGO

0   100
Miles

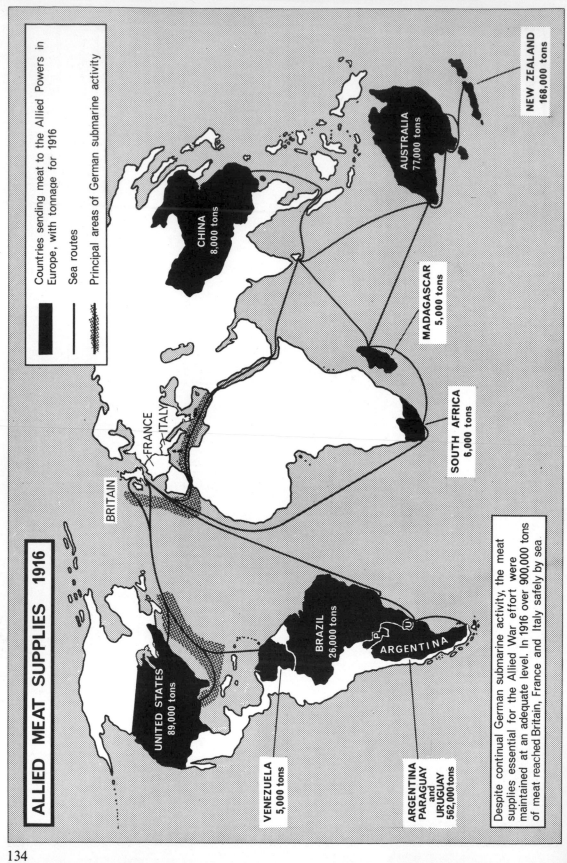

ALLIED MEAT SUPPLIES 1916

Countries sending meat to the Allied Powers in Europe, with tonnage for 1916

Sea routes

Principal areas of German submarine activity

BRITAIN

FRANCE

ITALY

UNITED STATES
89,000 tons

VENEZUELA
5,000 tons

BRAZIL
26,000 tons

ARGENTINA

ARGENTINA
PARAGUAY
and
URUGUAY
562,000 tons

CHINA
8,000 tons

AUSTRALIA
77,000 tons

MADAGASCAR
5,000 tons

SOUTH AFRICA
6,000 tons

NEW ZEALAND
168,000 tons

Despite continual German submarine activity, the meat supplies essential for the Allied War effort were maintained at an adequate level. In 1916 over 900,000 tons of meat reached Britain, France and Italy safely by sea

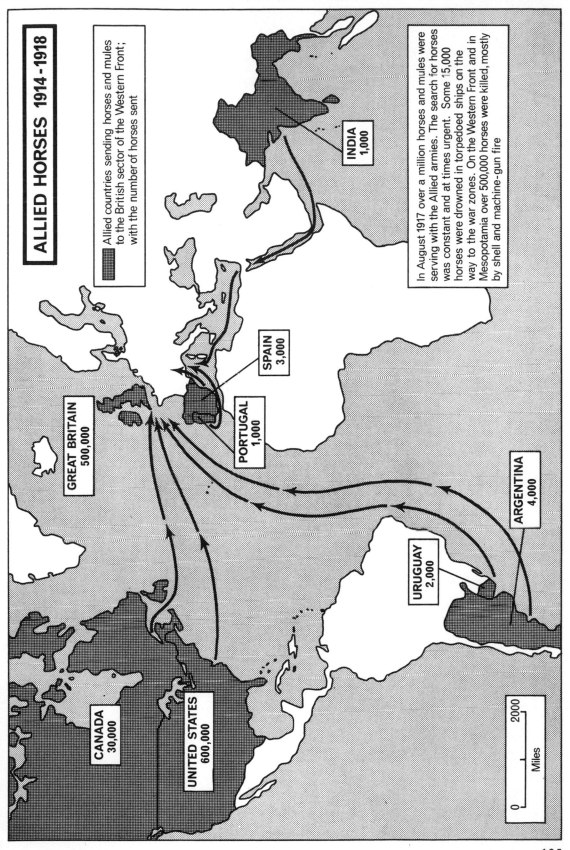

ALLIED HORSES 1914-1918

Allied countries sending horses and mules to the British sector of the Western Front; with the number of horses sent

INDIA
1,000

In August 1917 over a million horses and mules were serving with the Allied armies. The search for horses was constant and at times urgent. Some 15,000 horses were drowned in torpedoed ships on the way to the war zones. On the Western Front and in Mesopotamia over 500,000 horses were killed, mostly by shell and machine-gun fire

SPAIN
3,000

PORTUGAL
1,000

GREAT BRITAIN
500,000

ARGENTINA
4,000

URUGUAY
2,000

CANADA
30,000

UNITED STATES
600,000

0   2000
Miles

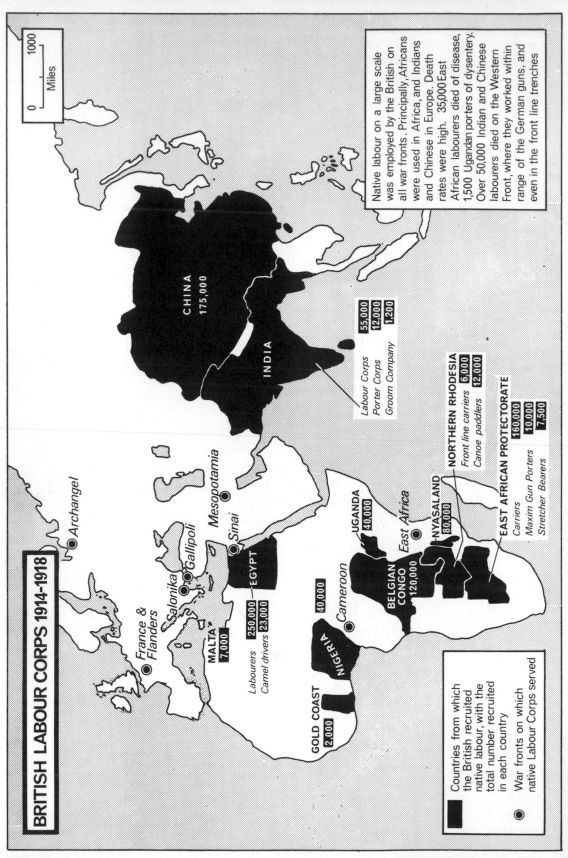

BRITISH LABOUR CORPS 1914-1918

Native labour on a large scale was employed by the British on all war fronts. Principally, Africans were used in Africa, and Indians and Chinese in Europe. Death rates were high. 35,000 East African labourers died of disease, 1,500 Ugandan porters of dysentery. Over 50,000 Indian and Chinese labourers died on the Western Front, where they worked within range of the German guns, and even in the front line trenches

CHINA 175,000

INDIA

Labour Corps	55,000
Porter Corps	12,000
Groom Company	1,200

NORTHERN RHODESIA
| Front line carriers | 6,000 |
| Canoe paddlers | 12,000 |

EAST AFRICAN PROTECTORATE
Carriers	160,000
Maxim Gun Porters	10,000
Stretcher Bearers	7,500

Archangel

France & Flanders

Salonika

Gallipoli

Mesopotamia

Sinai

EGYPT
| Labourers | 250,000 |
| Camel drivers | 23,000 |

MALTA 7,000

UGANDA 40,000

East Africa

NYASALAND 80,000

BELGIAN CONGO 120,000

Cameroon

NIGERIA 40,000

GOLD COAST 2,000

Countries from which the British recruited native labour, with the total number recruited in each country

War fronts on which native Labour Corps served

0   1000
Miles

136

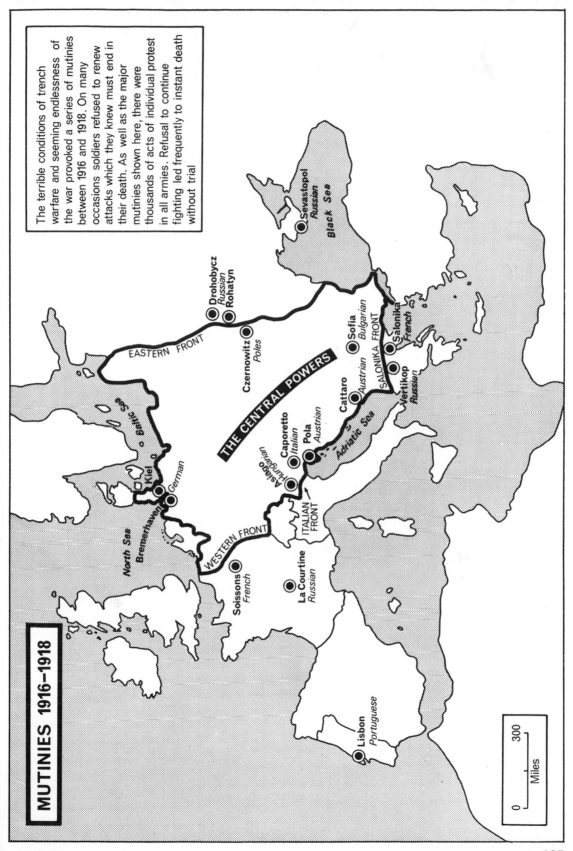

MUTINIES 1916–1918

The terrible conditions of trench warfare and seeming endlessness of the war provoked a series of mutinies between 1916 and 1918. On many occasions soldiers refused to renew attacks which they knew must end in their death. As well as the major mutinies shown here, there were thousands of acts of individual protest in all armies. Refusal to continue fighting led frequently to instant death without trial

Black Sea

Sevastopol
Russian

Drohobycz
Russian
Rohatyn

EASTERN FRONT

Czernowitz
Poles

Baltic Sea

Salonika
French

Sofia
Bulgarian

SALONIKA FRONT

Vertikop
Russian

THE CENTRAL POWERS

Cattaro
Austrian

Caporetto
Italian

Pola
Austrian

Adriatic Sea

Asiago
Hungarian

Kiel
German

ITALIAN FRONT

WESTERN FRONT

North Sea
Bremerhaven

Soissons
French

La Courtine
Russian

Lisbon
Portuguese

300

0 Miles

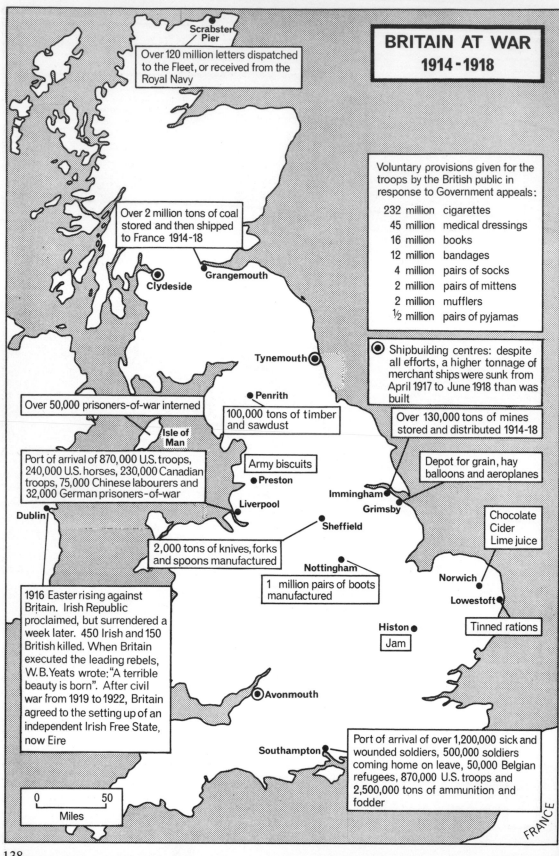

Scrabster Pier

Over 120 million letters dispatched to the Fleet, or received from the Royal Navy

BRITAIN AT WAR
1914 - 1918

Over 2 million tons of coal stored and then shipped to France 1914-18

Clydeside

Grangemouth

Voluntary provisions given for the troops by the British public in response to Government appeals:

232 million	cigarettes
45 million	medical dressings
16 million	books
12 million	bandages
4 million	pairs of socks
2 million	pairs of mittens
2 million	mufflers
½ million	pairs of pyjamas

Tynemouth

Shipbuilding centres: despite all efforts, a higher tonnage of merchant ships were sunk from April 1917 to June 1918 than was built

Penrith

Over 50,000 prisoners-of-war interned

100,000 tons of timber and sawdust

Over 130,000 tons of mines stored and distributed 1914-18

Isle of Man

Army biscuits

Depot for grain, hay balloons and aeroplanes

Port of arrival of 870,000 U.S. troops, 240,000 U.S. horses, 230,000 Canadian troops, 75,000 Chinese labourers and 32,000 German prisoners-of-war

Preston

Immingham

Grimsby

Liverpool

Dublin

Sheffield

Chocolate
Cider
Lime juice

2,000 tons of knives, forks and spoons manufactured

Nottingham

Norwich

1 million pairs of boots manufactured

Lowestoft

1916 Easter rising against Britain. Irish Republic proclaimed, but surrendered a week later. 450 Irish and 150 British killed. When Britain executed the leading rebels, W.B. Yeats wrote: "A terrible beauty is born". After civil war from 1919 to 1922, Britain agreed to the setting up of an independent Irish Free State, now Eire

Histon

Jam

Tinned rations

Avonmouth

Port of arrival of over 1,200,000 sick and wounded soldiers, 500,000 soldiers coming home on leave, 50,000 Belgian refugees, 870,000 U.S. troops and 2,500,000 tons of ammunition and fodder

Southampton

FRANCE

0   50
Miles

138

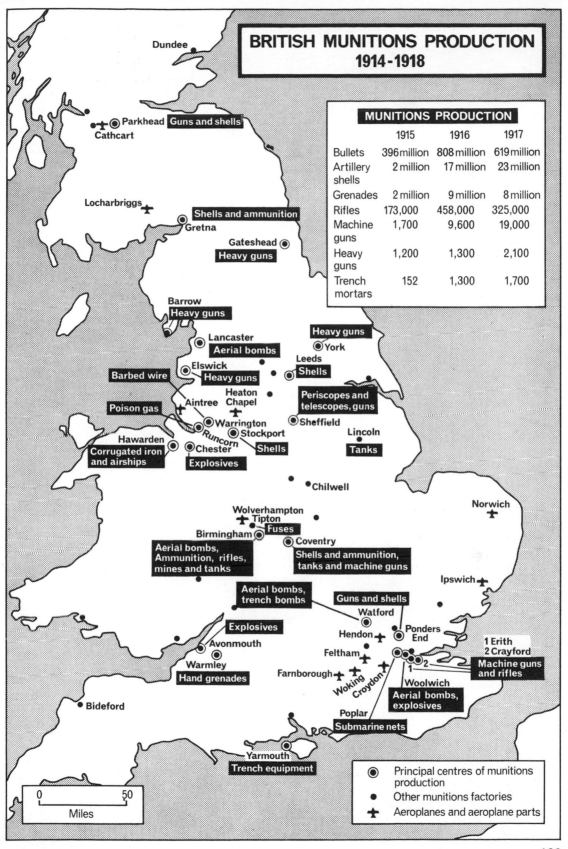

BRITISH MUNITIONS PRODUCTION 1914-1918

Dundee

Parkhead **Guns and shells**
Cathcart

Locharbriggs

Shells and ammunition
Gretna

Gateshead
Heavy guns

Barrow
Heavy guns

Lancaster
Aerial bombs

Heavy guns
York

Elswick
Heavy guns

Leeds
Shells

Barbed wire

Poison gas

Aintree
Heaton
Chapel

Periscopes and telescopes, guns

Warrington
Runcorn Stockport
Shells

Sheffield

Hawarden
Corrugated iron and airships
Chester
Explosives

Lincoln
Tanks

Chilwell

Norwich

Wolverhampton
Tipton
Fuses
Birmingham

Aerial bombs, Ammunition, rifles, mines and tanks

Coventry
Shells and ammunition, tanks and machine guns

Ipswich

Aerial bombs, trench bombs

Guns and shells
Watford

Hendon
Ponders End

Explosives

Feltham

Avonmouth

Warmley
Hand grenades

Farnborough

Woking
Croydon

1 Erith
2 Crayford
Machine guns and rifles

Woolwich
Aerial bombs, explosives

Bideford

Poplar
Submarine nets

Yarmouth
Trench equipment

MUNITIONS PRODUCTION

	1915	1916	1917
Bullets	396 million	808 million	619 million
Artillery shells	2 million	17 million	23 million
Grenades	2 million	9 million	8 million
Rifles	173,000	458,000	325,000
Machine guns	1,700	9,600	19,000
Heavy guns	1,200	1,300	2,100
Trench mortars	152	1,300	1,700

◉ Principal centres of munitions production

● Other munitions factories

✈ Aeroplanes and aeroplane parts

0   50
Miles

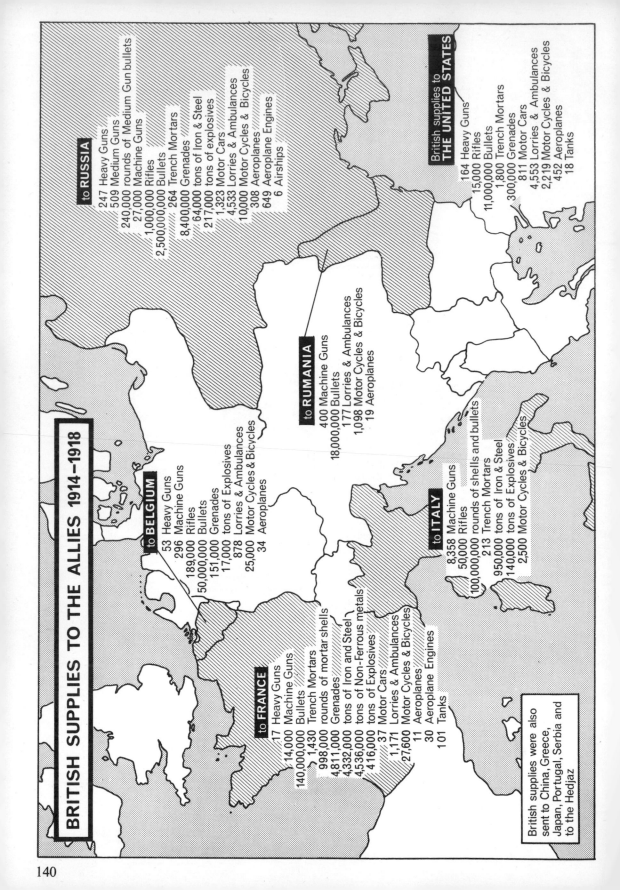

BRITISH SUPPLIES TO THE ALLIES 1914–1918

to RUSSIA
- 247 Heavy Guns
- 509 Medium Guns
- 240,000 rounds of Medium Gun bullets
- 27,000 Machine Guns
- 1,000,000 Rifles
- 2,500,000,000 Bullets
- 264 Trench Mortars
- 8,400,000 Grenades
- 64,000 tons of Iron & Steel
- 217,000 tons of explosives
- 1,323 Motor Cars
- 4,533 Lorries & Ambulances
- 10,000 Motor Cycles & Bicycles
- 308 Aeroplanes
- 649 Aeroplane Engines
- 6 Airships

British supplies to THE UNITED STATES
- 164 Heavy Guns
- 15,000 Rifles
- 11,000,000 Bullets
- 1,800 Trench Mortars
- 300,000 Grenades
- 811 Motor Cars
- 4,553 Lorries & Ambulances
- 2,219 Motor Cycles & Bicycles
- 452 Aeroplanes
- 18 Tanks

to BELGIUM
- 53 Heavy Guns
- 296 Machine Guns
- 189,000 Rifles
- 50,000,000 Bullets
- 151,000 Grenades
- 17,000 tons of Explosives
- 878 Lorries & Ambulances
- 25,000 Motor Cycles & Bicycles
- 34 Aeroplanes

to RUMANIA
- 400 Machine Guns
- 18,000,000 Bullets
- 177 Lorries & Ambulances
- 1,098 Motor Cycles & Bicycles
- 19 Aeroplanes

to ITALY
- 8,358 Machine Guns
- 50,000 Rifles
- 100,000,000 rounds of shells and bullets
- 213 Trench Mortars
- 950,000 tons of Iron & Steel
- 140,000 tons of Explosives
- 2,500 Motor Cycles & Bicycles

to FRANCE
- 17 Heavy Guns
- 14,000 Machine Guns
- 140,000,000 Bullets
- 1,430 Trench Mortars
- 998,000 rounds of mortar shells
- 4,811,000 Grenades
- 4,332,000 tons of Iron and Steel
- 4,536,000 tons of Non-Ferrous metals
- 416,000 tons of Explosives
- 37 Motor Cars
- 1,171 Lorries & Ambulances
- 27,600 Motor Cycles & Bicycles
- 11 Aeroplanes
- 30 Aeroplane Engines
- 101 Tanks

British supplies were also sent to China, Greece, Japan, Portugal, Serbia and to the Hedjaz.

140

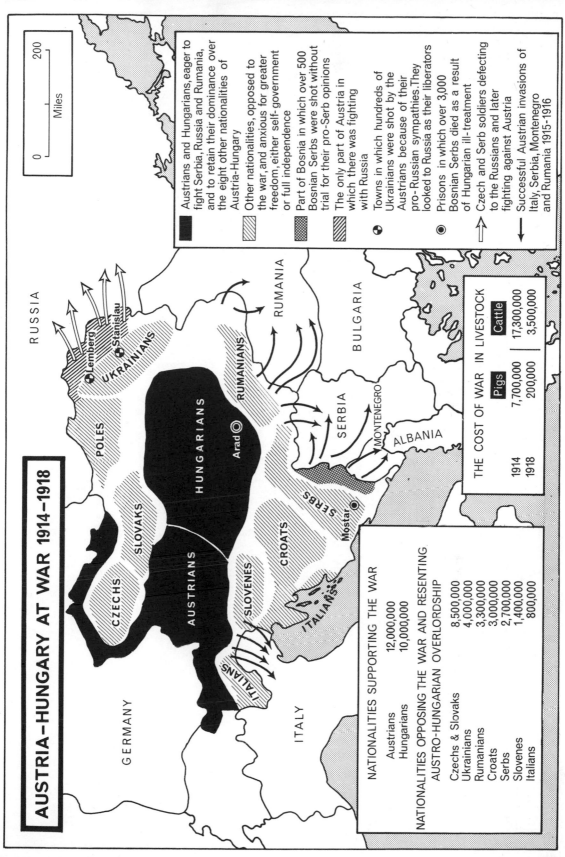

AUSTRIA–HUNGARY AT WAR 1914–1918

GERMANY

RUSSIA

Lemberg
Stanislau

UKRAINIANS

POLES

CZECHS

SLOVAKS

AUSTRIANS

HUNGARIANS

Arad ◎

RUMANIANS

RUMANIA

SLOVENES

CROATS

SERBS

Mostar ◉

SERBIA

MONTENEGRO

ALBANIA

BULGARIA

ITALIANS

ITALY

Legend:

- ■ Austrians and Hungarians, eager to fight Serbia, Russia and Rumania, and to retain their dominance over the eight other nationalities of Austria-Hungary
- ▨ Other nationalities, opposed to the war, and anxious for greater freedom, either self-government or full independence
- ▩ Part of Bosnia in which over 500 Bosnian Serbs were shot without trial for their pro-Serb opinions
- ▨ The only part of Austria in which there was fighting with Russia
- ◐ Towns in which hundreds of Ukrainians were shot by the Austrians because of their pro-Russian sympathies. They looked to Russia as their liberators
- ◉ Prisons in which over 3,000 Bosnian Serbs died as a result of Hungarian ill-treatment
- ⇧ Czech and Serb soldiers defecting to the Russians and later fighting against Austria
- ⬇ Successful Austrian invasions of Italy, Serbia, Montenegro and Rumania 1915-1916

NATIONALITIES SUPPORTING THE WAR

Austrians	12,000,000
Hungarians	10,000,000

NATIONALITIES OPPOSING THE WAR AND RESENTING AUSTRO-HUNGARIAN OVERLORDSHIP

Czechs & Slovaks	8,500,000
Ukrainians	4,000,000
Rumanians	3,300,000
Croats	3,000,000
Serbs	2,700,000
Slovenes	1,400,000
Italians	800,000

THE COST OF WAR IN LIVESTOCK

	Pigs	Cattle
1914	7,700,000	17,300,000
1918	200,000	3,500,000

Scale: 0 — 200 Miles

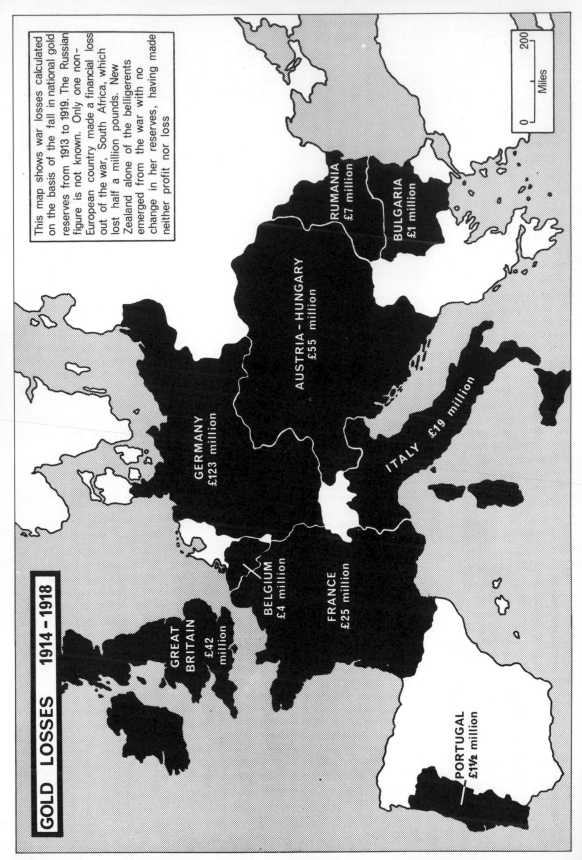

GOLD LOSSES 1914–1918

This map shows war losses calculated on the basis of the fall in national gold reserves from 1913 to 1919. The Russian figure is not known. Only one non-European country made a financial loss out of the war, South Africa, which lost half a million pounds. New Zealand alone of the belligerents emerged from the war with no change in her reserves, having made neither profit nor loss

GREAT BRITAIN £42 million

BELGIUM £4 million

FRANCE £25 million

PORTUGAL £1½ million

GERMANY £123 million

AUSTRIA – HUNGARY £55 million

RUMANIA £7 million

BULGARIA £1 million

ITALY £19 million

Miles
0 200

142

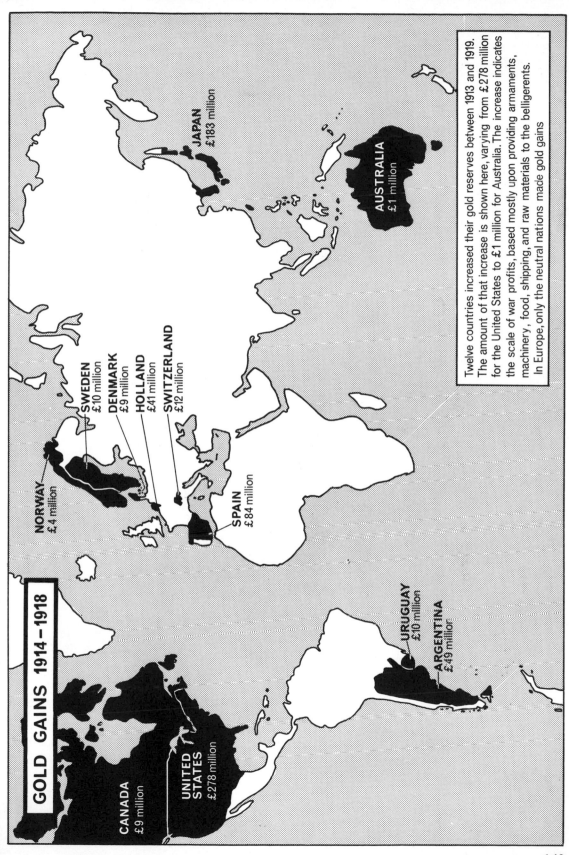

GOLD GAINS 1914–1918

CANADA
£9 million

UNITED STATES
£278 million

NORWAY
£4 million

SWEDEN
£10 million

DENMARK
£9 million

HOLLAND
£41 million

SWITZERLAND
£12 million

SPAIN
£84 million

URUGUAY
£10 million

ARGENTINA
£49 million

JAPAN
£183 million

AUSTRALIA
£1 million

Twelve countries increased their gold reserves between 1913 and 1919. The amount of that increase is shown here, varying from £278 million for the United States to £1 million for Australia. The increase indicates the scale of war profits, based mostly upon providing armaments, machinery, food, shipping, and raw materials to the belligerents. In Europe, only the neutral nations made gold gains

143

Section Ten

AFTERMATH

Too much blood had been spilt. Too much life-essence had been consumed. The gaps in every home were too wide and empty. The shock of an awakening and the sense of disillusion followed swiftly upon the poor rejoicings with which hundreds of millions saluted the achievement of their hearts' desire. There still remained the satisfactions of safety assured, of peace restored, of honour preserved, of the comforts of fruitful industry, of the home-coming of the soldiers; but these were in the background; and with them all there mingled the ache for those who would never come home.

WINSTON S. CHURCHILL
"THE WORLD CRISIS: THE AFTERMATH"

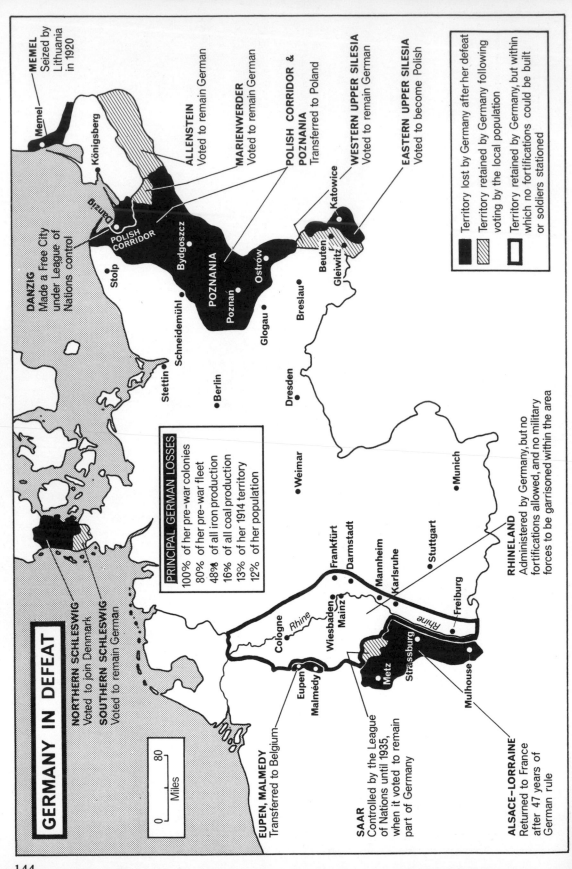

GERMANY IN DEFEAT

MEMEL Seized by Lithuania in 1920

DANZIG Made a Free City under League of Nations control

ALLENSTEIN Voted to remain German

MARIENWERDER Voted to remain German

POLISH CORRIDOR & POZNANIA Transferred to Poland

WESTERN UPPER SILESIA Voted to remain German

EASTERN UPPER SILESIA Voted to become Polish

Territory lost by Germany after her defeat

Territory retained by Germany following voting by the local population

Territory retained by Germany, but within which no fortifications could be built or soldiers stationed

Memel

Königsberg

Danzig

POLISH CORRIDOR

Stolp

Bydgoszcz

Schneidemühl

POZNANIA

Poznań

Ostrow

Glogau

Breslau

Katowice

Beuten

Gleiwitz

Stettin

Berlin

Dresden

PRINCIPAL GERMAN LOSSES
100% of her pre-war colonies
80% of her pre-war fleet
48% of all iron production
16% of all coal production
13% of her 1914 territory
12% of her population

Weimar

Munich

NORTHERN SCHLESWIG Voted to join Denmark

SOUTHERN SCHLESWIG Voted to remain German

Frankfürt

Darmstadt

Cologne

Rhine

Wiesbaden

Mainz

Mannheim

Karlsruhe

Stuttgart

Freiburg

Rhine

Eupen

Malmédy

Metz

Strassburg

Mulhouse

RHINELAND Administered by Germany, but no fortifications allowed, and no military forces to be garrisoned within the area

EUPEN, MALMEDY Transferred to Belgium

SAAR Controlled by the League of Nations until 1935, when it voted to remain part of Germany

ALSACE–LORRAINE Returned to France after 47 years of German rule

0   80
Miles

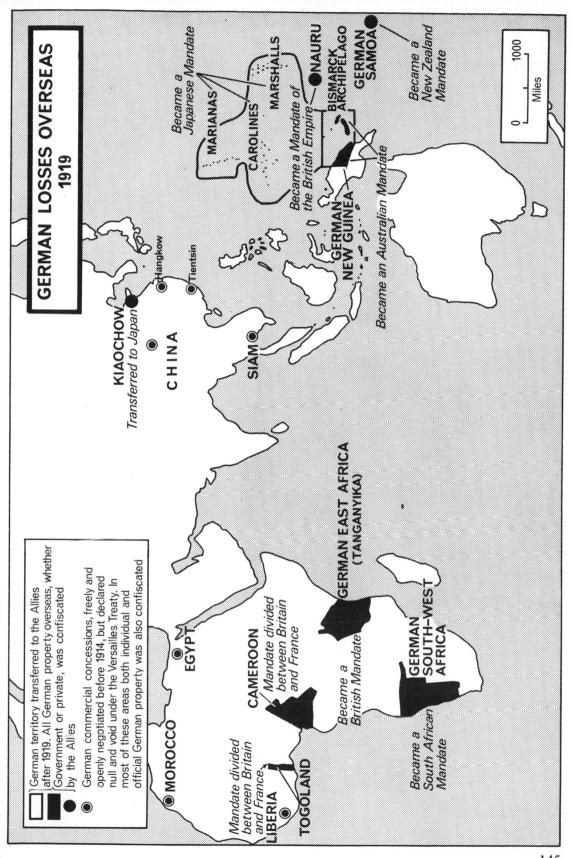

GERMAN LOSSES OVERSEAS
1919

German territory transferred to the Allies after 1919. All German property overseas, whether Government or private, was confiscated by the Allies

German commercial concessions, freely and openly negotiated before 1914, but declared null and void under the Versailles Treaty. In most of these areas both individual and official German property was also confiscated

1000
0
Miles

MARIANAS
CAROLINES
MARSHALLS
NAURU
Became a Japanese Mandate

BISMARCK ARCHIPELAGO
Became a Mandate of the British Empire

GERMAN SAMOA
Became a New Zealand Mandate

GERMAN NEW GUINEA
Became an Australian Mandate

Hangkow
Tientsin

KIAOCHOW
Transferred to Japan

CHINA

SIAM

MOROCCO
Mandate divided between France and Britain

EGYPT

LIBERIA
TOGOLAND
Mandate divided between Britain and France

CAMEROON
Mandate divided between Britain and France

GERMAN EAST AFRICA (TANGANYIKA)
Became a British Mandate

GERMAN SOUTH-WEST AFRICA
Became a South African Mandate

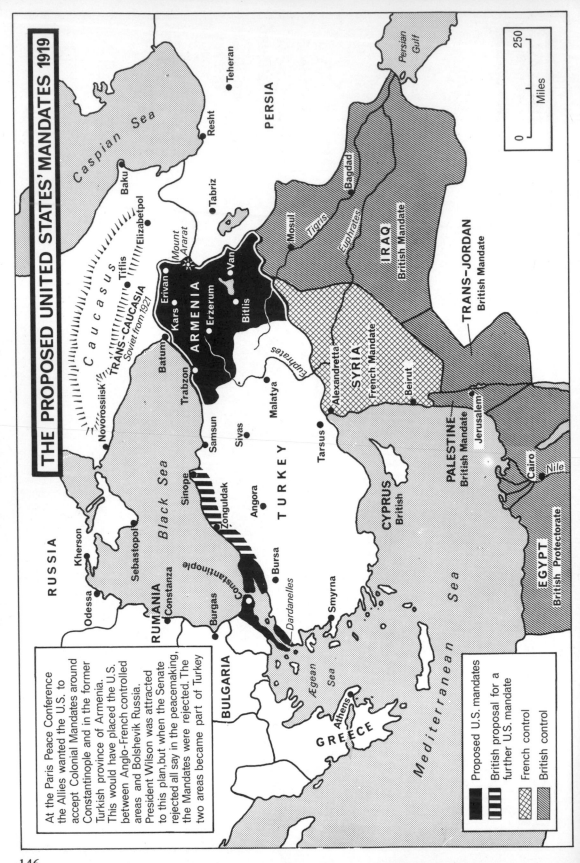

THE PROPOSED UNITED STATES' MANDATES 1919

250

0

Miles

Persian Gulf

PERSIA

Caspian Sea

Teheran

Resht

Baku

Tabriz

Elizabetpol

Mount Ararat

Tiflis

TRANS-CAUCASIA
Soviet from 1921

Mosul

Tigris

Euphrates

IRAQ
British Mandate

TRANS-JORDAN
British Mandate

Caucasus

Erivan

Van

ARMENIA

Kars

Erzerum

Bitlis

Battum

Novorossiisk

Trabzon

Euphrates

Alexandretta

SYRIA
French Mandate

Beirut

PALESTINE
British Mandate

Jerusalem

Cairo

Nile

EGYPT
British Protectorate

Samsun

Sivas

Malatya

Tarsus

TURKEY

Angora

Bursa

Sinope

Zonguldak

CYPRUS
British

Sebastopol

Kherson

RUSSIA

Odessa

RUMANIA

Constanza

Burgas

Black Sea

Constantinople

Dardanelles

Smyrna

Aegean Sea

BULGARIA

GREECE

Athens

Mediterranean Sea

At the Paris Peace Conference
the Allies wanted the U.S. to
accept Colonial Mandates around
Constantinople and in the former
Turkish province of Armenia.
This would have placed the U.S.
between Anglo-French controlled
areas and Bolshevik Russia.
President Wilson was attracted
to this plan, but when the Senate
rejected all say in the peacemaking,
the Mandates were rejected. The
two areas became part of Turkey

Proposed U.S. mandates

British proposal for a
further U.S. mandate

French control

British control

146

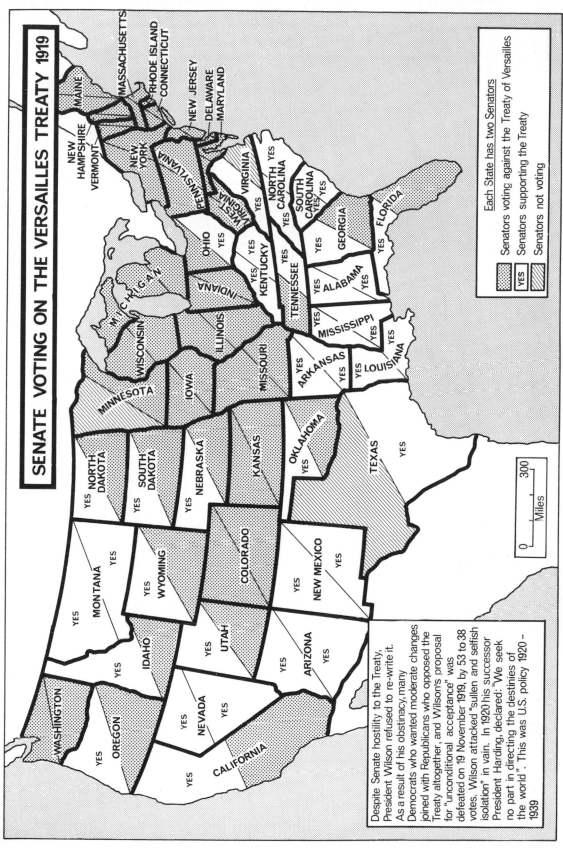

SENATE VOTING ON THE VERSAILLES TREATY 1919

Each State has two Senators

Senators voting against the Treaty of Versailles

YES Senators supporting the Treaty

Senators not voting

MAINE
MASSACHUSETTS
RHODE ISLAND
CONNECTICUT
NEW JERSEY
DELAWARE
MARYLAND
NEW HAMPSHIRE
VERMONT
NEW YORK
PENNSYLVANIA
VIRGINIA   YES
WEST VIRGINIA   YES
NORTH CAROLINA   YES YES
SOUTH CAROLINA   YES YES
GEORGIA   YES
FLORIDA   YES
OHIO   YES
KENTUCKY   YES YES
TENNESSEE   YES YES
ALABAMA   YES YES
MICHIGAN
INDIANA   YES
ILLINOIS   YES
MISSISSIPPI   YES
LOUISIANA   YES YES
WISCONSIN
MISSOURI
ARKANSAS   YES YES
MINNESOTA
IOWA
NORTH DAKOTA   YES
SOUTH DAKOTA   YES
NEBRASKA   YES
KANSAS
OKLAHOMA   YES
TEXAS   YES
MONTANA   YES
WYOMING   YES
COLORADO   YES
NEW MEXICO   YES
WASHINGTON   YES
OREGON   YES
IDAHO   YES
UTAH   YES
ARIZONA   YES
NEVADA   YES YES
CALIFORNIA

300
0
Miles

Despite Senate hostility to the Treaty,
President Wilson refused to re-write it.
As a result of his obstinacy, many
Democrats who wanted moderate changes
joined with Republicans who opposed the
Treaty altogether, and Wilson's proposal
for "unconditional acceptance" was
defeated on 19 November 1919, by 53 to 38
votes. Wilson attacked "sullen and selfish
isolation" in vain. In 1920 his successor
President Harding, declared: "We seek
no part in directing the destinies of
the world". This was U.S. policy 1920 –
1939

147

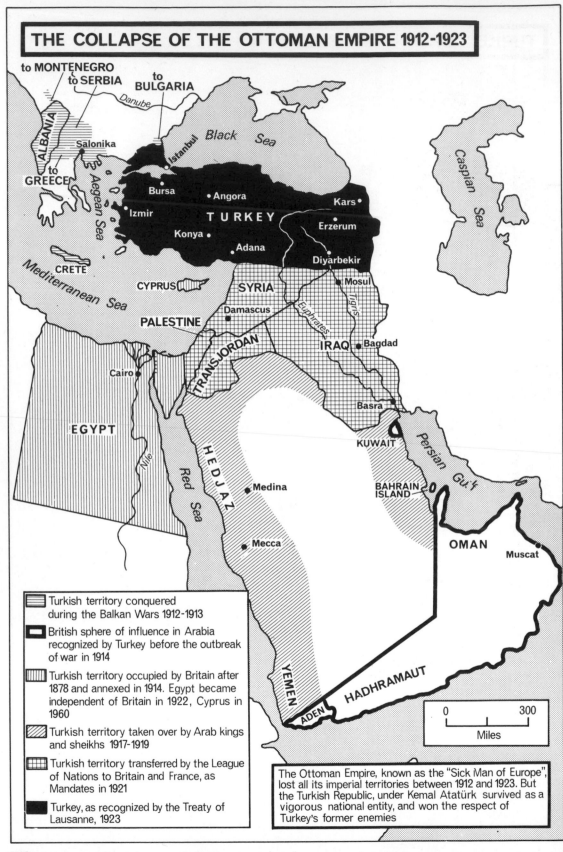

THE COLLAPSE OF THE OTTOMAN EMPIRE 1912-1923

to MONTENEGRO
to SERBIA
to BULGARIA

Danube

ALBANIA

Salonika

to GREECE

Black Sea

Istanbul

Caspian Sea

Bursa

Angora

Kars

Izmir

T U R K E Y

Erzerum

Konya

Adana

Diyarbekir

Aegean Sea

CRETE

CYPRUS

Mediterranean Sea

Mosul

SYRIA

Damascus

PALESTINE

Euphrates

Tigris

IRAQ

Bagdad

TRANSJORDAN

Cairo

EGYPT

Basra

KUWAIT

Persian Gulf

HEDJAZ

Red Sea

Nile

Medina

BAHRAIN
ISLAND

Mecca

OMAN

Muscat

YEMEN

ADEN

HADHRAMAUT

0	300

Miles

Turkish territory conquered
during the Balkan Wars 1912-1913

British sphere of influence in Arabia
recognized by Turkey before the outbreak
of war in 1914

Turkish territory occupied by Britain after
1878 and annexed in 1914. Egypt became
independent of Britain in 1922, Cyprus in
1960

Turkish territory taken over by Arab kings
and sheikhs 1917-1919

Turkish territory transferred by the League
of Nations to Britain and France, as
Mandates in 1921

Turkey, as recognized by the Treaty of
Lausanne, 1923

The Ottoman Empire, known as the "Sick Man of Europe",
lost all its imperial territories between 1912 and 1923. But
the Turkish Republic, under Kemal Atatürk survived as a
vigorous national entity, and won the respect of
Turkey's former enemies

148

TURKEY, GREECE, AND BRITAIN 1919-1922

0 — 60 Miles

BULGARIA

Black Sea

Adrianople (Edirne)
Midia
Bosphorus
Rodosto (Tekirdağ)
Constantinople
Ismit
Dedeagatch
Keshan
Kavala
Salonika
SAMOTHRACE
Sea of Marmora
Dardanelles
Biga
Bandirma
Mudania
Bursa
Chanak
IMBROS
Kum Kale
LEMNOS
İnönü
Eskisehir
MITYLENE
Aegean Sea
T U R K E Y
Kütahya
Manisa
Dumlupiner
Afionkarahissar
Athens
Smyrna (İzmir)
Denizli
DODECANESE ISLANDS
RHODES
CRETE

G R E E C E

	Greece in 1914
	Bulgarian territory ceded to Greece in 1919
	Turkish territory occupied by Greece in 1919 with British encouragement
– – –	The "Zone of the Straits" occupied by Britain 1919 - 1922
←	Turkish forces defeated the Greeks in August 1922. Hostilities ended at the Mudania Convention, and Greece withdrew from all Turkish territory occupied in 1919
⇐	Turkish advance towards British forces at Chanak halted on the verge of war in October 1922. Britain then agreed to evacuate the "Zone of the Straits", including Constantinople, which had been under British occupation since 1919

•°• Occupied by Italy in 1912. Claimed by Greece 1920. Formally annexed by Italy, 1923. Transferred to Greece 1948

149

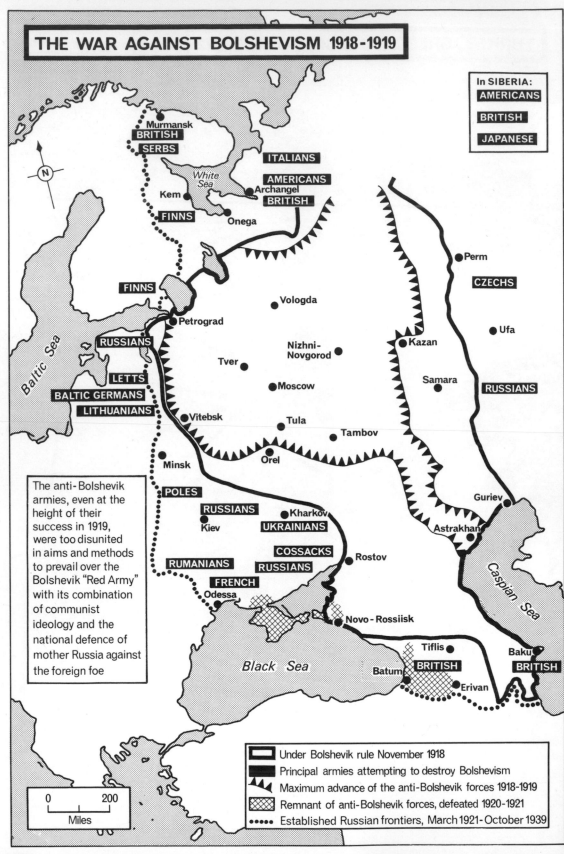

THE WAR AGAINST BOLSHEVISM 1918-1919

In SIBERIA:
AMERICANS
BRITISH
JAPANESE

Murmansk
BRITISH
SERBS
ITALIANS
White Sea
AMERICANS
Kem
Archangel
BRITISH
FINNS
Onega
Perm
CZECHS
FINNS
Vologda
Ufa
Petrograd
RUSSIANS
Nizhni-Novgorod
Kazan
Tver
Samara
LETTS
Moscow
RUSSIANS
BALTIC GERMANS
LITHUANIANS
Vitebsk
Tula
Tambov
Orel
Minsk
POLES
Guriev
RUSSIANS
Kharkov
Kiev
UKRAINIANS
Astrakhan
COSSACKS
Rostov
RUMANIANS
RUSSIANS
FRENCH
Odessa
Novo-Rossiisk
Caspian Sea
Tiflis
Baku
Black Sea
Batum
BRITISH
BRITISH
Erivan

Baltic Sea

The anti-Bolshevik armies, even at the height of their success in 1919, were too disunited in aims and methods to prevail over the Bolshevik "Red Army" with its combination of communist ideology and the national defence of mother Russia against the foreign foe

0   200
Miles

Under Bolshevik rule November 1918
Principal armies attempting to destroy Bolshevism
Maximum advance of the anti-Bolshevik forces 1918-1919
Remnant of anti-Bolshevik forces, defeated 1920-1921
Established Russian frontiers, March 1921 - October 1939

150

THE RUSSO-POLISH WAR 1920

Legend:

- ━━━━ Poland's established frontiers, June 1920
- •••••• The eastern extent of Polish conquests, April, May and June 1920
- ⟵ Russian attacks following the Polish occupation of Kiev in June 1920
- Polish lines of defence, August 1920
- ⊕ The 'Miracle of the Vistula'. Russian armies were defeated; they retreated to Russia
- ▨ Seized by Poland from Lithuania, October 1920
- ▨ Annexed by Poland from Russia, Treaty of Riga, March 1921
- ┅┅┅ Poland's eastern frontier from 1921 to 1939

ESTONIA

LATVIA

Baltic Sea

LITHUANIA

RUSSIA

•Vilna

•Minsk

DANZIG

EAST PRUSSIA

Grodno

GERMANY

Vistula

Bialystok

Plotzk

Pinsk

•Poznan

Warsaw

POLAND

Radom

GERMANY

Lublin

Kholm

Kiev

Vistula

Lvov

•Cracow

Kamenets Podolsk

CZECHOSLOVAKIA

0   100

Miles

HUNGARY

RUMANIA

151

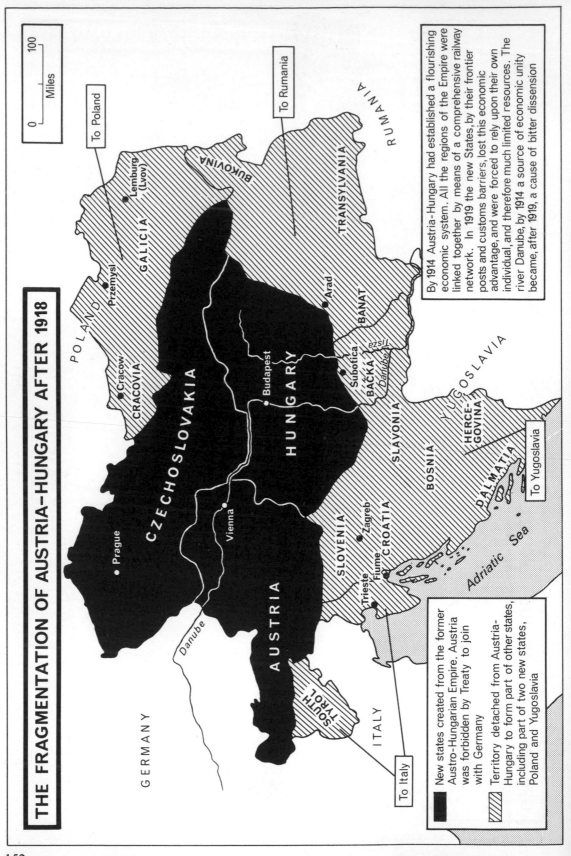

THE FRAGMENTATION OF AUSTRIA–HUNGARY AFTER 1918

100

0

Miles

To Poland

To Rumania

To Italy

To Yugoslavia

GERMANY

POLAND

GALICIA

Lemburg (Lvov)

Przemysl

Cracow

CRACOVIA

BUKOVINA

RUMANIA

TRANSYLVANIA

Arad

BANAT

Subotica

BAČKA

Tiszá

Danube

CZECHOSLOVAKIA

Prague

Vienna

Budapest

HUNGARY

AUSTRIA

SOUTH TYROL

ITALY

Danube

SLOVENIA

Zagreb

Trieste

Fiume

CROATIA

SLAVONIA

BOSNIA

HERCE-GOVINA

YUGOSLAVIA

DALMATIA

Adriatic Sea

By 1914 Austria-Hungary had established a flourishing economic system. All the regions of the Empire were linked together by means of a comprehensive railway network. In 1919 the new States, by their frontier posts and customs barriers, lost this economic advantage, and were forced to rely upon their own individual, and therefore much limited resources. The river Danube, by 1914 a source of economic unity became, after 1919, a cause of bitter dissension

New states created from the former Austro-Hungarian Empire. Austria was forbidden by Treaty to join with Germany

Territory detached from Austria-Hungary to form part of other states, including part of two new states, Poland and Yugoslavia

152

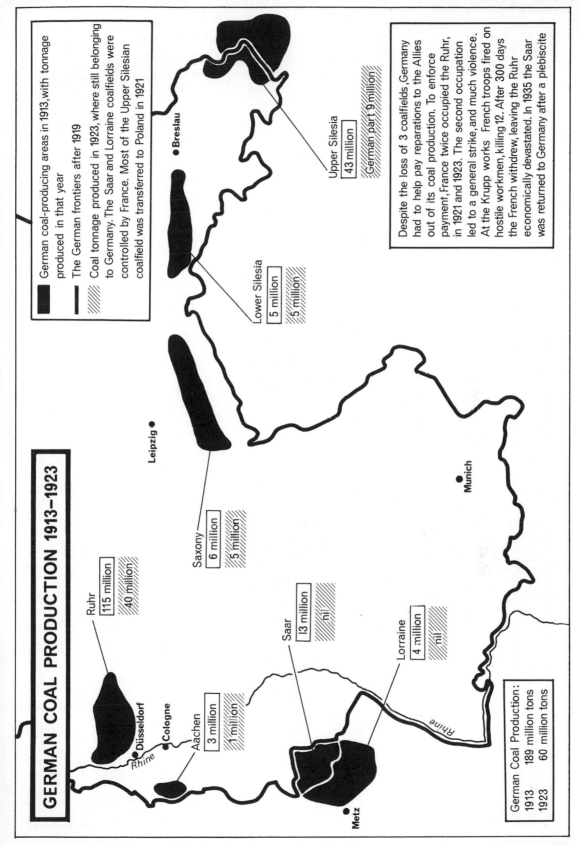

GERMAN COAL PRODUCTION 1913–1923

German coal-producing areas in 1913, with tonnage produced in that year

The German frontiers after 1919

Coal tonnage produced in 1923, where still belonging to Germany. The Saar and Lorraine coalfields were controlled by France. Most of the Upper Silesian coalfield was transferred to Poland in 1921

Despite the loss of 3 coalfields, Germany had to help pay reparations to the Allies out of its coal production. To enforce payment, France twice occupied the Ruhr, in 1921 and 1923. The second occupation led to a general strike, and much violence. At the Krupp works French troops fired on hostile workmen, killing 12. After 300 days the French withdrew, leaving the Ruhr economically devastated. In 1935 the Saar was returned to Germany after a plebiscite

Upper Silesia
43 million

German part 9 million

● Breslau

Lower Silesia
5 million
5 million

Leipzig ●

Saxony
6 million
5 million

Ruhr
115 million
40 million

● Düsseldorf
● Cologne

Rhine

Aachen
3 million
1 million

Saar
13 million
nil

Lorraine
4 million
nil

Rhine

● Metz

Munich ●

German Coal Production:
1913   189 million tons
1923   60 million tons

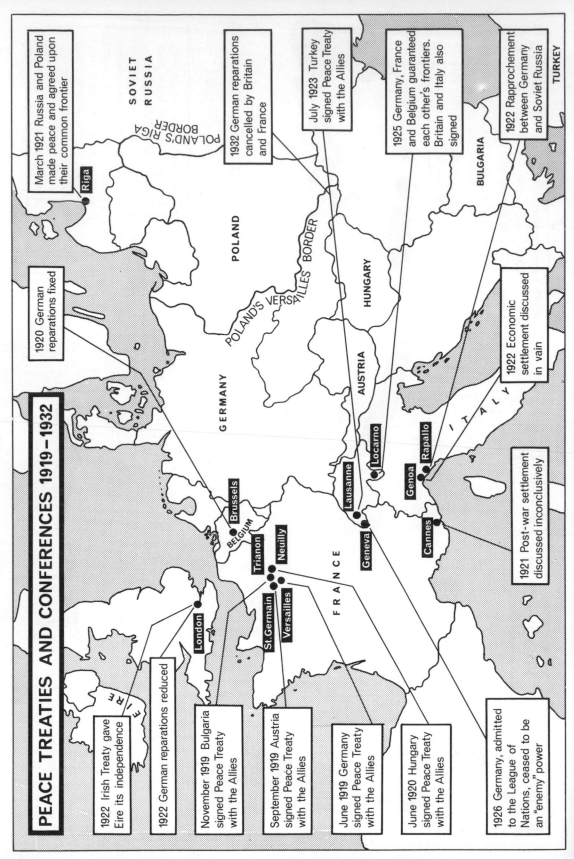

PEACE TREATIES AND CONFERENCES 1919–1932

March 1921 Russia and Poland made peace and agreed upon their common frontier

1932 German reparations cancelled by Britain and France

July 1923 Turkey signed Peace Treaty with the Allies

1925 Germany, France and Belgium guaranteed each other's frontiers. Britain and Italy also signed

1922 Rapprochement between Germany and Soviet Russia

1920 German reparations fixed

1922 Economic settlement discussed in vain

1921 Post-war settlement discussed inconclusively

1922 Irish Treaty gave Eire its independence

1922 German reparations reduced

November 1919 Bulgaria signed Peace Treaty with the Allies

September 1919 Austria signed Peace Treaty with the Allies

June 1919 Germany signed Peace Treaty with the Allies

June 1920 Hungary signed Peace Treaty with the Allies

1926 Germany, admitted to the League of Nations, ceased to be an "enemy" power

SOVIET RUSSIA

POLAND'S RIGA BORDER

Riga

POLAND

VERSAILLES BORDER

POLAND'S

GERMANY

AUSTRIA

HUNGARY

BULGARIA

TURKEY

ITALY

Locarno

Rapallo

Genoa

Lausanne

Brussels

BELGIUM

Geneva

Cannes

Trianon

Neuilly

London

St. Germain

Versailles

FRANCE

EIRE

THE NEW STATES OF CENTRAL EUROPE 1920

■	New states established by 1920 with the encouragement of the Allied powers
░	The remnant of Austria-Hungary, two independent and separate states established by the Allied powers
▨	Austro-Hungarian territory added to Rumania and Serbia by the Allied powers. The enlarged Serbia became the Serb-Croat-Slovene kingdom, later known as Yugoslavia
▤	Former Russian territory joined to Rumania

POPULATIONS IN 1920

Poland	27,000,000
Rumania	17,400,000
Czechoslovakia	14,600,000
Yugoslavia	12,000,000
Hungary	8,700,000
Austria	6,500,000
Finland	3,600,000
Lithuania	2,400,000
Latvia	1,800,000
Estonia	1,000,000
Danzig	400,000
Fiume	50,000

FINLAND

ESTONIA

LATVIA

LITHUANIA

RUSSIA

FREE CITY OF DANZIG

EAST PRUSSIA

Baltic Sea

POLAND

GERMANY

CZECHOSLOVAKIA

AUSTRIA

HUNGARY

BESSARABIA

FREE CITY OF FIUME

YUGOSLAVIA

RUMANIA

ITALY

Adriatic Sea

ALBANIA

BULGARIA

Black Sea

GREECE

TURKEY

0   300
Miles

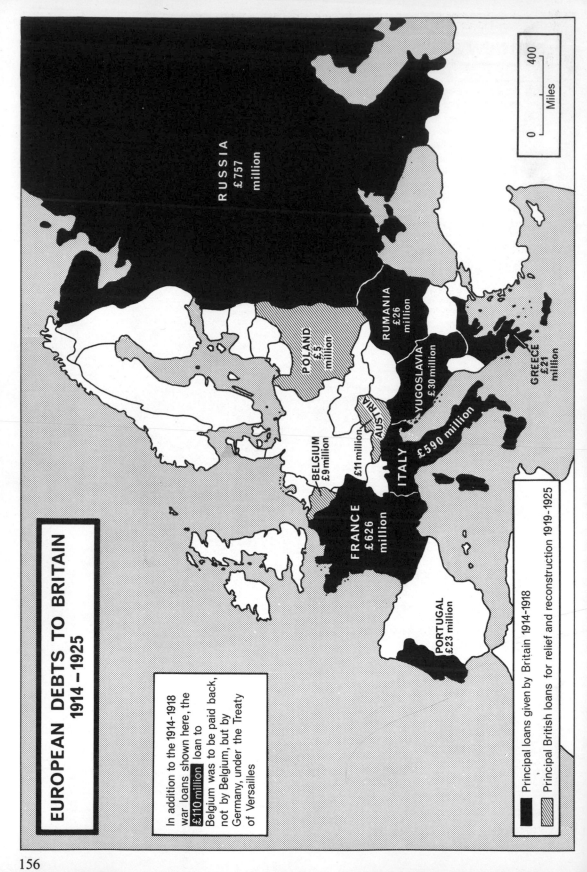

EUROPEAN DEBTS TO BRITAIN
1914–1925

In addition to the 1914–1918 war loans shown here, the £110 million loan to Belgium was to be paid back, not by Belgium, but by Germany, under the Treaty of Versailles

RUSSIA £757 million

POLAND £5 million

RUMANIA £26 million

YUGOSLAVIA £30 million

GREECE £21 million

ITALY £590 million

AUSTRIA £11 million

BELGIUM £9 million

FRANCE £626 million

PORTUGAL £23 million

400
0
Miles

■ Principal loans given by Britain 1914-1918
▨ Principal British loans for relief and reconstruction 1919-1925

156

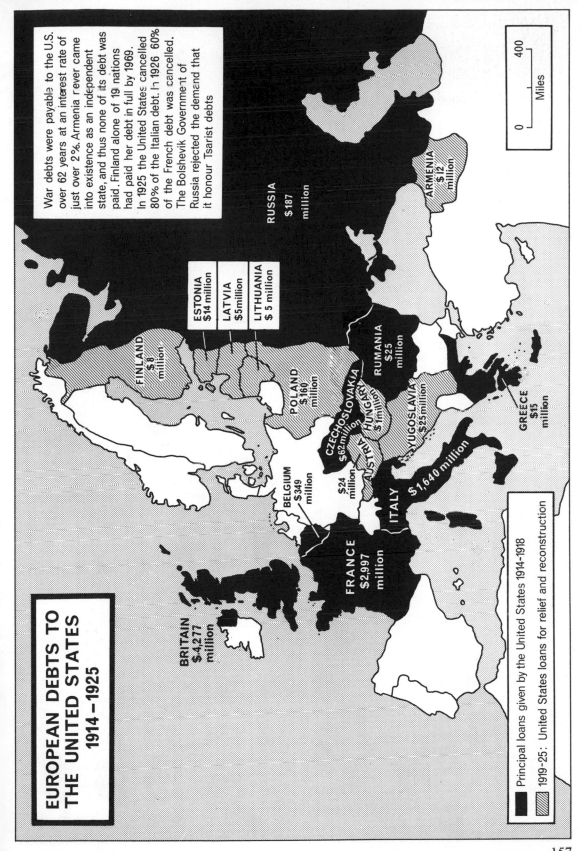

EUROPEAN DEBTS TO THE UNITED STATES
1914–1925

War debts were payable to the U.S. over 62 years at an interest rate of just over 2%. Armenia never came into existence as an independent state, and thus none of its debt was paid. Finland alone of 19 nations had paid her debt in full by 1969. In 1925 the United States cancelled 80% of the Italian debt. In 1926 60% of the French debt was cancelled. The Bolshevik Government of Russia rejected the demand that it honour Tsarist debts

RUSSIA
$187 million

ARMENIA
$12 million

ESTONIA $14 million

LATVIA $5million

LITHUANIA $5 million

FINLAND $8 million

POLAND $160 million

RUMANIA $25 million

CZECHOSLOVAKIA $62million

HUNGARY $1million

AUSTRIA

YUGOSLAVIA $25million

GREECE $15 million

BELGIUM $349 million

$24 million

ITALY $1,640 million

FRANCE $2,997 million

BRITAIN $4,277 million

0   400
Miles

Principal loans given by the United States 1914-1918

1919-25: United States loans for relief and reconstruction

157

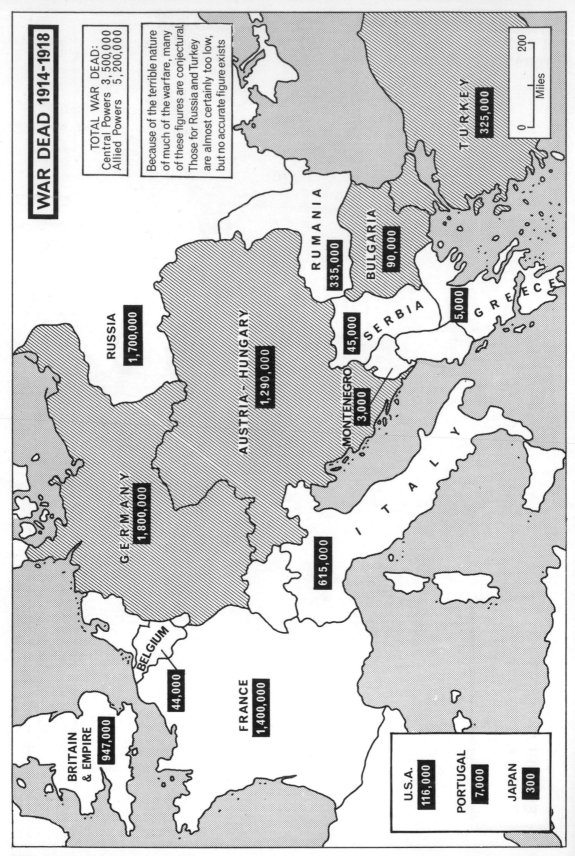

WAR DEAD 1914-1918

TOTAL WAR DEAD:
Central Powers 3,500,000
Allied Powers   5,200,000

Because of the terrible nature of much of the warfare, many of these figures are conjectural. Those for Russia and Turkey are almost certainly too low, but no accurate figure exists

200
Miles
0

TURKEY
325,000

RUSSIA
1,700,000

RUMANIA
335,000

BULGARIA
90,000

SERBIA
45,000

GREECE
5,000

AUSTRIA-HUNGARY
1,290,000

MONTENEGRO
3,000

GERMANY
1,800,000

ITALY
615,000

BELGIUM
44,000

BRITAIN & EMPIRE
947,000

FRANCE
1,400,000

U.S.A.
116,000

PORTUGAL
7,000

JAPAN
300

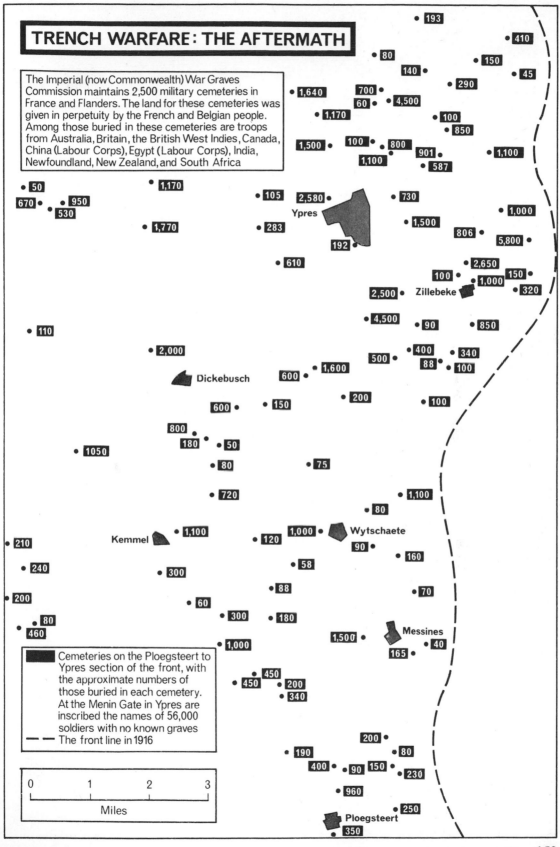

TRENCH WARFARE: THE AFTERMATH

The Imperial (now Commonwealth) War Graves Commission maintains 2,500 military cemeteries in France and Flanders. The land for these cemeteries was given in perpetuity by the French and Belgian people. Among those buried in these cemeteries are troops from Australia, Britain, the British West Indies, Canada, China (Labour Corps), Egypt (Labour Corps), India, Newfoundland, New Zealand, and South Africa

193
410
80
150
140
45
290
1,640
700
60
4,500
1,170
100
850
1,500
100
800
1,100
901
1,100
1,100
587

50
1,170
105
2,580
730
670
950
530
1,500
1,770
283
1,000
806
5,800
192
610
2,650
100
150
1,000
320
2,500
Zillebeke
Ypres

110
4,500
90
850
2,000
400
340
500
88
100
Dickebusch
600
1,600
600
150
200
100
800
180
50
1050
80
75
720
1,100
80
Kemmel
1,100
1,000
Wytschaete
210
120
90
240
58
160
300
200
88
70
60
80
300
180
1,000
1,500
Messines
40
165
450
450
200
340

200
80
190
400
90
150
230
960
250
Ploegsteert
350

■ Cemeteries on the Ploegsteert to Ypres section of the front, with the approximate numbers of those buried in each cemetery. At the Menin Gate in Ypres are inscribed the names of 56,000 soldiers with no known graves
– – – The front line in 1916

0   1   2   3
Miles

Bibliographical Note

The following bibliography is strictly selective, consisting principally of those books which I personally found most useful, both for preparing individual maps and for background knowledge about many diverse aspects of the war: its campaigns, its diplomacy, its men and its moods. It ranges from the multi-volume official histories replete with documents and maps, to much briefer narratives of particular events. Put together, I hope that these books provide a useful and varied introductory survey of the war.

GENERAL WORKS

As an introductory guide I have frequently consulted several contemporary works of reference and encyclopaedias, of which three were of particular value: *The Annual Register*, 5 vols, covering the years 1914 to 1919 (London, 1915–1920); *The Times History of the War*, 21 vols, covering 1914 to 1920 (London, 1914–1920), which contains, for example, the fullest account I have seen of America's shipbuilding crusade (map 87), and has informative articles on every theatre of war, and every aspect of the conflict, social, political, medical, the role of women, etc; and the *Encyclopaedia Britannica*, the thirteenth edition of which contains three extra volumes, numbers 29, 30 and 31, which deal with the war years and immediate post-war period (London and New York, 1926).

THE PRELUDE TO WAR

A stimulating survey of the long-term and immediate origins of the war, together with a full bibliography, is A. J. P. Taylor, *The Struggle for Mastery in Europe* (Oxford, 1954). Also of importance are Luigi Albertini, *The Origins of the War of 1914*, 3 vols (Oxford, 1952–1957) and F. H. Hinsley, *Power and the Pursuit of Peace* (Cambridge, 1963).

For diplomatic activity in Berlin on the eve of war, as well as a reflective view of events leading up to war, Sir Horace Rumbold, *The War Crisis in Berlin July to August 1914* (London, 1940) is of interest. A recent German view of responsibility is Gerhard Georg B. Ritter, *The Schlieffen Plan: Critique of a Myth* (London, 1958). For an account of the final steps to war, there is R. W. Seton-Watson, *Sarajevo: A Study in the Origin of the Great War* (London, 1926).

THE WAR IN OUTLINE

Of the many general histories of the war, three of the most readable are A. J. P. Taylor, *The First World War, An Illustrated History* (London, 1963) which has the added merit of excellent pictures; C. R. M. F. Cruttwell, *A History of the Great War, 1914 to 1918* (Oxford, 1934); and Vincent J. Esposito (ed), *A Concise History of World War One* (London, 1964). Despite its British, and at times personal bias, Winston S. Churchill, *The World Crisis*, 6 vols (London, 1923–1931) has a superb first chapter on the coming of war, and many insights into different phases of the war itself; its penultimate volume, *The Aftermath*, deals with the peace treaties and other post-war problems.

THE WAR IN THE AIR

A good general survey is R. H. Kiernan, *The First War in the Air* (London, 1934). The Official British History, extremely rich in maps, is Walter Raleigh and H. A. Jones, *The War in the Air,* 6 vols text (including many maps), 2 vols maps (Oxford, 1922–1937). The German story is told in Georg Paul Neumann, *The German Airforce in the Great War* (London, 1921); and the effect of German activity in Joseph Morris, *The German Air Raids on Great Britain 1914–1918* (London, 1926) and Kenneth Poolman, *Zeppelins Over England* (London, 1960).

Two recent books of interest are Douglas H. Robinson, *The Zeppelin in Combat* (London, 1962) and Arch Whitehouse, *The Zeppelin Fighters* (London, 1968). An important study of the most serious phase of the aerial war is Raymond H. Fredette, *The First Battle of Britain 1917–1918 and the Birth of the Royal Air Force* (London, 1966). Early methods of dealing with this new method of warfare are described in E. B. Ashmore, *Air Defence* (London, 1929).

THE WAR AT SEA

A useful introduction is Thomas G. Frothingham, *The Naval History of the World War,* 3 vols (Cambridge Mass., 1924, 1925, 1926). The British story was first told, with copious documentation and excellent maps, in Sir Julian S. Corbett and Henry Newbolt, *Naval Operations,* 5 vols text plus 5 vols maps (London, 1920–1931). A work of high scholarship which combines this material with the results of much patient research into British and German naval archives is Arthur J. Marder, *From the Dreadnought to Scapa Flow,* 5 vols (London, 1961–1970).

The story of merchant shipping and oceanic trade routes is as full of interest and drama as that of the fighting navies, and can be read in C. Ernest Fayle, *Seaborne Trade,* 4 vols (London, 1920, 1920 (maps), 1923, 1924) and Archibald Hurd, *The Merchant Navy,* 3 vols (London, 1921, 1924, 1929).

The literature is as voluminous for underwater activity as for that on the surface. Two interesting introductory books on this aspect of the war are R. H. Gibson and Maurice Prendergast, *The German Submarine War* 1914–1918 (London, 1931) and Robert M. Grant, *U-Boats Destroyed* (London, 1964).

Specific topics covered in this Atlas can be explored further in Richard Hough, *The Pursuit of Admiral von Spee* (London, 1969) and Edwin P. Hoyt, *The Last Cruise of the Emden* (London, 1967). A member of the Imperial Royal Family who was on the *Emden* has also told his story: Prince Franz Joseph of Hohenzollern, *Emden* (London, 1928). For the naval and diplomatic aspects of the war in the Italian and Adriatic zones I have consulted Archibald Hurd, *Italian Sea-Power and the Great War* (London, 1918) and P. H. Michel, *La Question de l'Adriatique 1914–1918* (Paris, 1938).

One of the most significant aspects of the war at sea was the Allied naval blockade of Germany. This can be studied in detail in H. W. C. Davis, *A History of the Blockade* (London, 1920), M. W. W. P. Consett, *The Triumph of Unarmed Force* (London, 1928), A. C. Bell, *The Blockade of Germany* (London, 1937) and Marion C. Siney, *The Allied Blockade of Germany 1914–1916* (Ann Arbor, 1957). A lesser known aspect of the blockade is given detailed study by S. L. Bane and R. H. Lutz (eds), *The Blockade of Germany After the Armistice* (Stanford, 1942).

METHODS OF WAR

There are many interesting volumes on the different methods employed during the war by the opposing armies. Their attempts to burrow underneath each other are well described in W. Grant Grieve and Bernard Newman, *Tunnellers* (London, 1936) and Alexander Barrie, *War Underground* (London, 1962). The attempt to break through the barbed-wire by mechanical means is told by J. F. C. Fuller, *Tanks in the Great War 1914–1918* (London, 1920) and B. H. Liddell Hart, *The Tanks* (London, 1959).

Some idea of the extent of the dependence of the belligerents on transport and communications can be seen in the Official British History, A. M. Henniker, *Transportation on the Western Front 1914–1918* (London, 1937) and W. J. K. Davies, *Light Railways of the First World War* (London, 1967).

BRITAIN

A good introductory history of British policy during the war is Sir Llewellyn Woodward, *Great Britain and the War of 1914–1918* (London, 1967). A voluminous compendium of statistics among which the curious reader could spend many hours is the War Office publication, printed by His Majesty's Stationery Office, *Statistics of the Military Effort of the British Empire During the Great War 1914–1920* (London, 1922). Among the many fascinating regimental histories is one of particular interest because of its author, who lost his son in the war: Rudyard Kipling, *The Irish Guards in the Great War* (London, 1923). "The only wonder to the compiler of these records," wrote Kipling in his introduction, "is that any sure fact whatever should be retrieved out of the whirlpools of war."

The munitions story, one of the most fascinating of the domestic issues of the war, can be followed in detail in the Ministry of Munitions publication, *The History of the Ministry of Munitions,* 12 vols (London, 1920–1924). A more personal aspect of the munitions struggle, together with an account of his two years as Prime Minister, is in the *War Memoirs of David Lloyd George,* 6 vols (London, 1933–1936).

Lloyd George's predecessor also left memoirs which deal with war policy: H. H. Asquith, *Memories and Reflections,* 2 vols (London, 1928). Two contemporary diarists with close contacts at the centre of events are Christopher Addison, *Politics from Within* (London, 1924), and *Lord Riddell's War Diary* (London, 1933). A graphic political narrative of this period is in Lord Beaverbrook's two volumes, *Politicians and the War 1914–1916*, 2 vols (London, 1928, 1932) and *Men and Power 1917–1918* (London, 1956). A scholarly examination of Britain's decision for war, and the nine succeeding months in British politics is Cameron Hazlehurst *Politicians at War* (London, 1971). British strategy is examined critically by Paul Guinn, *British Strategy and Politics 1914–1918* (Oxford, 1965). Both Hazlehurst and Guinn have excellent bibliographies.

Social and domestic scenes from the war are presented in a fascinating volume, Mrs C. S. Peel, *How We Lived Then 1914–1918* (London, 1929).

THE BRITISH EMPIRE

The Imperial aspects of the war are told in outline by Sir Charles Lucas (ed), *The Empire at War,* 5 vols (Oxford, 1921–1926). The Australian story has been told in detail, and with some passion, by C. E. W. Bean and others, *Official History of Australia in the War of 1914–1918*, 12 vols (Canberra, 1921–1934). A rich fund of statistics is the Government of India's official publication, *India's Contribution to the Great War* (Calcutta, 1923). A future Lord Chancellor was co-author of the well-mapped official volume, J. W. B. Merewether and Sir Frederick Smith, *The Indian Corps in France* (London, 1917). The first volume of the official story of the Canadian Expeditionary Force is a small but fascinating volume by the future Lord Beaverbrook: Sir Max Aitken, *Canada in Flanders* (London, 1916).

Two British Official Histories which cover aspects of the war in Africa are C.

Hordern, *Military Operations, East Africa* (London, 1941) and F. J. Moberly, *Military Operations, Togoland and the Cameroons 1914–1916* (London, 1931). Other useful Imperial war histories are H. T. B. Drew (ed) *The War Effort of New Zealand* (Auckland, 1924), G. W. L. Nicholson, *Official History of the Canadian Army* (Ottawa, 1962) and John Buchan, *The History of the South African Forces in France* (London, 1920).

FRANCE, BELGIUM AND THE WESTERN FRONT

A compelling account of the opening phase of the war is Major-General Sir Edward Spears, *Liaison 1914* (London, 1930). The story of the German advance has been told by its commander, Alexander von Kluck, *The March on Paris and the Battle of the Marne 1914* (London, 1920). One of the most interesting of the French military memoirs is Maréchal Foch, *Memoires Pour Servir A L'Histoire De La Guerre De 1914–1918* (Paris, 1931). A useful supplement and addition to these memoirs is Liddell Hart, *Foch* (London, 1931). Clemenceau has given his own account both of the war and post-war period in Georges Clemenceau, *Grandeur and Misery of Victory* (London, 1930). A more humble, but highly entertaining picture of the war by a young French painter serving in the British army is Paul Maze, *A Frenchman in Khaki* (London, 1934).

One of the most terrible of all the battles of the war is described in Alistair Horne, *The Price of Glory: Verdun 1916* (London, 1962). The French mutinies have been the subject of frequent accounts, of which the following two are among the more recent and more useful: Richard M. Watt, *Dare Call It Treason* (London, 1953) and John Williams, *Mutiny 1917* (London, 1962). The destructiveness of the war on the western front is shown in Charles Gide (ed), *Effects of the War Upon French Economic Life* (Oxford, 1923), and something of the efforts to restore the damage by William MacDonald, *Reconstruction in France* (London, 1922).

The rapid conquest of Belgium is told in a short Belgian publication, *Military Operations of Belgium* (London, 1915). Something of the nature of the German occupation was described at the time by two books by Jean Massart, *Belgians Under the German Eagle* (London, 1916) and *The Secret Press in Belgium* (London, 1918). There is also some disturbing evidence in Arnold J. Toynbee, *The German Terror in Belgium* (London, 1917).

British military operations on the western front are treated exhaustively and copiously mapped, by J. E. Edmonds (and others), *France and Belgium*, with several volumes of text and maps for each year of the war (London, 1922–1947). It would be invidious to select books on individual campaigns, of which there are several thousand; nor is there a good select bibliography dealing with the more recent of these. An introduction to this enormous literature can be made through two particular studies of merit, A. H. Farrar-Hockley, *The Somme* (London, 1964) and Major-General Sir Edward Spears, *Prelude to Victory* (London, 1939), which deals with the French offensive of 1917. A stimulating critique of the German, British and French naval and military commanders is Corelli Barnett, *The Swordbearers* (London, 1963).

THE FIGHTING MEN

It was the experiences of the ordinary soldiers, rather than the decisions of their commanders, which ensured that the First World War influenced men long after the Armistice. A varied and moving idea of these experiences can be gained from: Bruce Bairnsfather, *Bullets & Billets* (London, 1917) and *From Mud to Mufti* (London, 1919); Philip Gibbs, *Realities of War* (London, 1920); Edmund Blunden, *Undertones of War* (London, 1930); Brian Gardner (ed), *Up The Line To Death: The War Poets 1914–*

1918 (London, 1964); Robert Graves, *Goodbye To All That* (London, 1929); Erich Maria Remarque, *All Quiet on the Western Front* (London, 1929); Siegfried Sassoon, *Counterattack* (London, 1917), some of the most bitter poems of the war; and Siegfried Sassoon, *Memoirs of an Infantry Officer* (London, 1930).

The songs of the war with their terrifying progress from the gay to the grotesque can be heard on the Decca recording *Oh What A Lovely War* (London, 1963; mono LK 4542). Another moving record of contemporary poetry and letters is provided on *Wilfred Owen (1893–1918)* (London, 1968) published by the Argo Record Company on mono RG 593.

For a poignant survey of the British cemeteries whose ground was presented to the British people in perpetuity by the Governments of Belgium and France, and as an indispensable handbook for any visit to the western front, there is a publication by the Imperial (now Commonwealth) War Graves Commission, Sidney C. Hurst, *The Silent Cities* (London, 1929).

ITALY AND THE ITALIAN FRONT

A useful general introduction is Thomas Nelson Page, *Italy and the World War* (London, 1921). For the military story there is a fascinating account by an Italian historian who served on the Army Staff, Luigi Villari, *The War on the Italian Front* (London, 1932). A British historian who also wrote an interesting account of the Italian front, where he was serving in an ambulance unit, is G. M. Trevelyan, *Scenes From Italy's War* (London, 1919).

The British military operations in Italy are described in detail by Sir James E. Edmonds and H. R. Davies, *Military Operations, Italy 1915–1919* (London, 1949). There is an interesting eye-witness account by a future Chancellor of the Exchequer, Hugh Dalton, *With British Guns in Italy* (London, 1919). Among the most famous of all the literary works of the First World War is one which is set on the Italian front, Ernest Hemingway, *A Farewell to Arms* (New York and London, 1929).

For the broader aspects of Italian war policy, there is a useful account in M. H. H. Macartney and P. Cremona, *Italy's Foreign and Colonial Policy 1914–1937* (New York, 1938). An Italian Prime Minister's record is in Giovanni Giolitti, *Memoirs of My Life* (London, 1923).

THE SALONIKA FRONT

One of the most recent and most readable accounts, which also contains a comprehensive bibliography, is Alan Palmer, *The Gardeners of Salonika* (London, 1965). The Italian representative with the Allied forces, who has left a vivid account of this zone of war, was Luigi Villari, *The Macedonian Campaign* (London, 1922). As so often the British Official History combines detailed research with a lively style and copious maps, C. Falls, *Military Operations, Macedonia,* 2 vols (London, 1933, 1935).

RUSSIA AND THE EASTERN FRONT

A good general introduction to the period is to be found in Sir Bernard Pares, *The Fall of the Russian Monarchy* (London, 1939). The Russian defeat in East Prussia is described in detail, and with an excellent series of maps, in Sir Edmund Ironside, *Tannenberg* (Edinburgh and London, 1925). The most successful of all the Russian Generals has left his own account, A. A. Brussilov, *A Soldier's Note-Book 1914–1918* (London, 1930). Another General whose memoirs are extremely informative is General N. M. Golovin, *The Russian Army in the World War* (London, 1931). A British Officer attached to the Russian Army, who has left his own vivid account, is General Sir A. Knox, *With the Russian Army 1914–1917,* 2 vols (London, 1921).

A useful survey of Russian policy and foreign aspirations from the outbreak of war to the Revolution is to be found in C. Jay Smith, *The Russian Struggle For Power 1914–1917* (Athens, Georgia, 1956). For the Revolution itself, and the ensuing civil war and Allied intervention, the most useful account is still W. H. Chamberlin, *The Russian Revolution,* 2 vols (New York, 1935). A recent and enthralling description of the February Revolution is George Katkov, *Russia 1917* (London, 1967).

The treaty signed between the Bolsheviks and the Germans, to Russia's inevitable and enormous disadvantage, is described in detail by John W. Wheeler-Bennett, *Brest-Litovsk* (London, 1938). For British policy towards Russia after the Revolution, and a documentary account of the Allied attempt to crush the new Bolshevik state, see Richard H. Ullman, *Intervention and the War* (Princeton and London, 1961). Two earlier volumes of much value are George F. Kennan, *Russia Leaves the War* (London, 1956) and *Decision to Intervene* (London, 1956).

GERMANY

A penetrating account of German war aims during the war is Fritz Fischer, *Germany's Aims in the First World War* (London, 1967). The documentary background to the disintegration of Germany during the war is to be found in Ralph Haswell Lutz (ed), *Fall of the German Empire 1914–1918,* 2 vols (Stanford, 1932). A recent study of internal German affairs based upon much further detailed research is Gerald D. Feldman, *Army, Industry and Labor in Germany 1914–1918* (Princeton, 1966).

Among contemporaries who left accounts of their activities was General Ludendorff, *My War Memories 1914–1918,* 2 vols (London, 1933). Also of interest for the German view are Th. Von Bethmann Hollweg, *Reflections on the World War* (London, 1920) and Prince von Bülow, *Memoirs of Prince von Bülow* (Boston, 1932); volume 3, "The World War and Germany's Collapse," covers the years 1909 to 1919. Hindenburg's story has been told most effectively in J. W. Wheeler-Bennett, *Hindenburg: The Wooden Titan* (London, 1936).

One of the most stimulating of all recent historical works, based upon a careful study of the newly-opened British archives, is Wm. Roger Louis, *Great Britain and Germany's Lost Colonies 1914–1919* (Oxford, 1967). Dr Louis records that E. S. Montagu, when Secretary of State for India, declared that it would be difficult to find "some convincing argument for not annexing *all* the territories in the world". His book is both an essential introduction to British imperial policy and a model of historical research.

RUMANIA

The best introductory study is R. W. Seton-Watson, *A History of the Roumanians* (Cambridge, 1934).

Two pro-Rumanian accounts produced during the First World War are R. W. Seton-Watson, *Roumania and the Great War* (London, 1915) and D. Mitrany, *Greater Rumania: A Study in National Ideals* (London, 1917). Rumania's war effort and diplomacy is examined in detail by Pamfil Seicaru, *La Roumanie dans la Grande Guerre* (Paris, 1968).

The Rumanian Foreign Minister, Take Jonescu, published his memoirs immediately after the war as *Souvenirs* (Paris, 1919).

TURKEY, MESOPOTAMIA AND THE MIDDLE EAST

There is a discussion of German pre-war influence over Turkey in Morris Jastrow, *The War and the Bagdad Railway* (Philadelphia, 1918). The leading Turkish Minister to have left a record of political and military affairs is Djemal Pasha, *Memories of a Turkish Statesman 1913–1919* (London, 1922).

The Mesopotamian campaign is extremely well documented; and a recent general work, with much fascinating detail, is A. J. Barker, *The Neglected War: Mesopotamia 1914–1918* (London, 1967). The Official British History is once again a model of detail and exposition, F. J. Moberly, *The Campaign in Mesopotamia 1914–1918*, 4 vols (London, 1923–1927).

For the war in Arabia and Palestine, T. E. Lawrence, *The Revolt in the Desert* (London, 1927) is a graphic personal account. The defeat of Turkey in Palestine is dealt with in a short volume, Cyril Falls, *Armageddon 1918* (London, 1964). Cyril Falls was also one of the authors of the longer Official History of this campaign, Sir G. Macmunn and C. Falls, *Egypt and Palestine,* 3 vols and 2 vols maps (London, 1928–1930).

There is a good biography of the Turkish national leader by Lord Kinross, *Atatürk* (London, 1964). For a discussion of some of the plans to defeat the Turkish Empire, an early but informative work is H. N. Howard, *The Partition of Turkey 1913–1923* (Norman, Oklahoma, 1931); but this subject still awaits its historian. The best general work on British policy in the Middle East is Elizabeth Monroe, *Britain's Moment in the Middle East 1914–1956* (London, 1963). The Palestine question is best followed in Leonard Stein, *The Balfour Declaration* (London, 1961) and Christopher Sykes *Cross Roads to Israel* (London, 1965).

THE DARDANELLES AND GALLIPOLI

The attempt to defeat Turkey by an attack on Constantinople lasted for only ten months, but has been responsible for more literature than any other campaign of the war. Two good introductory works are Robert Rhodes James, *Gallipoli* (London, 1965) and John North, *Gallipoli: The Fading Vision* (London, 1936). The Official British History is the most readable and most critical of all those produced after the war, C. F. Aspinall-Oglander, *Military Operations, Gallipoli,* 2 vols (London, 1929, 1932). There is much pungent comment also in C. E. W. Bean's Australian Official History already cited.

The naval campaign is described in the Official British Naval History cited above and in Admiral of the Fleet Lord Wester-Wemyss, *The Navy in the Dardanelles Campaign* (London, 1924). There is a useful French account in A. Thomazi, *La Guerre Navale aux Dardanelles* (Paris, 1926). There is also an interesting German record by a German General, Hans Kannengiesser Pasha, *The Campaign in Gallipoli* (London, 1927).

A moving account of the campaign as seen from the trenches is A. P. Herbert's novel, *The Secret Battle* (London, 1919), of which Winston Churchill wrote: "It was one of those cries of pain wrung from the fighting troops by the prolonged and measureless torment through which they passed; and like the poems of Siegfried Sassoon should be read in each generation, so that men and women may rest under no illusion about what the war means."

AUSTRIA–HUNGARY

The best general surveys are A. J. P. Taylor, *The Habsburg Monarchy 1815–1918* (London, 1949) and A. J. May, *The Habsburg Monarchy 1867–1914* (Cambridge Mass., 1951). There is a full account of Britain's attitude towards the Habsburg monarchy in an excellent recent study, which has the added merit of a comprehensive bibliography, Harry Hanak, *Great Britain and Austria–Hungary During the First*

World War (London, 1962). The memoirs of the Austrian Foreign Minister are also of interest, Count Ottokar Czernin, *In the World War* (London, 1919); but of greater historical importance is the superb account of the final decade of Habsburg foreign policy, A. F. Pribram, *Austrian Foreign Policy 1908–1918* (London, 1923).

For the disintegration of the Empire two standard works are Oskar Jászi, *The Dissolution of the Habsburg Monarchy* (Chicago, 1929) and J. Andrássy, *The Collapse of the Austro–Hungarian Empire* (London, 1930). A recent scholarly account, which supersedes these in many ways, is Z. A. B. Zeman, *The Break-up of the Habsburg Empire 1914–1918* (London, 1961).

EASTERN EUROPE AND THE BALKANS

The best general survey, covering both world wars, and with an excellent bibliography, is C. A. Macartney and A. W. Palmer, *Independent Eastern Europe* (London, 1962). An interesting account of American policy towards central Europe can be found in V. S. Mamatey, *The United States and East Central Europe 1914–1918* (Oxford, 1958).

A wartime appraisal of the national potential of eastern Europe by a British diplomatic historian is G. P. Gooch, *The Races of Austria–Hungary* (London, 1917). For the Balkans, R. W. Seton-Watson, *The Rise of Nationality in the Balkans* (London, 1917) is a plea in favour of Balkan nationalism, particularly of the Serb variety; while M. E. Durham, *Twenty Years of Balkan Tangle* (London, 1920) is less impressed with the Serb case.

The story of the war in Montenegro can be read in Alexander Devine, *Montenegro* (London, 1918). A somewhat obscure corner of the Balkans is dealt with in detail by Edith P. Stickney, *Southern Albania or Northern Epirus in International Affairs 1912–1923* (Stanford, 1926).

SERBIA AND YUGOSLAVIA

For Serbia's war effort a useful general survey is W. H. Crawfurd Price, *Serbia's Part in the War* (London, 1918). Two British ladies have left eye-witness accounts of the débâcle: Lady Ralph Paget, *With Our Serbian Allies,* 2 vols (London, 1915, 1916), and Caroline Matthews *Experiences of A Woman Doctor in Serbia* (London, 1918). The Cambridge historian G. M. Trevelyan contributed to the pro-Serbian polemic in a pamphlet *The Serbians and Austrians* (London, 1915).

The Jugoslav Committee in London produced a series of pamphlets and appeals in favour of a South Slav state, the first of which was *Appeal to the British Nation and Parliament* (London, 1915). The best account of the formation of Yugoslavia is Henry Baerlein, *The Birth of Yugoslavia,* 2 vols (London, 1922).

GREECE

Two books written from opposing view-points give a glimpse of the complexities and antagonisms of Greek politics during the First World War: P. N. Ure, *Venizelos and his Fellow-Countrymen* (London, 1917) and George M. Melas, *Ex-King Constantine and the War* (London, 1920). There is a perceptive study of Graeco–Turkish national problems by A. J. Toynbee, *The Western Question in Greece and Turkey* (London, 1922).

CZECHOSLOVAKIA

Two wartime pleas for statehood by two future Presidents are T. G. Masaryk, *Austrian Terrorism in Bohemia* (London, 1916) and E. Beneš, *Bohemia's Case for*

Independence (London, 1917). A future distinguished British historian who entered into the argument in favour of the small nations was L. B. Namier in two booklets, *The Czecho-Slovaks, an Oppressed Nationality* (London, 1917) and *The Case for Bohemia* (London, 1917).

Somewhat more reflective accounts by the Czechoslovak statesmen themselves are T. G. Masaryk, *The Making of A State* (London, 1927) and E. Beneš, *My War Memoirs* (London, 1928). The fullest general history is R. W. Seton-Watson, *History of the Czechs and Slovaks* (London, 1943).

BULGARIA

An attempt to win British support for the Bulgarian case was made by Stojan Protić, *The Aspirations of Bulgaria* (London, 1915). A more general survey of Bulgarian history and claims, intended to influence Bulgaria's position as an enemy power at the Paris peace conference, was published by D. Mishew, *The Bulgarians in the Past* (Lausanne, 1919). There is a useful recent atlas of Bulgarian history compiled by D. Kosev and others, *Atlas po Bulgarska Istoria* (Sophia, 1963).

POLAND

Two wartime pamphlets seeking to enlist British support for Poland are Arnold J. Toynbee, *The Destruction of Poland* (London, 1916) and H. N. Brailsford, *Poland and the League of Nations* (London, 1917). The fullest account of Poland's emergence to nationhood as a result of the war can be found in T. Komarnicki, *The Rebirth of the Polish Republic* (London, 1957). A most useful recent historical atlas is W. Czaplinśky and T. Ladogórski, *Atlas Historyczny Polski* (Warsaw, 1968).

THE UNITED STATES OF AMERICA

A useful introductory survey is John Bach McMaster, *The United States in the World War 1914–1918* (New York and London, 1927). There is an interesting chapter on the First World War in George F. Kennan, *American Diplomacy 1900–1950* (London, 1952). The German attempt to persuade Mexico to declare war on the United States is described in Barbara Tuchman, *The Zimmerman Telegram* (London, 1957). Woodrow Wilson's policy can best be followed in his as yet uncompleted five-volume biography, Arthur S. Link, *Wilson* (Princeton, 1960–   ). A useful general study is E. R. May, *The World War and American Isolation* (Cambridge, 1959). For diplomatic aspects of the war, and of the peacemaking, the Department of State has published, as a supplement to *Papers Relating to the Foreign Relations of the United States,* two comprehensive documentary volumes, *The World War* (Washington, 1933) and *Papers Relating to the Foreign Relations of the United States: The Paris Peace Conference 1919,* 13 vols (Washington, 1942–1947). The most detailed account of America at war is in F. H. Simonds, *History of the World War,* 5 vols (New York, 1917–1920).

The American Ambassador in London has left an interesting account of the wartime period which forms a part of Burton J. Hendrick, *The Life and Letters of Walter H. Page,* 3 vols (London, 1925). The American Ambassador in Berlin likewise left an account of his experiences, James W. Gerard, *My Four Years in Germany* (London, 1917), as did his colleague in Constantinople, Henry Morgenthau, *Secrets of the Bosphorus* (London, 1918). The German Ambassador in Washington also wrote his story, Johann H. Von Bernstorff, *My Three Years in America,* (New York, 1920).

The Peace negotiations dominate American writings on the war. Three useful volumes covering this aspect are Robert Lansing, *The Big Four and Others of the Peace Conference* (Boston, 1921), and *The Peace Negotiations: A Personal Narrative* (Boston, 1921); and J. T. Shotwell, *At the Paris Peace Conference* (New York, 1937).

TREATIES AND REPARATIONS

The wartime secret treaties were made public by the Bolsheviks immediately they seized power, and were first published in English by F. S. Cocks, *The Secret Treaties and Agreements* (London, 1918). There is a recent scholarly study of both the Constantinople agreements and the Treaty of London by W. Gottlieb, *Studies in Secret Diplomacy* (London, 1957). For the Peace Treaties themselves the most comprehensive account is still Sir H. W. V. Temperley (ed), *A History of the Peace Conference of Paris,* 6 vols (London, 1920–1924). This contains a superb essay by L. B. Namier on the disintegration of the Habsburg monarchy.

For specific treaties I have consulted F. Deak, *Hungary at the Paris Peace Conference* (New York, 1942); R. H. Lutz and G. Almond, *The Treaty of Saint Germain* (Stanford, 1935); I. F. D. Morrow, *The Peace Settlement in the German–Polish Borderlands* (Oxford, 1936); Sherman David Spector, *Rumania at the Peace Conference* (New York, 1962); and George Louis Beer, *African Questions at the Paris Peace Conference* (New York, 1923). The complexities of Italian policy during the peace negotiations are unravelled by R. Albrecht-Carrié, *Italy at the Paris Peace Conference* (New York, 1938).

A literary masterpiece, which also includes some contemporary diary material, is Harold Nicolson, *Peacemaking 1919* (London, 1933). The British Prime Minister defended and explained his policy with characteristic vigour in David Lloyd George, *The Truth About the Peace Treaties,* 2 vols (London, 1938). A recent study of the evolution of the controversial war guilt clause, and of the part which the Treaty played in influencing the British policy of appeasement between the wars is to be found in Martin Gilbert, *The Roots of Appeasement* (London, 1966). The Treaty of Versailles itself can be read in a small and useful edition of primary material, Arthur Berriedale Keith (ed), *Speeches and Documents on International Affairs 1918–1937* (London, 1938).

The story of reparations has not yet been given a full scholarly study. The British Prime Minister put his case in David Lloyd George, *The Truth about Reparations and War Debts* (London, 1932). A British Treasury official who had taken part in the negotiations in Paris was responsible for the most outspoken and most influential criticism of reparations, J. M. Keynes, *The Economic Consequences of the Peace* (London, 1919). This was answered by Etienne Mantoux, *The Carthaginian Peace* (London, 1952). The American view was given by one of the American architects of the settlement, Bernard M. Baruch, *The Making of Reparations and the Economic Sections of the Treaty* (New York, 1920).

Index

88; and battle of Vimy Ridge, 89; and battle of Messines, 90; and life under Arras, 91; and the Allies in July 1917, 95; driven back by Germany on western front, 110; heavy casualties during counter-attack, 119; troops active on Italian front, 122; and her Empire war effort, 130; and the Near East, 132; and the search for horses, 135; uses native labour from Asia and Africa, 136; her war effort, 138, 139; aid to her Allies, 140; the cost of the war to, 142; and the Treaty of Versailles, 144, 145; and the partition of the Turkish Empire, 146, 148; and the war between Greece and Turkey, 149; and the war against Bolshevism, 151; European war debts to, 156; war dead, 158; losses on a short sector of the western front, 159

BRUSSELS   German plan to drive through during attack on France, 10; occupied by the Germans, 17; and the communications system of the Central Powers, 61; still under German occupation at the time of the Armistice, 117

BRUSSILOV   his attack against Austria–Hungary and Germany on the eastern front, 104

BULGARIA   suspicious of Austria–Hungary, 2; neutral on the outbreak of war, 12; Allies hope to win over to their cause, 33; abandons neutrality in order to attack Serbia, 48; invades Rumania and occupies corner of Greece, 62; base for German Zeppelin flight for Africa, 72; Allied advances through, 120; surrenders to Allies, 123; German wartime economic plans for, 127; loses outlet on Aegean Sea, 149; war dead, 158

CAMBRAI   occupied by the Germans, 18; British attempt to capture, 93; German looting in, 98; Germans driven from defensive positions of, 117; part of reparations zone, 125

CANADA   shipping losses off the coast of, 86; troops active in assault on Vimy Ridge, 89; and at Passchendaele, 103; her contribution to the Empire war effort, 130; sends horses to British sector of the western front, 135

CAPORETTO   Italian defeat at, 122

CHANAK   British aim to seize by naval attack alone, 33; the attack fails, 35; part of territory promised to Russia, 37, 40; part of proposed United States mandate, 146; occupied by British troops, 149

CHEMIN DES DAMES   heavy French losses at, 89; Germans occupy, 110

CHINA   growing Russian influence in, 23; an Allied Power by July 1917, 95; sends meat to Europe, 134; supplies Britain with large coolie labour force, 136; Germany deprived of all commercial possessions in, 145

CHURCHILL   sees battle of Marne as decisive for Allies, 16; fights for five months on the western front, 59; accuses Allied offensives as being needless operations of infinite cost, 93

CONSTANTINOPLE   European terminus of Berlin–Bagdad railway, 4; German cruisers escape to, 13; part of territory promised to Russia, 37, 40; and communications system of the Central Powers, 61; Allied fleet anchors off, 120; offered to the United States as a mandate, 146; British occupation of, 149

GALLIPOLI PENINSULA   part of territory promised to Russia, 37; Allied attack on, 38; Allied trenches on, 39

GAMBETTA   his advice to France, 1

GENEVA   Germany ceases to be an enemy power at, 154

GERMAN SUBMARINES   sunk by Britain, 78; active against British merchant ships, 79; in the Dover Strait, 80; in the Mediterranean, 81; cheated of their prey by the convoy system, 82, 83; the extent of their success, 84, 85, 86; bring the United States into the war, 94; surrender to the Allies, 118

GERMANY   fears British naval supremacy, 1; her growing isolation, 2; controls Berlin–Bagdad railway, 4; plans the swift defeat of France, 10; her cruisers escape to Constantinople, 13; declares war on France and invades Belgium, 14; advances across France, 15; halted at battle of Marne, 16; and race to the sea, 18, 19; her Far Eastern Empire, 23; her Pacific squadron defeated, 25; advances against Russia, 27; war aims in Africa, 30; loses her African Empire, 31; British naval defences against possible invasion from, 44; British invasion plans against, 45; war aims in Eastern Europe, 46; military successes against Russia in 1915, 47; fails to capture Verdun, 53; effective trench defences of, 54, 55; driven back by the Allies on the Somme, 56; repels British attack at Gommecourt, 57; excellent communications system with the other Central Powers, 61; Zeppelin raids over Britain, 64; air attacks on Paris, 66; fires shells at Paris, 67; Zeppelin raid of 19 October 1917, 68; air raids over London, 70; naval battles in the North Sea, 75; effect of naval blockade on, 76, 77; vigorous submarine activity against Britain, 78, 79; and against the Allies, 81; tactical withdrawal on the western front, 88; withstands Allied attack of April to June 1917, 89; forced to withdraw from Messines, 90; and battle of Cambrai, 93; at war with the United States, 94; her vandalism in France and Belgium, 98; strikes and social unrest in, 99; trench system on the western front, 100; successful Baltic blockade against Russia, 104; war aims in the Near East, 105; occupies western Russia, 109; advances against Britain and France, 110; driven back on the western front, 112, 113, 117, 118; revolutionary activity in, 114; Allied occupation of, 118; and Bulgaria, 120; revolution of November 1918 in, 121; total isolation of, 123; war aims in the west during the war, 124; French war aims towards, 125; her wartime diplomacy, 126; her economic aspirations, 127; her war aims in Africa, 128; her control of Persian towns in 1915, 132; driven from German East Africa, 133; mutinies in, 137; enormous fall in gold reserves as a result of the war, 142; and the Treaty of Versailles, 144, 145; coal production of before and after the war, 153; nearly two million war dead, 158

GOEBEN and BRESLAU   German cruisers escaping to Constantinople, 13

GREECE   neutral on the outbreak of war, 12; Allies hope to win over to their cause, 33; promised Albanian territory, 37; promised Turkish territory, 40; allows Serb soldiers refuge in Corfu, 49; Bulgarian attack on, 62; shipping losses, 84; joins Allies in 1917, 96; German economic plans for, 127; her forces driven from Turkey, 149; war debts to Britain and the United States, 156, 157; war dead, 158

HINDENBERG LINE   Germans withdraw to, 88

HITLER   serves throughout the war on western front, 59

NORTHERN RHODESIA German troops surrender in, 97; German war aims in, 128; native labour of, 136

NORTH SEA British naval preparations in, 14; British blockade of, 74, 76; naval battles in, 75

NORWAY neutral throughout the war, 12; her ships intercepted by the Allies, 74; shipping losses, 84; German economic plans for, 127; increase in gold reserves as a result of the war, 143

ODESSA bombarded by German ships flying the Turkish flag, 13, 32; Ukranians hamper Russian war effort in, 106; Jews welcome liberation from Russian tyranny in, 108; Bolsheviks seize power in, 109; Germans encourage revolution in, 126; becomes a French base during the war against Bolshevism, 150

OTTOMAN EMPIRE *see* TURKEY

OXFORD target of a German Zeppelin raid, 68

PALESTINE Turkish province, seen as under possible British or United States control, 34; promised by Britain as national home for the Jews, 40

PARIS German plan to encircle, 10; German failure to encircle, 15; Germans driven away from, 16; air raids on, 66; gun bombardment of, 67; final German threat to, 110

PASSCHENDAELE scene of intense fighting during 1917, 21, 102, 103; Germans drive Allies from in 1918, 111

PERSIA proposed railway to, 4; Russian and British spheres of influence in, 9; Turkish attack on Russian sphere, 32; proposed Russian attack on Turkey through, 43; German war aims in, 105; Turkish occupation of north-west corner of, 109; British attack Turks in, 116; German diplomatic activity in, 126; British and Russian control extended in, 132

PERSIAN GULF Turkish Empire and, 5; British influence in, 9; British plan to extend influence over, 34; British landings at head of, 43; British defensive perimeter on, 132

PETAIN describes effect of battle of Verdun, 53

PETROGRAD (formerly ST PETERSBURG) Russian capital and communications centre, 60, 104; Bolsheviks seize power in, 108, 109; anti-Bolshevik forces fail to capture, 150

PLOEGSTEERT a village in the Ypres salient, 20, 21; British underground tunnels near, 51; Churchill fights in trenches of, 58; mines exploded near, 90; Imperial (now Commonwealth) War Graves in region of, 159

POISON GAS used on the western front, 50; used at Verdun, 53; becomes a part of trench warfare, 54, 55; Hitler a victim of, 59; used during battle of the Lys in 1918, 111